INSTITUTIONAL ADJUSTMENT FOR ECONOMIC GROWTH

Institutional Adjustment for Economic Growth

Small scale industries and economic transition in Asia and Africa

Edited by
PER RONNÅS
ÖRJAN SJÖBERG
MAUD HEMLIN
Stockholm School of Economics

Routledge
Taylor & Francis Group

LONDON AND NEW YORK

First published 1998 by Ashgate Publishing

Reissued 2018 by Routledge
2 Park Square, Milton Park, Abingdon, Oxon, OX14 4RN
711 Third Avenue, New York, NY 10017, USA

Routledge is an imprint of the Taylor & Francis Group, an informa business

Notice:
Product or corporate names may be trademarks or registered trademarks, and are used only for identification and explanation without intent to infringe.

Publisher's Note
The publisher has gone to great lengths to ensure the quality of this reprint but points out that some imperfections in the original copies may be apparent.

Disclaimer
The publisher has made every effort to trace copyright holders and welcomes correspondence from those they have been unable to contact.

A Library of Congress record exists under LC control number: 97077531

ISBN 13: 978-1-138-33863-0 (hbk)
ISBN 13: 978-0-429-44156-1 (ebk)

Contents

Tables

Acknowledgements

As a result of a collaborative effort, the present volume is in many ways the result of contributions by a number of people and institutions. The Department for Research Cooperation (SAREC) of the Swedish International Development Agency (SIDA) provided generous financial support. However, their role went beyond the mere pecuniary as Dr. Malur Bhagavan at SAREC took a keen interest in all aspects of the implementation of the project and provided both encouragement and intellectual stimulation. Special thanks are due to the staff and the Director, Mr. V.P. Diejomaoh, of the ILO-EAMAT office in Addis Ababa for generous logistic support to many of the activities in the field. Dr. Rizwanul Islam, Director of the ILO-SAAT office in New Delhi had the overall responsibility as coordinator of the project within the frame of which the present volume was produced and also provided valuable comments and suggestions. A number of people provided intellectual feedback on the framework employed throughout this research effort or inputs into the individual studies. Ms. Gun Eriksson Skoog, Mr. R. Kombo, Professor Teshome Mulat, Professor S.R. Osmani, Mr. F. Parry, Mr. G Riugu and Mr. M.K. Kabundi deserve special mention in this regard. Ms. Sue Svedäng polished the English of the various manuscripts. The editors alone bear the full responsibility for any remaining errors, omissions or other shortcomings.

1 Introduction

Per Ronnås

This volume owes its existence to a comprehensive research project on 'Small Scale Industries in Africa: Lessons from the Asian Experience' undertaken jointly by the interdisciplinary teams of the International Labour Organisation for South Asia and East Africa in New Delhi and Addis Ababa,[1] respectively, and the Centre of International Economics and Geography at the Department of Economics at Stockholm School of Economics, with generous financial support from the Swedish Agency for Research Cooperation with Developing Countries.

The rationale behind this project can be summarised as follows: (i) Small and medium sized enterprises (SMEs) play a crucial role in economic development and in translating economic growth into improved standards of living; (ii) there is a glaring difference between the dynamic development of SMEs in many Asian countries and their near absence in most African countries; (iii) differences in economic policies are likely to explain a significant part of these differences in SME performance; and, consequently (iv) African countries may be able to draw valuable lessons from the Asian experiences.

The present volume, produced by members of the research team at Stockholm School of Economics, focuses on the special category of countries popularly referred to as 'transition economies'. That is, countries which supposedly are undergoing a comprehensive and fundamental societal transformation, which will bring them from a monolithic society focused on the mobilisation of resources and the control of minds with a view to create an utopian communist society within the frame of a centrally administered economy, to a pluralistic society based on a market economy and the rule of law. It may convincingly be argued that only a handful countries, mainly in East Central Europe are undergoing sufficiently fundamental change to qualify for the epithet transition economies. In China and Vietnam the old political system remains in place as does, at least formally, the socialist ideology. Economic reforms and the introduction of elements of a market economy are not seen as part of an overall societal transformation, as is the case in East Central Europe, but as a necessity to revitalise stagnant economies and achieve economic growth. In the case of Vietnam, it may be argued that economic liberalisation and increased tolerance of private economic agents is officially seen as an expedient, if

---

[1] Formerly the Asian Regional Team for Employment Promotion (ARTEP) and the Jobs and Skills Programme for Africa (JASPA).

1

ideologically somewhat unorthodox, way to move from one stage of socialism to another, materially more advanced, stage of socialism. Reality may of course turn out otherwise, but this does not alter the fact that these countries may at best be termed 'partial transition economies'. The two main transition economies in Africa, Ethiopia and Tanzania, differ from their European, as well as Asian, counterparts by their low level of overall economic and social development. Economies largely based on subsistence agriculture and with low levels of literacy do not easily lend themselves to centralised administration of the economy and the creation of the socialist man. Hence, societal transformation becomes, in a sense, easier. A complete change of the political regime in Ethiopia and, somewhat less pronounced, in Tanzania, also makes them different from China or Vietnam.

However, the fact that the countries under study hardly deserve the epithet of fullfledged transition economies matters little to the studies in this volume.[2] The focus is not on transition economies *per se*, but on the institutional particularities and peculiarities which these economies display. Although in this regard, too, there are large differences between individual countries, the common features are sufficiently prominent to set this group of countries apart.

Within the frame of the overall rationale for the project as outlined above, the conceptual starting point of the present volume is provided by the following beliefs:

- Proliferation and endogenous growth of small and medium scale industries are of fundamental importance for sustainable economic development as well as for efficiently translating growth into enhanced employment opportunities and incomes.

- Small and medium scale industries are particularly dependent upon sound economic policies and a conducive institutional setting. They lack the security inherent in the size of large scale industries as well as the latters' ability to internalise transactions and to exercise pressure on policy makers. At the same time they do not have the possibility of informal micro enterprises to confine their activity to a small and well-known world of neighbourhood customers and to temporarily disappear if the economic and political environment becomes too hostile.

- The institutional setting is as important as the economic regime and macroeconomic policies to a sound development of small and medium scale industries. Hence, the animated discussion on the pros and cons of economic structural adjustment in Africa somewhat misses the point.[3]

---

[2] If the radical nature or speed of reform had been our main concern, Mozambique had arguably been a better choice for inclusion than the two now chosen.

[3] In a truly voluminous literature see, e.g., World Bank (1994) and Stein (1992), the two of which may be seen as representative of the two dominant (and polarised) strands of the debate. For a recent survey of the literature, see Gibbon (1996).

2

While none of the Asian countries provide unqualified success stories with regard to sound and dynamic development of small and medium sized industries, most of them vastly outperform the average African country. Although an examination of the Asian experiences will hardly provide a holy grail, readily applicable on African countries, it is reasonable to assume that such an examination can reveal ingredients for success, which may be generalised and provide valuable lessons for African countries.

The present volume is of course not the first one to propose that Asia and Africa are appropriate objects of study for comparative purposes or that Asia can usefully be held up as a model for African economies to emulate.[4] What is more, we would go along with observers who argue that Africa, in comparison with Asia, has been dealt a weak hand. From a geographical point of view, factors as diverse as lower population densities, which imply higher costs per capita for infrastructure and the like,[5] poorer soils and greater exposure to the adverse effects of tropical climates and disease or a higher incidence of countries being landlocked[6] plausibly add to Africa's burden. The political economy adds further strains as Africa has had more than its share of weak government and bad governance, expressed among other things through widespread systems of patronage, rent seeking and downright destructive entrepreneurship.[7] Under such conditions also those African countries that would seem well-placed to profit from a generous endowment of natural riches easily fall prey to the pitfalls of the so called resource curse.[8]

Accepting the above, in full or in part, is not tantamount to endorsing blanket claims that above all Africa needs to be protected from the real or imagined onslaught of structural adjustment programmes sponsored by the International Monetary Fund or the World Bank. Nor does it necessarily imply an acceptance of the proposition that Africa not only needs good governance and a stronger state, but also would stand to benefit from interventionist or *dirgiste* industrial policies of the type often observed to have been pursued in Asia's successful economies.[9] Rather, there is a range of policy measures that are worthwhile, that do not presuppose the existence of a sophisticated developmental state, and that do not run the risk of resulting in gross allocative inefficiencies. Restricting our attention to one particular sector, that of formal, small scale manufacturing firms, and one generally neglected type of problems they face, ours is of course not a new panacea for changing everything for the better. Giving some thought to this rather restricted domain of inquiry may, however, serve to highlight some of the problems associated with low levels of entrepreneurship and a lack of viable and growing small scale firms.

---

[4] Stein (1995a).
[5] Osmani (1995).
[6] Kamarck (1976); and ADB (1997), pp. 321-333.
[7] For a useful and easily accessible tract on such vices, see Krueger (1993).
[8] Auty (1995), pp. 18-20.
[9] Both propositions of which appear in, e.g., Stein (1995b).

In fact, the past few decades have seen a surge in the importance attached to small and medium scale industries in economic development in Asia and elsewhere. Increased concern for satisfaction of basic needs and equitable growth combined with a disenchantment with the ability of large scale industry to serve as a vehicle for employment and income generation and as a means to alleviate poverty, and a need to relieve agriculture of its traditional role as the primary source of livelihood and perennial employment buffer prompted a search for more employment intensive growth strategies. In Asia, the impressive growth and role of SMEs in Meiji Japan and, later, in Taiwan and Hong Kong provided inspiration for those who argued for a more prominent role for SMEs in economic development. Elsewhere, the dynamic development of SMEs in industrial districts, such as Emilia-Romagna in Italy, Baden-Württemberg in Germany and Northwest Jutland in Denmark, clearly suggested that also in industrially advanced economies small was not only beautiful, but also possible and even desirable.

Small and medium scale industries are seen to have a number of palatable properties.[10] First and foremost of these is their ability to generate employment and incomes, alleviate poverty and contribute towards a more equitable distribution of income. However, while several Asian countries, such as Taiwan and China, provide irrefutable empirical evidence of the impressive capacity of not least rural industries to generate employment and incomes, these attributes need to be qualified. It is not employment *per se*, but the productivity and incomes associated with the employment that is relevant. While the levels of labour income and productivity in SMEs in East Asia generally seem to be well above baseline incomes in agriculture, the picture in South Asia is more mixed. Yet, on balance the importance of SMEs as a means of employment and income generation can hardly be questioned.

Secondly, SMEs permit a geographically more dispersed pattern of industrial development than a reliance on large scale industries would. This is important for several reasons. Given that the geographical mobility of factors of production is imperfect, dispersed industrial development will enhance the degree of utilisation of the available productive resources of the country through improved resource mobilisation. It will also counteract migration to large urban centres and ensuant social and economic problems. Lastly, it creates conditions for a broad based cumulative development through a symbiotic development of agriculture and local industry. A diversification of the local economic base is conducive to agricultural development through improved backward and forward linkages, while a prospering agriculture provides a favourable environment for local industrial development.

Thirdly, it is often argued that SMEs provide a breeding ground for entrepreneurial talent and skills. This argument rests on intuitive reasoning rather than on solid empirical evidence. Yet, it would appear to be rather uncontroversial.

---

[10] de Soto (1989).

The fact that small is not only beautiful, but can also be highly efficient, did for a long time receive surprisingly scant attention. The improved utilisation of productive resources, which is likely to follow from dispersed industrial development, has already been mentioned above. The use of more labour intensive technology and a generally lower capital/labour ratio in SMEs than in large scale manufacturing is clearly more in line with the relative resource endowment and comparative advantages of the developing countries in Asia and Africa. Small scale production is in most instances also more flexible and better able to adapt to changing economic circumstances than large scale production. However, small scale production is by itself no guarantee for flexibility. Managerial competence, sufficiently skilled labour and an efficient flow of information is also needed. Still, by way of summing up, it may be concluded that proliferation and endogenous growth of SMEs are essential ingredients in long term sustainable economic development.

It is no coincidence that the increased attention paid to SMEs in economic development has appeared in tandem with a shift from economic policies favouring import substitution and protection of domestic industry against foreign competition to a policy of export led growth and increased exposure of the domestic economy to external competition. The former policy often went hand in glove with a development strategy based on capital intensive large scale industries and discriminated against SMEs in several ways.[11] Trade regulations were usually discriminatory as large firms were better placed to obtain import permits than small firms. Subsidised credits invariably implied some form of rationing and easier access for large scale industries than for SMEs to credit. Furthermore, investment incentives as a rule also discriminated against small industries as tax incentives and other concessions and subsidies typically were geared to large scale industries. Lastly, government investments in industry were almost invariably in large scale units. Hence, economic liberalisation, deregulation and opening up of the domestic economy to the outside world intuitively worked in favour of SMEs by diminishing discrimination against them.

However, the institutional setting is at least as important as macro-economic policies for a sound development of SMEs through its implications on the transaction costs of small firms.[12] These lack the ability of large scale industries to internalise transactions at the same time as they are in a weaker position to search for information, enforce contracts and property rights and protect themselves against rent seeking and predatory behaviour based on might. At the same time they do not have the possibility of informal micro enterprises to reduce transaction costs and protect property rights by confining their activity to the immediate neighbourhood and withdraw if the economic and political environment becomes too threatening. The institutional setting, that is the set of effective rules within which economic agents act, has a strong bearing on transaction costs. Well-

---

[11] Eloquently and persuasively covered by Osmani (1995).

[12] For a full discussion see Chapter Three.

defined, impartial and universal rules designed to facilitate protection of property rights and to provide a legal and normative framework for market transactions can go a long way towards reducing transaction costs, not least for SMEs.[13]

Seen against this backdrop, the flourishing informal sector in many African countries may be interpreted as symptoms of profound institutional weaknesses, rather than, as has often been the case, a promising source of employment and income generation and proof of entrepreneurial spirit in general. The near absence of formal SMEs and the poor record of graduation from informal to formal and of endogenous enterprise growth only serve to reinforce this interpretation of the informal sector. Institutional restructuring as a prerequisite for sound economic development attains a crucial importance and may go a long way to explain why singular focus on structural adjustment in the narrow sense of economic policy change has frequently failed to deliver the expected results, not least in Africa.

The experiences of the transition economies highlight the supreme importance of institutional change as part and parcel of the transformation from command to market economy. Indeed, there is a sound empirical basis for suggesting that successful institutional change is proving to be a *sine qua non* to the success of the societal transformation as a whole. This should not come as a surprise. The institutional setting of the classical socialist command economies could hardly be more inimical to market based economic development. The absence of rule of law combined with a refusal to recognise private property rights (except in its most limited form), horizontal economic contacts between economic agents and the assignment of but the most peripheral role to market and prices, resulted in very high transaction costs for economic activities outside the plan.

It is against this background that the focus on the two main transition economies in Africa should be seen. They are examined against the backdrop of the experiences of four Asian countries - China, Taiwan, India and Vietnam - each of which has a unique story to tell. China and Vietnam, provide interesting case studies as they have, at least so far, managed to combine market economic reforms with growth despite seemingly modest restructuring of the institutional setting. In the case of China this performance is all the more remarkable as the economic growth has to a large extent been spearheaded by SMEs. India, too, is in the midst of a process of deregulation, liberalisation and reduced direct government involvement in the economy. However, in the case of India, this structural adjustment takes place against a backdrop of a long tradition of strong overt, if not always very effective, government support to small scale industries. The case of Taiwan is interesting as a classical success story, in which the government has played anything but a passive role.

The present volume thus approaches the Asian experiences and the African record to date with regard to SME development by combining the insights provided by transaction costs economics with a thorough understanding of the nature

---

[13] This is not to deny the importance of other factors, such as a high level of literacy and education, efficient transportation and communications, to transaction costs.

of socialist command economies and the problems associated with their transformation into market economies.[14] The individual country experiences are described and analysed with a view to identify transactional inefficiencies and their impact on small scale manufacturing enterprises. As well as devoting attention to existing obstacles to the establishment and growth of small scale industry, this volume also points to some lessons that can be learnt with respect to possible ways and means available to individual firms and policy makers to overcome existing impediments. In particular, the need for, and successes and tribulations often associated with, thorough institutional adjustment are detailed at some length.

Apart from the introductory chapter, the volume is composed of six in-depth country studies; China and Taiwan in Chapter Four, Vietnam and India in Chapter Five, Ethiopia in Chapter Six and Tanzania in Chapter Seven. These studies are built around core concepts and ideas derived from a discussion of the institutions typical of, if not necessarily singular to, socialist economies (Chapter Two) and the specific transactional characteristics of small scale enterprises (Chapter Three). As such, the research reported here is primarily concerned with a reinterpretation of existing scholarship. Yet, the case studies are informed by direct personal experiences on part of the authors and editors with and in the individual countries under study. The main lines of the picture emerging from the case studies and the lessons that may be drawn from them are outlined in the concluding chapter.

---

[14] Apart from the present volume, a number of working papers and other studies were also produced under the project, viz.: Teshome Mulat (1994), *Institutional Reform, Macroeconomic Policy Change and the Development of Small-Scale Industries in Ethiopia*, Working Paper Series in Economics and Finance No. 23, Stockholm School of Economics; Sara Johansson and Per Ronnås (1995) *Rural Industrialization: A Review of Selected Asian Experiences*, Working Paper Series in Economics and Finance No. 46, Stockholm School of Economics; Kristina Kurths (1995), *Private Small Scale Industries in Vietnam: Development Environment and Empirical Results*, Working Paper Series in Economics and Finance No. 57, Stockholm School of Economics; Mboya Bagachwa (1994), *Small-Scale Industries in Asian and African Transition Economies: The Case of Tanzania*, manuscript; Xiaomin Pang (1995), *Linkages, Agglomeration Economics and Rural Industrialization: Industrial Districts in China*, manuscript.

2 Institutional adjustment: reforming the developing socialist economy

Örjan Sjöberg

Introduction

'Centrally planned economies', Polish economist Jan Winiecki once argued, 'are going to remain *permanently developing countries* (PDCs) severely constrained in their attempt to return to the normal pattern of development'.[1] Whether because of 'micro level import substitution',[2] and hence the inability to derive benefits from the division of labour and economies of scale, or for reasons associated with allocative inefficiencies created by a system characterised by administrative pricing, soft budget constraints and chronic shortages,[3] the result has been little short of disastrous. Also economies that started out from an advanced position soon found that they were rapidly falling behind their peers. The emergence elsewhere of the Newly Industrialised Economies served to highlight this precarious situation, as did the increasing inability to meet reasonable expectations for improving standards of living at home. If not earlier, then at least by the late 1980s it had become abundantly clear also to the leaders of many of the socialist economies that traditionally conceived precepts led nowhere.

As a result, half a decade or so later few centrally planned economies remain. Although the immediate reasons for their disappearance, and the dispatch by which they have been relegated to the dustbin of history, differ, the effect has been a movement towards the market. The same is true of a number of states that attempted the transition to socialism, but never managed to implement central planning in full before they had run up against the imperatives of economic development.

Instead, marketisation, liberalisation and privatisation have come to dominate an agenda which once was dedicated to socialist ends. By encouraging a more efficient allocation of resources, based on scarcity pricing, and the removal of monopolies former centrally planned economies hope to achieve a decisive move away from central planning. Privatisation is usually seen as integral to this process, as property rights have to be redesigned with reduced transaction costs in mind. Expectations are that, as a result, incentives will become conducive to achieving eco-

---

[1] Winiecki (1989), p. 380; emphasis in the original.
[2] Ibid. p. 366.
[3] Kornai (1980), and (1992).

9

nomic growth and that the structure of the economy will change in a favourable direction. This is as true of the structure of industries as of the configuration of enterprises sizes, the current status of both of which are widely regarded as hampering sound economic development.

The transition from a command to a market economy, however, is fraught with difficulties and uncertainty. Not only is there, despite occasional claims to the contrary, no generally accepted theory laying out the particulars of the transition; views also differ with regard to the desired end result. At best, there are a number of insights derived from normative theories pertaining to existing industrialised economies, as tempered by the track record of the early movers.[4]

Nowhere is this more apparent than in societies that also have to contend with all the ordinary problems that we have come to associate with the least developed economies. It can be argued that countries such as China, Ethiopia, Tanzania and Vietnam - not to speak of those also ravaged by domestic strife during most of their existence as independent states, such as Angola and Mozambique - have been particularly hard hit by ill-conceived economic policies. As a result, they invariably face a formidable challenge. Standard recipes on how to run, let alone create, a market economy may not apply, and there is precious little leeway in trying out a new model. Problems relating to the sheer survival often need to be urgently solved, while at the same time resources are extremely thin on the ground.

It is against the above background that the value of assessing the experience of the relatively successful among formerly socialist economies attempting the transition to a market economy becomes clear. After all, there may be lessons to be learnt, both in terms of positive examples to follow and misguided policies to be avoided rather than repeated. To this end, this chapter tries to highlight the reasons for lacklustre performance on part of centrally planned economies, and the implications for reform. Setting out from some general insights regarding obstacles to economic development inherent in the centrally planned economy, the aim is not only to provide for a background for the case studies to follow but also to identify useful foci for these studies.

The section immediately below provides the background. Ideological imperatives and the consequences of production and investment planning as typically conceived are briefly outlined. The next section reviews the case for structural adjustment in reforming (formerly) socialist economies, noting in particular the need to forestall (or do something about) high levels of inflation. It is argued, however, that the importance of macro-economic stability extends beyond keeping economic aggregates in check. It is as much a question of credibility, towards which end structural adjustment is but one step. The penultimate section therefore addresses the exigency of institutional adjustment, arguing that the lowering of transaction costs is as important to the success of reform as are the more frequently voiced concerns about production costs not properly reflecting comparative advantage.

---

[4] E.g., Åslund (1994).

10

Ideological imperatives and the logic of planning

Socialist economies have often been seen as a world apart. Listings of the distinguishing features of socialist economies, not least those among developing countries, abound. State control of the commanding heights of the economy, and possibly the nationalisation of land and strategic industries to go with it, is one such trait frequently identified. A heavy presence of the public sector in domestic wholesaling and foreign trade is another. Yet others could easily be added.

The very existence of such compendia of traits points to the difficulty of reaching an agreement as to what a socialist economy is. This no doubt reflects attempts to reconcile self-description on part of governments and ruling parties, the use of 'socialism' both as an ideological and social science concept, and conflicts over the essence of the term as used in political discourse or the social sciences. Even so, most observers would agree that central planning/management of the economy, or an attempt to introduce it, is part of the picture. The primacy of political objectives over narrowly economic ones is another, the substitution of direct bureaucratic control of markets to coordinate economic activities being a typical outcome at least in the so called classical socialist system.

Indeed, the classical socialist system is seen as embodying all of these traits. This is true irrespective of whether it is viewed as a historically given manifestation - for which the Soviet Union of the late 1930s or early 1950s would be the prototype - or as an ideal model in the sense employed by Max Weber (but again based on the experience of historically existing centrally planned economies). As such, it is arguably the most frequently used point of departure for analysis. Later 'versions', or the impact of contingent factors including national and historical specificity, provide for considerable variation, but may for most purposes be seen as deviations (but not necessarily aberrations) from the Soviet experience or the ideal model.[5] This is the cue taken here.

More specifically, the classical model is seen as having a number of fundamental characteristics, partly derived from considerations not immediately associated with issues of economics. The resulting system, developed around normative propositions on how the world ought to be ruled, tends to give rise to a host of intended and unintended consequences. This is not least true of the economy, and these consequences are well-known and widely accepted to conform to the notion of a 'shortage economy'.[6]

Following Kornai's seminal *The Socialist System*, where both the classical model and the resulting shortage economy have been most effectively and thoroughly outlined, the system rests upon a particular combination of the structure of power, ideology, property and coordination mechanisms.[7] Power refers to the one party

---

[5] Conversely, should modifications or anomalies no longer make the classical model useful as a heuristic device or a point of reference, that is, should shortages no longer make themselves felt, then the socialist nature of the economy can at least for analytical purposes be called in doubt.

[6] Kornai (1979), and (1980).

[7] Kornai (1992), Part Two, esp. Chapters 3-6.

state and its monopolistic or near-monopolistic claim to political and ideological control of society. Ideology can be seen as a codification of values that shape the world outlook of those in power or, at times and somewhat more modestly, the values and promises alluded to in trying to legitimise the existing order. Property takes its forms partly in response to power and ideology: power, because of the need to vest control with the ruling party; ideology, because it provides the rationale for state ownership and control. 'The nature of political power, the prevailing ideology, and the property relations', Kornai maintains, 'determine jointly the part (or at least the main feature of the role) that various coordination mechanisms can play in society',[8] each conceivable such mechanism coordinating the various economic activities of individuals, groups of individuals or organisations in society. In the socialist economy, coordination is typically conducted by recourse to administrative decision making.

'Direct bureaucratic coordination' is thus the key means to the ideologically and politically motivated ends of the classical socialist system. Under this system, the preferred mode of management, usually referred to as 'centralised planning', is made up by a number of institutions and procedural norms handed down from Soviet experience, including administrative pricing, money as a mere accounting unit in production, full bureaucratic control over entry and exit, procedures of investment allocation, and so forth. Only a few select areas are to some extent intentionally left open to influences of 'the law of value', that is, market allocation and scarcity pricing, the demand side of markets for consumer goods and labour at times being among them.

While planning and direct bureaucratic coordination are buttressed by concerns of power and ideology, for analytical purposes it is nevertheless useful to distinguish these concepts from the strategy of development. The latter can be thought of as being derived from ideological considerations (e.g., the promise to develop fast) and reinforced by the behavioural norms of the preferred system of coordination.[9] It includes a proclivity for high levels of investment (and correspondingly low levels of consumption), a specific set of sectoral priorities, some of which are derived from the thinking of the founding fathers, others from the exigencies of the moment, and an inclination to make use of opportunities for resource mobilisation rather than productivity growth.[10]

Hence, for the purposes of the volume of which this chapter is a part it is important to note that beyond bureaucratic coordination of the economy, common denominators of socialist economies also include a strategy of development based on various degrees of self-reliance. Although but seldom taken to conceivable

---

[8] Ibid., p. 91.

[9] Ibid., pp. 160-63. It should be noted, however, that Kornai (1992) explicitly eschews the term 'growth strategy' to describe this phenomenon. This is done on grounds of it not being a strategy (which would imply conscious choice); rather 'the elements of conscious choice in forced growth are diluted with spontaneous, concomitant phenomena, and even trends that develop in spite of the leadership's wishes' (p. 197).

[10] Ibid., p. 197.

extremes, self-reliance is often pursued with autarky in mind and invariably translates into strict import substitution at the national level. As a result socialist economies are often characterised by many of the traits usually associated with import substitution, such as low (or negative) real interest rates and financial repression, overvalued currencies and foreign exchange rationing, inappropriately high levels of capital intensity and, inadvertently, a heavy dependence on imports of raw materials and intermediate goods - only more so, the cynic might add, than the average import substituting non-socialist economy.

Import substitution, as Osmani has cogently argued,[11] does not in and of itself necessarily discriminate against small scale industrial enterprises. Some policies intended to support import substitution may be of a discriminating nature, however, and the above list of characteristics are indicative of what this may entail. Under normal circumstances many of these adverse effects could perhaps be avoided, but in the classical socialist economy the existence of ideology decisively shifts the balance in favour of larger units. Both by asserting the superiority of large scale, capital intensive plants - market size, the major constraint to returns to scale, is after all not considered an obstacle[12] - and in setting sectoral priorities import substitution has tended to be accompanied by policies discriminating against small scale enterprises.

Ironically, the adopted mode of economic management has much the same effect, but at the level of the enterprise or plant. In order to ensure that the enterprise, and its ability to fulfil assigned plans, is not made hostage to shortages, inhouse production is much preferred to having to rely on external suppliers of goods and producer services. A proliferation of ancillary and auxiliary activities is often observed - Winiecki's micro level import substitution, or 'do-it-yourself-bias', alluded to in the opening paragraph of this chapter - as is the hoarding of factor and other inputs. As a consequence, whereas considerations of the impact of linkage effects and a strong belief in economies of scale have typically prompted socialist governments to opt for the establishment of large scale production units, the manner in which planning operates has served to erode or prevent precisely these linkage effects and the reaping of returns to scale.

Combining such unintended consequences with an appreciation of the imperatives inherent in any attempt to monitor and plan it is easy to see why the enterprise structure under the classical socialist model has led to a domination of large scale enterprises - without, therefore, being able to enhance productivity. It is also easy to recognise the rigors such economies have in meeting consumer demand.

---

[11] Osmani (1995).

[12] Nor are other obstacles such as transportation costs (often heavily subsidised) or customer preferences, the latter of which is often a major consideration when choosing to locate close to markets.

Economic and political environment during reform

Although the classical model has not outlived its usefulness as a starting point or a heuristic device, it no longer exists as an empirical fact, save perhaps for in North Korea. Early on several socialist countries started experimenting with less rigid models of central planning, some of them giving up a considerable part of previously centralised economic decision making to the market. The experiences of early reformers such as Hungary, Poland and Yugoslavia stand out, while the concessions granted to the so-called non-state sector (i.e., those enterprises and collectives not under central planning) in China by the mid-1980s emerged as the perhaps most powerful shift yet to appear within a basically unaltered political framework.

With the notable exception of the Asian socialist countries and Cuba, by the late 1980s reformers and laggards alike had reached the point where the domestic political order no longer could be maintained. The reasons for this need not detain us here, but the consequences were far-reaching. Central planning was given up, reluctantly in some places, more decisively in others, some of the reformers no doubt helped by the fact that under the pressure of lacklustre performance their economies had started dismantling themselves from within.[13]

As this happened, some of the characteristic features of the shortage economy reasserted themselves or took on a new appearance. Whereas political change may have been quick to materialise in many of the formerly socialist polities, this was nowhere the case with respect to the economy. Also under ideal circumstances, economies need a set of organisational structures and supporting institutions - formal rules and informal norms - which are not easily introduced overnight. Furthermore, not only does it take time to put new institutions in place, pre-existing organisational frameworks, old practices and other legacies of the centrally planned past are not readily removed. Rather, resilience is to be expected even if previous regulatory frameworks can be abrogated with the stroke of a pen or at least a vote in parliament.[14] Not surprisingly, the more entrenched direct bureaucratic coordination was, the harder to abolish it.

One such resilient feature which, as events came to pass, proved critical to the early post-planning era was the monetary overhang frequently developed under central planning. This typically helped to reinforce the processes that created the shortage economy in the first place. As reforms were now initiated, repressed inflation came out in the open, additionally fuelled in many an instance by drastic shortfalls of government revenue (partly due to its reliance on transfer of profits from state owned enterprises) and hence increasing budget deficits. This was made worse for the pressure put on the budget by enterprises nurtured on soft budget

---

[13] As one would indeed expect, if one were to subscribe to the widely held view that '[t]he germs of collapse had been embedded in the socialist economic systems at their very inception,' with the economic crisis of the mature centrally planned economy being 'the terminal stage of a process of gradual deterioration' (Major 1994, p. 322).

[14] Kornai (1995a), and (1995b).

14

constraints and the need to institute social safety nets where none previously existed or were the responsibility of now ailing enterprises. In fact, much of the debate on the contents, sequencing and not least speed of reforms in formerly socialist countries has focused on the measures made necessary by this highly destabilising situation.[15]

As a result of this experience with inflation - whether as inherited or as created anew - it is somewhat besides the point to argue that several transition economies would have done well to emulate China's guarded approach to economic reform. Being gradual and piecemeal, with a notable element of experimentation, it has proved very successful without having to contend with the immediate and easily seen social costs often associated with a radical break with the past. Critically, China has had a clear advantage, or so Sachs and Woo argue, in that the heavily subsidised sectors made up a rather small portion of the economy.[16]

Much the same could be said to apply to most of the less developed among the formerly centrally planned economies. Even so, also with a benevolent situation with respect to the structure of the economy prevailing as they set out to reform, many of them have come to experience high levels of inflation, while China did not. It has been argued by McKinnon that this, rather than the possibility of China being inherently more successful at preventing falling government revenues or heavy borrowing from the state banking system, is largely due to a high level of households savings in the Chinese economy.[17] Perkins, for his part, points out that at least initially China did run a balanced budget and had accumulated little foreign debt. In addition, he notes, China, having realigned its trade already in the 1960s, was not forced to act on the basis of a rapidly disintegrating trading system.[18]

Be that as it may, the experience to date points to macro-economic balance, rather than an optimal sequence of reforms *per se*, as the constraining factor. Irrespective of whether reforms have been gradual, as in China, or radical it is probably fair to say that once in the quandary of high levels of inflation, there are few options but to stabilise the economy.[19] Without it, domestic liberalisation of the economy, opening up to the outside world of trade and investment, the intro-duction of new institutions and so forth will be to little avail no matter how well-conceived. Examples abound. Not only have those among the formerly centrally

---

[15] In what has increasingly become something of a caricature, two schools of thought are often iden-tified: 'gradualism' and 'shock therapy'. A good introduction is provided by the uncharacteristically civilised exchange of arguments in Brada (1993); and Murrell (1993).

[16] Sachs and Woo (1994); also Woo (1994). Having such an advantage does of course not invalidate the Chinese experience. This type of reform is clearly feasible (Brus 1993, pp. 439-40), but not neces-sarily replicable. Yet, it is the contention of the present author that lessons can be drawn from its track record, if not actually 'transferred'.

[17] McKinnon (1994).

[18] Perkins (1994), pp. 180-82. A further advantage was the labour intensive nature of Asian agricul-ture, maintained throughout much of China during the post-war period, making it easier to revert to family based farming.

[19] Recent theoretical work appears to bear this out (e.g., Friedman and Johnson 1995), as do several empirical investigations, including Åslund et al. (1996); and de Melo and Gelb (1996).

planned economies which have been successful in maintaining macro stability, or else have achieved it following early bouts of hyperinflation, typically done better than those which have not been able to contain inflation.[20] Cases also exist where institutional reform has failed to take off until macro-economic stability has been attained. Vietnam is a case in point, where agricultural reforms and foreign investment legislation not dissimilar from that of China were on the books for a number of years before they made an impact - which they did once inflation had been brought down from close to 700, and later a more modest 200+ per cent a year, to about 30 per cent.[21]

Inflation, overvalued currencies and current account deficits inducing governments to introduce administrative measures on foreign exchange allocation all have, as do several other expressions of untoward macro-economic policy, implications for small scale enterprises. For the most part, they are less likely to cope than are their large scale counterparts. But it would appear that there is more to the recent experience of reforming socialist economies than this.

As is well-known, inflation can have considerable corrosive effects on rational decision making through the volatility and obscurity it brings to the price signals that are the heart of the market process. Macro-economic stability on the other hand is likely to introduce a measure of confidence in the economy, thereby making life simpler for economic agents. Indications are, however, that this may not be enough.[22] Uncertainty regarding the designs of government, and its ability and willingness to interfere does not necessarily disappear simply because it gets its act together with respect to relevant economic aggregates. Similarly, while macro-economic stabilisation and structural adjustment programmes may help 'get the prices right', many of the former centrally planned economies have to make prices matter in the first place. This is largely a question of disposing of the institutions and procedures that nurture the shortage economy. But getting rid of past practices is not identical to replacing them with markets, regulations, norms and attitudes conducive to future growth. And, as argued up to this point, while the record to date suggests that this process is much enhanced by sound macro policies, such policies alone will not guarantee the emergence of a rational set of institutions to replace those discarded. In short, macro-economic stability is a necessary but not sufficient condition; institutional adjustment is also a component crucial to the success of reform in formerly centrally planned economies.

---

[20] E.g., Åslund (1994). The implication of this observation, that stabilisation was necessary and on balance beneficial, stands in stark contrast to the view, common among critics of 'shock therapy' (e.g., Schmieding 1993; and Rosati 1994) that stabilisation may actively contribute to the recession experience by many countries in the early stages of transition. Although quite possibly the case, governments most seriously pursuing stabilisation remain those which have performed the best with respect not only to inflation but also growth, incomes and unemployment.

[21] E.g., Wood (1989); and Drabek (1990).

[22] E.g., Weingast (1993); and Brunetti and Weder (1994).

Institutional adjustment and transaction costs

What makes institutional adjustment critical is the fact that the set of regulations that comes with bureaucratic coordination and central planning does not provide an enabling environment for economic activities. The track record shows that this was already the case under the orthodox economic order - after all, the classical precepts for a socialist economy were mostly given up before long and reforms instituted - but it becomes still more compelling as a move away from a command economy is being made. This is so on several counts, the most basic of which is the lingering influence of a number of institutions generic to central planning as exercised in the economies under consideration here. Most of these institutions share the quality of contributing to high transaction costs. Some do so on account of being removed from the context where they previously served a purpose, others were an impediment to development all along.

Transaction costs, which may be defined as the costs of operating in the market, are inherently a part of any exchange of goods and services. Information asymmetries, lack of perfect foresight and the existence of moral hazards invariably translate into risk and uncertainty. As information comes at a cost, economic agents can only be expected to remain boundedly rational. The institutional setting within which economic agents operate can be more or less conducive to the reduction of transaction costs, however. Faced with a high level of such costs, entrepreneurs may try their hand at developing mitigating strategies much in the same way as they strive for the lowering of direct costs of production. But, as with production costs, entrepreneurs face a set of institutions, and hence transaction costs, that are given at least for the short term. And while their cost reducing strategies may prove beneficial to society at large - that is, yielding positive externalities - chances are that their preferred game plans or ploys are only limitedly helpful or rational. Conversely, organisational structures, procedures, formal rules and informal norms external to the entrepreneur and her or his immediate sphere of influence may help reduce the risks and uncertainty inherent in market operations.

If so, then there is some scope for proactive policies in this regard. At the very least, a strong case can be made for the need of reviewing current practices, legal provisions and societal norms with a view of smoothing the way for business transactions. Setting out from the combined insights of transaction costs economics[23] and Kornai's analysis of the shortage economy, a number of transaction cost increasing traits of the centrally planned economy will be identified. The resilience of individual features in face of the attempted transition to a market economy may differ, as it may also differ between countries struggling to implement thorough reform. The transition itself may create new obstacles to the aspiring entrepreneur. But the enumeration should go a considerable way towards detailing and specify-

---

[23] As codified in works by, e.g., Williamson (1975), and (1985); North (1981), and (1990); Eggertsson (1990) and kindred theorists.

ing the nature of transaction costs in the formerly centrally planned economy. As such, it will serve as a point of departure for the case studies to follow in Chapters Four to Eight.

At its most fundamental, the major drawback of the classical or reformed model of central planning with respect to transaction costs is its predilection for instrumentalism and discretion in policy implementation. The structure of power and nature of ideology have conspired to push aside the rule of law in favour of, as the Chinese put it, 'the rule of man'. Any legal provision may be disregarded, should the representatives of the one party state consider it convenient or necessary. Since the separation of constitutional powers is inadequate or absent, there is no organisational unit outside the ruling party charged with the task of maintaining a semblance of legality; at least, there is no one in possession of the power needed to do so, unless done at the behest of the ruling elite.

This is of some consequence, not least in view of the fact that the lack of universal rules and an independent judiciary to enforce those rules make for high levels of uncertainty at every turn of the business transaction - from contact to contract and control.[24] In short, because of a low level of 'institutional efficiency'[25] the enforcement of contracts is as problematic and fraught with uncertainty as the chance of third part encroachment is real.

Furthermore, the fact that direct bureaucratic coordination implies that economic decisions are taken in the offices of bureaucrats rather than in the market place also has a negative effect on the workings of the economy. Besides the well-known outcome as far as allocative efficiency is concerned, the level and structure of transaction costs facing economic agents are likely to be higher than need be. Central planning is built around vertical links at the expense of lateral ones. One consequence of this organisational feature is the risk for information overload at the centre, yet the centre as likely as not will feel severely constrained by a lack of appropriate information from which to proceed with the planning of production.[26] At all levels the system is replete with incentives and opportunities for shirking. Indeed, as Major puts it, 'the ways and means of processing, withholding, and utilising information in a command economy have always been among the most essential areas of the "power game" between the rulers and the ruled'.[27] This state of affairs is particularly troubling as, in the absence of competition, and hence in the absence of a restraint prompted by the need to build and maintain a reputation, moral hazard is given a free rein. As a result, although in the absence of markets vertical integration has much to commend for it - this, after all, is the trade-off central to the choice between markets or hierarchies - USSR, Inc., is obviously

---

[24] To paraphrase Nooteboom et al. (1992), p. 141.

[25] To use the terms favoured by Major (1994) to distinguish macro level characteristics from transaction costs arising from the transactional particulars of an exchange at the micro level (in particular as regards informational asymmetry and the effects of property rights).

[26] The standard description of investment and production planning of a Soviet type, its problems and the measures taken to rectify the problems encountered, is provided by Nove (1986).

[27] Major (1994), p. 322.

going several steps too far.

It is not easily remedied, however. Although marketisation is the obvious answer, lateral, or horizontal, links between enterprises are as a rule under-developed. Sources of information on potential trading partners are therefore, as reformers have come to realise, few and the habits of surveying existing and potential markets are a novelty to managers nurtured in a supply restrained econo-my. Search and other transaction costs are high, and may reach such heights so as to impede entrepreneurial efforts altogether. The changing nature of the allocation of factors of production, and then not only in markets for capital and labour but also land and physical infrastructure, is also likely to confound economic agents. As with input and output markets, the transition from shortages to demand con-straints under competition puts a premium on a new range of talents, and on the organisational and institutional structures to support them.

For all of the obstacles created during the transition, these changes of course also offer prospective merchants and industrialists plenty of new opportunities; daring entrepreneurs will often find the rewards alluring. Niche markets are easily identified where new needs arise or where state owned enterprises are incapable of entering - or never bothered to. As many learn to their regret, however, without the appropriate regulatory framework little can be achieved on a sustained basis. Legislation guiding entry and exit in markets, forms of governance, sanctions and enforcement of contracts, and so forth, are not seldom found wanting or non-existent.

Existing informal institutions, that is, norms and codes of behaviour, may serve as workable substitutes, but again experience suggests that this cannot be taken for granted. For a start, also informal institutions take time to evolve and come into their own. And even though new appropriate informal institutions may answer widely felt needs, there is little to suggest that they will be optimal. Rather, strategies such as networking and relational contracting, not seldom relying on bonds of kinship or ethnicity, derive their strength from being exclusive and small. In such a setting the parties to an agreement may enjoy the benefits of conditions conducive to minimising moral hazard and free riding, the monitoring of progress and ease of contract enforcement. However, the fact that they are based on particularistic rather than generalised trust does impose a considerable constraint upon the usefulness of such institutional development.[28] To use Casson's line of reasoning, they are characteristic of societies with a 'low-trust culture', while in a 'high-trust culture' transaction cost reducing institutions and sentiments permeate society at large.[29]

---

[28] Platteau (1994a), and (1994b).

[29] Casson (1991), p. 12. In fact, Casson goes one step further, suggesting that 'the extensive reliance on law, and on the view that competition is the only real safe-guard against being cheated over price' (p. 12) is indicative of a low trust society. The economy would be better served by norms, the superi-ority of which as compared to a monitoring system 'is that it turns to advantage the natural infor-mation asymmetry which is the cause of the difficulty in monitoring' (p. 17). Put differently, it is better to rely on a mechanism under which 'people punish themselves for anti-social behaviour, rather

Instead, in the vacuum created between legitimate, but overly uncertain or risky, business deals and traditional forms of economic governance, opportunities for rent seeking may arise. Indeed, rent seeking and directly unproductive profit seeking (DUP) activities thrive in such an environment. This is especially so if unsuccessful macro policies have maintained or reinforced distortions introduced in the past through central planning, or created them anew. Opportunities for unproductive, even destructive, ventures are ample and chances are that lobbying for preferential treatment, such as licenses or access to government resources, will pay off handsomely. In an environment characterised by a low level of institutional efficiency and hence high transaction costs, the probability that such innovative unproductive operations will work out more favourably to individual economic agents than honest entrepreneurial activities are not to be ignored.

On a perhaps not as pessimistic, but still troubling, note, recent literature on the reasons for the existence of informal or micro enterprises identifies transaction costs - stemming from information asymmetries, market failures, government policies and regulations - as a possible root cause.[30] Seen as an organisational response to high costs of operating in the market, informal status and small size both have distinct advantages. This is as true of the hiring of labour as the ability to solve problems of management, including not only the monitoring of production but also organisation and marketing. As long as the informational advantages of informal status and small size are not compensated for by returns to size, one should not expect entrepreneurs to opt for formal recognition or, for that matter, that informal enterprises will 'graduate' to formal or large size entities.[31]

All of the above is illustrative of the need to move beyond debates over the pros and cons of structural adjustment programmes, or gradualism and shock treatment. Although macro-economic issues are obviously important, also transaction costs do have a rightful claim to our attention. This is in particular true of economies in transition from central planning to a market economy. However, this must not be construed as a question of either or. The structure of transaction costs is closely linked to sound macro-economic management. Not only does inflation add to uncertainty, but new transaction cost reducing institutions suited for normalcy will only be accepted should there be a widely felt need for them.[32] Else they may well be turned on their head and used for other purposes, such as rent seeking and DUP activities, in the process becoming discredited with adverse consequences for their

---

than relying on a third party, such as the legal system, to do it for them. The moral mechanism turns people into self-monitoring agents and so avoids the costs of external monitoring' (p. 17).

[30] Fafchamps (1994), pp. 6-14.

[31] As a consequence of this line of reasoning, and although there are sound practical reasons to apply the criterion of size (e.g., Ngwira 1995), for the purposes of this project we favour legal approval and registration as the distinguishing traits separating the formal from the informal enterprise. For, even though size and legal status often go hand in hand, the latter and not the former is the more likely to decide the nature and magnitude of transaction costs facing the individual enterprise.

[32] This proposition does not represent an unquestioning acceptance of the framework proposed by North (1990). Rather, our formulation stops short of the supposition that transaction cost mitigating institutions arise in response to high transaction costs as surely as night follows day.

future efficacy. This would be especially detrimental against the background that we might expect that some transaction costs may rise substantially, and perhaps to forbidding levels, as central planning is discarded in favour of the market.

Concluding remarks

Whereas there is no denying the usefulness of macro-economic stabilisation, which is often a necessary but not sufficient condition for a successful transition from a command to a market economy, this chapter has also identified some of the institutional biases inherent in central planning which have to be contended with. This in turn points to the need to specify existing and potential sources of high transaction costs, and how these are best mitigated or avoided. Also in the case of African (formerly) socialist economies it would seem most useful to move beyond the debate over the advantages and adverse effects of structural adjustment programmes.

The emphasis in subsequent chapters will be on the challenges facing those economies in promoting the growth of the perhaps most severely neglected part of the socialist economy (besides agriculture, that is), namely the small scale industrial sector. This is of considerable consequence, since it is widely held that the promotion of small scale industry represents an untapped opportunity - indeed forms the backbone of a viable development strategy - for the average developing economy. Given the inherited structure of enterprises by industry and size, small scale enterprises would also appear to offer some of the best opportunities to successfully making the transition from a command to a market economy.

3 Small industries and institutional framework: a transaction costs approach

Bhargavi Ramamurthy

Introduction

It has been established beyond doubt that small industries are *sine qua non* to the overall industrial development of any country. The major arguments in favour of small industries range from employment generation to their unmatched sensitivity to the discipline of the market. This range covers all attributes of collective efficiency,[1] entrepreneurial innovation,[2] flexibility,[3] labour intensive production,[4] and better exploitation of networks.[5] Starting from a general premise that small is beautiful, the next important task is that of helping them thrive in a world of varying industrial organisations and institutions. Whether small firms perform well or not and, more importantly, whether they yield prospects for economic and socially viable development, is largely a question of how they are organised and within what political and institutional setting they operate.[6] The institutional framework, particularly in the developing countries, has become an important focus of recent writings on small industry with de Soto's analysis of institutional constraints providing a useful point of departure.[7] Williamson argues that differences in the institutional environment are likely to be most important for explaining international and inter-temporal differences in organisational arrangements.[8] Much of the literature in this area is set in an economic environment of a mixed economy, more particularly the private small businesses operating in response to market signals in general with varying degrees of governmental regulation.[9] Continuing with the mainstream, analysis of the institutional framework can be done in two ways depending on the particular focus: the institutional

---

[1] Schmitz (1990).
[2] E.g., see ILO (1974); Pernia and Pernia (1986); Baumol (1988); and Ray (1990).
[3] See Piore and Sabel (1984); Schmitz (1989); Berry and Mazumdar (1991); Rasmussen et al. (1992); Pedersen et al. (1994); and van Dijk (1995).
[4] See Anderson (1982).
[5] See Sengenberger and Pyke (1991).
[6] Späth (1992).
[7] de Soto (1989).
[8] Williamson (1993).
[9] For a picture of the situation under central planning, see Ben-Ner and Neuberger (1988).

framework that is conducive to small enterprise operations; and the growth constraints to small enterprises and the institutional arrangements that can help overcome such obstacles, the latter approach being more dynamic than the former one. The present chapter, however, chooses a more eclectic approach, to incorporate factors, developed over time, that influence behaviour of small firms in addition to factors that in general are conducive to the proper functioning of small enterprises.

It is widely believed that small enterprises enjoy various advantages owing to their size, flexibility being one of these, but it is also recognised that they suffer from disadvantages precisely for reasons of being small. At this juncture then, it is necessary to distinguish between the disadvantages, especially cost disadvantages, arising out of their inability to utilise the economies of scale and those arising due to high transaction costs. The main argument for lack of economies of scale is the existence of indivisibilities in production, which yields 'threshold costs'.[10] Transaction costs come into the picture as and when they alter these threshold costs and place the small firm at an advantageous or disadvantageous position. The main purpose of this chapter is to identify this relationship between transaction costs, institutions and size of firms and point to the institutional factors that affect the direction of change of transaction costs, that is, the factors that increase or decrease transaction costs to small firms.

The remainder of this chapter is organised as follows: the next section contains the basic concepts of institutions and transaction costs and their relationship; the penultimate section contains the dynamics of small industry and its linkages with the institutional framework; and the concluding section draws the threads together.

Institutions, transaction costs and their relationship

Defining institutions and transaction costs

Firms choose a particular organisational form, but the political, social, legal and economic system within which firms make those choices is exogenous to them. Economies or nations determine the structure of rights or the 'rules of the game' in which individual economic actors make choices.[11] Put differently, the nature of the institutions and coordination mechanisms that make up the economic environment affects the choice of firms' organisational structure.[12] As a result, the institutional setting within which small firms operate becomes a crucial factor in ensuring economic efficiency of small scale production. Following neo-institutionalist economics, institutions can be defined as rules, both formal rules (such as statutes) and informal ones (such as norms), that constrain behaviour.[13] As the theory is con-

---

[10] Nooteboom (1993).
[11] Scully (1988).
[12] Ben-Ner et al. (1993).
[13] Eggertsson (1994).

cerned with behaviour, institutions are defined as effective rules, rather than nominal rules, with emphasis on enforcement.[14] It follows from this definition that, to a production unit, and more particularly to a small firm, the institutional setting becomes an exogenous factor. While conceiving of institutions as rules, we are logically led to examine the agencies through which these rules are operationalised. For the present purposes, if we focus on the institutional environment that specifically influences the economic performance of small firms, then the framework consists of three major agents: the government, the quasi-government and the private, non-governmental agencies. Apart from these, socio-cultural norms and standards also influence the behaviour of small firms. Next, in describing the link between efficiency in small scale production and the institutional framework, we are led to the related concepts of transaction costs, contracts and organisations.

Entrepreneurial activity, like all other human activities, relies heavily on the gains from exchanges or transactions. Market failures in perfect enforcement of property rights give rise to transaction costs, which are the costs incurred in enforcing internal property rights.[15] Two major definitions of transaction costs[16] are 'the costs of running the economic system',[17] and 'the costs of measuring the valuable attributes of what is being exchanged and the costs of protecting rights and policing and enforcing agreements'.[18] The concept of transaction costs follows from the non-existence of the perfect markets typical of neo-classical economics. The costs of transacting arise because information is costly and asymmetrically held by the parties to the exchange and also because the manner in which the actors develop institutions to structure human interaction results in some degree of imperfection of markets.[19] More specifically, Dahlman defines transaction costs in terms of three factors: search and information costs, bargaining and decision costs, and policing and enforcement costs.[20] Transaction cost theory presupposes that a transaction, contract or an exchange exists. In fact, the distinction between information costs and transaction costs is explicitly brought out by some commentators: when information is costly, various activities related to the exchange of property rights between individuals give rise to transaction costs.[21] Put differently, all transaction costs are not incurred at the point of exchange, and a distinction can be made between ex ante and ex post transaction costs. Ex ante transaction costs comprise the costs buyers and sellers incur in their search to identify a party with whom to transact. Ex post transaction costs comprise the costs to one party that

---

[14] Ibid.
[15] Ibid.
[16] Noted in Zhang and Sjöberg (1992), pp. 26ff.
[17] Williamson and Ouchi (1981), p. 388.
[18] North (1990), p. 270.
[19] Ibid., p. 108.
[20] Dahlman (1979).
[21] Eggertsson (1990), p. 15.

result from non-performance by the other.[22] Whereas information costs typically occur before exchange, monitoring costs typically occur after exchange.[23]

In this classification, the following are ex ante transaction costs: the search for information about the distribution of price and quality of commodities and labour inputs; the search for potential buyers and sellers and for relevant information about their behaviour and circumstances; and the bargaining that is needed to find the true position of buyers and sellers when prices are endogenous. Monitoring of contractual partners to see whether they abide by the terms of the contract; the enforcement of a contract and the collection of damages when partners fail to observe their contractual obligations; and the protection of property rights against third party encroachment (for example, protection against pirates or even against the government in the case of illegitimate trade) comprise ex post transaction costs. Nooteboom elaborates on this and states that transaction costs arise in three stages of transactions: contact, contract and control.[24] In the stage of contact are included search costs for the prospective buyer, marketing costs, search for size and kind of user demand, choice of the marketing instruments of the product, and so on. In the stage of contract, the costs incurred are towards setting up agreements to transact, and includes hedges against risks due to uncertainty, with asymmetric information between buyer and seller, and the possibility of opportunism. In the stage of control, there are costs of monitoring adherence to agreements, haggling, renegotiation, arbitration, litigation, loss of investments due to discontinuity of the transaction and so forth. The success of small enterprises is dependent on mechanisms which reduce these costs. The theory assumes that, given the institutional setting, people seek arrangements that minimise all costs, including transaction costs.[25] 'Economising on transaction costs incurred in market operations . . . is accomplished by replacing market transactions, in part or full, by direct governance within the firm, for instance through vertical integration'.[26] This is referred to as 'internalisation'.

As originally conceived by Ronald Coase,[27] and refined by Williamson,[28] transaction costs are 'an answer to the question why there are firms and why different activities are combined in one firm'.[29] Transaction cost economics (or TCE, for short) is based on the assumptions of bounded rationality (inability to foresee all possible contingencies in a transaction) and opportunism. Combined, these two factors may result in a sufficient degree of uncertainty over the execution of a contract. Bounded rationality is taken to arise from the scarcity or cost of information and limited capacity for information processing.[30] This makes it difficult to foresee

---

[22] Levy et al. (1994), p. 8; and Eggertsson (1990), p. 15.
[23] North and Wallis (1994).
[24] Nooteboom (1992).
[25] Eggertsson (1994).
[26] Williamson (1975), pp. 20-21, and (1981/82), p. 548.
[27] Coase (1937).
[28] Williamson (1975), and (1985).
[29] Nooteboom (1993).
[30] Ibid.

opportunism in the transacting partner and hence requires 'complete' contracts that protect against any possible opportunism. Asset specificity (or transaction specific investments in assets by the producer) is another dimension in TCE, in which case, transaction costs tend to be asymmetric between buyer and producer, so that both parties to the contract are 'locked in'.[31]

The amount of transaction costs incurred by a firm in this world of imperfect information depends on the strength of the institutional structures of society. Williamson, a transaction cost economist, holds that firms react to a given, existing institutional setup. From a different perspective, that of neo-institutionalism, North suggests that these measurement and enforcement costs are in fact the sources of social, political and economic institutions.[32] We need not go along with North as far as the unfailingly endogenous nature of institutions, however, to appreciate that

> [w]ith insecure property rights, poorly enforced laws, barriers to entry, and monopolistic restrictions, the profit-maximizing firms will tend to have short time horizons and little fixed capital and will tend to be small scale. The most profitable businesses may be in trade, redistributive activities or the black market. Large firms with substantial fixed capital will exist only under the umbrella of government protection with subsidies, tariff protection, and pay-offs to the polity - a mixture hardly conducive to productive efficiency.[33]

High transaction costs are often associated with weak institutions (weak public enforcement of rules), but high transaction costs can also be associated with strong institutions that leave the agent with few rights.[34] This, however, does not imply that institutions are the sole causes of high transaction costs. Costs of transacting are affected by several other factors, such as the technology of measurement and monitoring, the physical characteristics of assets, and the nature of the exchange.[35]

From the above it is clear that there is a two-way reinforcing, if not necessarily straight forward or determining in a strict sense of the word,[36] relationship between transaction costs and institutions. Firms adapt to these two components through the process of internalisation. Transaction costs are inevitable to a firm and the ways in which it works to reduce transaction costs depends on factors internal and external to the firm. In Third World countries telephone systems that do not work, the inability to get spare parts, endless production interruptions, long queues and waiting time to get permits and product variability are overwhelming indirect evidence that an effective institutional infrastructure does not exist.[37] These and other deficiencies in the institutional environment cause higher transaction costs to

---

[31] Ibid.
[32] North (1990), p. 27.
[33] Ibid.
[34] Eggertsson (1994).
[35] Ibid.
[36] As North (1990) at that point at least seemed to suggest. Cf Joskow (1995).
[37] North (1990), pp. 68-9.

a firm. The government, political parties or small firms collectively can try to reduce transaction costs - or the cost of governance schemes - by furthering norms that restrict opportunistic business conduct, by stabilising market conditions to reduce exogenous uncertainty, and by furthering technical standards or standardised procedures that reduce in particular the threshold costs of search, evaluation, contracting, monitoring and arbitration.[38]

Transaction costs and the size of the firm

Explaining the effects of firm size on transaction costs, Nooteboom shows that transaction costs are bound to be higher for the smaller firm, in its role as buyer and as seller, but also for the transaction partners.[39] This is because it is more sensitive to uncertainty, more vulnerable to opportunism, yield a greater risk of unintended discontinuity for their partners and raise possibilities of opportunism to a greater degree. Transaction costs are higher, either directly or indirectly, in that they raise the expenses required to compensate for greater risks to their partners. This is supported by Levy and associates who assert that large firms can use non-market mechanisms to internalise within the firm many of the functional technical and marketing skills that they need to conduct business.[40] 'SMEs (small and medium enterprises), by contrast, lack the resources and in-house functional diversification of their larger counterparts, and depend more on external sources to acquire technological and marketing capability. Acquiring the resources they need involves transaction costs. It follows that the less developed technical and marketing support systems are, the higher will be the transaction costs to SMEs, with a corresponding impairment in their competitive position'.[41] Further, transaction costs are higher when the status of law and related judicial practices is uncertain.[42] This fact has considerable bearing for the government and policy makers, and it is intuitively appealing to discern that suitable institutional structures would help reduce uncertainty and thereby the transaction costs to a small firm. However, the concept of a small firm is extremely heterogeneous and designing institutions to assist a heterogeneous group could entail high costs in its own right, and make a bias in policy issues unavoidable. This in no way negates the role of institutions; particularly if we are led to believe that individual small firms tend to minimise transaction costs by resorting to a better exploitation of their internal strengths or through collective action, with other firms; then institutions could very well play an effective, supportive role in assisting small firms in reducing transaction costs. While this would lead us to infer that institutions generally exist to minimise transaction costs, as North points out,

---

[38] Nooteboom (1993).
[39] Ibid.
[40] Levy et al. (1994), pp. 1-2.
[41] Ibid.
[42] Scully (1987).

rules that restrict entry, require useless inspections, raise information costs, or make property rights less secure - in fact raise transaction costs. The above-mentioned rules are made in the polity and reflect the bargaining strength of contractors, trade unions, and others in the political market. Because that market is *imperfect*, institutions everywhere are a mixed bag composed of those that lower costs and those that raise them.[43]

However, it is not a problem of intention in designing these institutions; changing the economic scenery requires a changing institutional structure. The point is that existing institutions may become hurdles as the structure of the economy changes. Unsuitable institutions could also be perpetuated by certain rent seekers, individuals or groups, who gain from such a perpetuation. Furthermore, this is compounded by the fact that in many developing countries, a large number of small firms operate on the borderline of legality. Indeed, or so North asserts, 'developing countries have dichotomized economies in the sense that in addition to the official (first) economy there is also a hidden (second) economy, the activities of which are concealed from the state for a variety of reasons'.[44]

In general the factors causing high transaction costs to small firms are: (i) information bottlenecks; (ii) unfavourable policy environment;[45] and (iii) the nature of the small business activity.[46] It is recognised that an unsuitable institutional framework would cause an increase in the number as well as volume of operations of the black economy, with higher transaction costs. In many countries, especially, in the Third World, entrepreneurs must make costly investments in a tortuous bureaucratic process which may take months or years, and sometimes pay bribes, in order to acquire the rights to establish a legitimate firm.[47] Under these conditions, transaction costs of the firm rise and would prevent the natural expansion orientation of its production. Since large firms on an average are better endowed in terms of resources, transaction costs to a small firm are higher than to its larger counterpart.

Dynamics of small firms

The concept of small firms or small scale enterprises is highly relative, and varies across time and space. Different countries have different cut-off points for the small scale sector. Even when defined, the small firm sector is extremely heterogeneous; technologically backward sweatshops exist alongside highly flexible and

---

[43] North (1990), p. 63; emphasis in the original.
[44] Clapham (1985), p. 8.
[45] Policy reform differs from institutional support and direct firm level assistance, because it affects enterprises generally rather than reaching only individual beneficiaries (Steel 1993).
[46] Here we are concerned with the legality of the small firm. The more non-compliant the firm is with rules and regulations, the higher its transaction costs (see Goss 1991).
[47] Eggertsson (1994).

innovative small firms.[48] Problems of heterogeneity are, however, overcome for the present purposes since the main focus here is on understanding the linkages between institutional framework and a specific size category.

The dynamics of small firms can be studied at a macro level, which gives an aggregate picture of small enterprises at the national level in terms of employment, output and incomes. Or they can be studied at a micro level, describing the life and activities of individual firms. Here we choose the latter approach with an emphasis on the kinds of decisions a small firm undertakes to remain in existence. Even entry into small scale production entails a considerable amount of transaction costs and depends critically on the micro and macro environment of the institutional framework within which it chooses to operate. The dynamics of small industry may be examined at five levels:

a) Organisation within the firm
b) Inter-firm linkages
c) Linkages with markets
d) Linkages with government
e) Linkages with other agencies

In the following, these will be examined in turn.

Organisation within the firm. Firms, operating on the cost minimisation principle, have diverse needs to be taken care of - pertaining to finance (working and fixed), labour and other inputs, technology, marketing, and others, not to exclude procurement of licenses and permits. Transaction costs are quite substantial in such kinds of decision making, especially to a typical small firm with a single entrepreneur with overall responsibility. The effectiveness of the small firms at this level depends a lot on the strength of the entrepreneur in his social, informal networking and formation of trust based relationships with providers of capital, labour and land. The internal organisation of the firm is affected by exogenous variables too, not least through the linkages of the firm with other agents in the economy. 'The Coasian view suggests that the internal organization of the firm is important and must be studied separately from, although in conjunction with, other micro- and macroeconomic coordination mechanisms. The extent to which a firm can transact more cheaply than the market or the plan therefore depends on the organizational structure of the firm itself and on various attributes of the market or plan mechanisms'.[49] Efficient internal organisation depends on the skills of the entrepreneur. The typical Schumpeterian innovative entrepreneur directs the firm toward exploring and exploiting new opportunities.

---

[48] Späth (1992).
[49] Ben-Ner et al. (1993), p. 203.

Whether the bulk of the entrepreneurial activity will be devoted to innovation and its dissemination or to undertakings that yield little benefit to society or are even damaging to its instruments, depends on the nature of the reward incentives offered by current laws and other institutions. The point is that such institutions are far more amenable to modification by deliberate policy than is the supply of individuals with the psychological make-up that renders them fit to serve as leader entrepreneurs.[50]

Schmitz distinguishes between external and internal constraints on small producers, suggesting a division of internal constraints into: (i) motivation, drive, adaptability; (ii) organisational skills; and (iii) technical skills.[51] He observes that most detailed descriptions of the urban small scale economy would certainly defy the first concern.[52] King concludes on the obstacles confronting the small producer, in his study on technical skills and training in East Africa, thus:

> there are presently severe structural problems restricting his development into an own-account worker capable of the production of high quality precision goods. It is not principally the technical dimension which constitutes the obstacle, but rather the lack of a basic credit infrastructure, security of tenure in the urban areas, and a technology policy that would support the very small scale entrepreneur.[53]

This would suggest that a better organisation within the firm could result from an institutional framework that would reduce the transaction costs to the small firm by reducing information bottlenecks and bettering its access to resources in the society.

Inter-firm linkages. Inter-firm linkages pertain to the location of the small firm in the hierarchy of industrial organisation and the diversity in the large-small firm relationships. While most writings on small firms lean towards a perspective of horizontal linkages, equally important are the small firm's linkages with the large sector. Inter-firm linkages also help describe the growth prospects for small firms, depending on the categories to which they belong. Various attempts have been made at categorising small scale firms. Saith notes three categories of small firms in the pre-industrial manufacturing activity:[54] (i) industries genuinely 'proto' in nature, in that they do develop into modern industrial firms with accompanying transformations of the technological and organisational framework, and of the labour process; (ii) 'inferior' industries, in that with expansion of modern industry

---

[50] Baumol (1988).
[51] Schmitz (1982).
[52] The sociology of entrepreneurship is another major issue in enterprise formation, and is beyond the scope of this paper to discuss the details. Literature on this is abundant. E.g., see articles in Leibenstein and Ray (1988).
[53] King (1979), p. 228.
[54] Saith (1992), p. 17.

31

they die out, from competition with modern substitutes or from a loss of demand arising from urbanisation and rising incomes leading to altered preferences; and (iii) rural craft industries which manage to survive through adopting new tools, sources of power and raw materials, and successfully reorient their traditional organisation, product quality and mix towards the new demands of modern industry and the new consumer preferences. The dynamics of the small firm depends on the category to which it belongs since the presence (or absence) of linkages with other units varies among them.

In a Marxist framework, Rainnie offers a four-fold classification of small firms:[55]

1. Dependent small firms. These complement and service the activities of larger firms (e.g., through subcontracting). The viability of dependent small firms is closely connected to the level of activity and the 'make or buy' decisions of their main or dominant customers. Such a situation places effective control in the hands of the large enterprise, a control which extends not only over financial matters but also over the organisation of the labour process, for instance, by forcing the minimisation of wage costs and the implementation of flexible working conditions.

2. Competitive independent small firms. These compete with large firms by intense exploitation of labour and of (often antiquated) equipment. Even here, however, the rules of existence are laid down, if possibly unwittingly and unintentionally, by the large firm. In terms of industrial relations the result is, more often than not, hyper-exploitation of labour.

3. Old independent small firms. These operate in niches of demand unlikely ever to be touched by large capital. This will often entail a hand-to-mouth existence, scraping around for a living. It is amongst this and the latter type of small business that sweatshops are most likely to be found.

4. New independent small firms. Small firms operating in (often founding and developing) specialised markets, but remaining open to the potentially fatal attentions of large firms. In other words, small firms which, within a very wide reading of the term, conduct the product and market research which large firms then step in and develop.

The life and growth of a small enterprise does not lend itself to any generalisation because of the diversity of its operations. There is thus a great deal of difficulty in explaining why firms come into existence and how they survive and why some of them die out. Describing a typical micro enterprise, Liedholm states 'the firm originates as a tiny enterprise - typically a one-person operation - with

---

[55] Rainnie (1989), p. 18.

three years of struggle, a high probability of failure, and little growth. If it survives these first three years, however, it is likely to experience a sudden spurt of growth, that will typically project it into one of the larger size categories of micro enterprises'.[56] However, transaction and transformation costs[57] vary with the type of small firm. Vertical linkages with large firms are found to have favourable effects in reducing transaction costs. 'Particular areas of economic activities apart, they need to link up with resource pools of others, be it large firms or small firms, to gain strategic options. Thus links and networks are paramount to small firm success'.[58] 'The relationship between small and large factories is not always competitive. In some industries, the relationship is complementary and indeed, even competitive'.[59]

Much of the literature on collective efficiency, flexible specialisation, industrial districts and so forth, address the horizontal linkages of small firms. These horizontal inter-firm flows of information, competition, and so on, are decisive factors in determining the survival of the small firm in production. Further they serve as means of reducing transaction costs to the small firm. Collectively, small firms can try to achieve advantages by cooperation[60] and this has been a major force in the formation of 'industrial districts'. The main problem for small firms is not being small but being lonely.[61] It can thus be inferred that strong inter-firm linkages have favourable effects on the transaction costs of small firms.

Linkages with markets. Small firms invariably incur substantial search costs, which could be recurring, in marketing their products, unless they establish themselves as ancillaries or have stable vertical linkages with large firms, such as in the form of subcontracting. Given the small scale of production, they may have to incur costs in convincing the buyers of their products, either standardised or tailor made. Substantial transaction costs are also to be incurred in ensuring upkeep of contracts. In a competitive environment, small firms confront other small and large firms in capturing market shares. The competition is more acute in the case of growth-oriented small firms aspiring to entrer into international markets. Small firms try to reduce transaction costs in this area by utilising their linkages with the government, other agencies and firms.

Linkages with government. The linkages of small firms with the government are among the most important factors affecting the dynamics. This linkage can exist at two levels: with government as the promoter of an economic environment, with its regulations and policies, and with government as a market for small industrial products. The regulatory environment comprises rules for registration, land use

---

[56] Liedholm (1993), p. 263. For a review of institutional support to micro enterprises in developing countries, see Levitsky (1989).

[57] Transformation costs broadly refer to the production costs of the firm.

[58] Pyke and Sengenberger (1992), p. 11.

[59] Ho (1980).

[60] Nooteboom (1993).

[61] Pyke and Sengenberger (1992), p. 11.

authorisation, labour laws, industrial safety and health standards, environmental regulations and so forth, which set legal limits for the pursuit of profits by the small firm. A further distinction is between macro-economic policies and other sector specific protectionary and promotional policies. The policy environment envelops the institutions that are designed to reduce transaction costs to economic agents in society in general, and the private small firms in particular. The broad macro-economic policies that would affect decision making in the small firm are finance and credit policies, government budget and taxation in particular, the foreign trade, exchange rate and balance of payments policies. These policies form the micro and macro environment of the small firm depending on the extent of impact they have. For instance, an exporting small firm would be directly affected by the foreign exchange and trade policies and this would therefore form the micro environment, while to a firm catering to a local market they would form the macro environment with more indirect effects. In many countries, there are specific policies to support small scale industry, providing special credit and technology for a few small scale firms.[62]

Yet legislation must not be construed as a means to the full removal of transaction costs. Norms and standards, not seldom tacit in nature, are often required as well. These may emerge and be maintained under the supervision of various voluntary or semi-official organisations or, for that matter, by extra-legal means such as reputation effects and ostracism. As Stewart notes, at times 'they are also embedded in norms of conduct that have become part of sub-cultures of cultures at large'. Similarly, as also most mainstream economists would accept, not all markets function properly. Whether for reasons of sunk costs, the existence of increasing returns or natural monopolies, markets may at times fail. To rectify such market failure, functional (or horizontal) industrial policy may be called for. However, mainstream economists typically see no reason why this line of reasoning should be extended to sectoral industrial policy, which aims to target selected industries for preferential treatment; this is tantamount to introducing distortions that are likely to undermine allocative efficiency. Rather, the role of government is to provide for the setting within which private agents are to operate.[63]

Policy choices are classified into two broad groups: fundamentals and selective interventions.[64] Among the most important of the former are macro-economic stability, high investments in human capital, stable and secure financial systems, limited price distortions and openness to foreign technology. Selective interventions include mild financial repression (keeping interest rates positive, but low), directed credit, selective industrial promotion, and export push trade policies. Attention to government's influence on the policy environment is warranted as highly profitable investment opportunities may be lost because of the anti-small bias in policies (e.g., import licenses that are difficult for small firms to obtain),

---

[62] Stewart (1990).
[63] Wade (1990).
[64] Page (1994).

34

market imperfections which constrain small firms' access to resources (e.g., the failure of financial intermediation to serve viable small investments), and social and cultural mores that inhibit the participation of certain groups (e.g., women) in small business.[65]

It is thus clear that the concrete contribution towards development made by a small or medium enterprise is the product of an intricate combination of behaviour patterns and the associated attitude and knowledge of the entrepreneur, and incentives or obstacles which give rise to a particular behaviour pattern. While entrepreneurial behavioural patterns can be influenced in the long run, the scheme of incentives and removal of obstacles can be influenced in the short run, through appropriate 'instrumental variables' in the form of specific policies.[66]

Linkages with other agencies. To overcome information bottlenecks, regarding financial assistance, marketing, training of workers, technical advice (like adoption of appropriate technology) and in contacts with other firms and markets, and so on, other quasi and non-governmental agencies also become useful.

However, the government's policies can affect the firm in any of the above mentioned five levels of operations. In general, five factors exert a particularly strong influence on the environment in which small and medium entrepreneurs operate:[67] resource endowment, size of the domestic market, level of income on the domestic market, industrial basis and politico-social organisation. With increasing attention being devoted to trade and macroeconomic policies in the last decade or so, students of small scale industry have more frequently criticised the pro-large bias of the tariff, other instruments of protection, and foreign exchange allocation, blaming some of the problems of small industry on the excessive support provided to large firms or to a sub-set of such firms.[68] Acknowledging the pro-large bias in policy formulations, Stewart opines that removing the privileges of the large scale is more important than special schemes and regulations to assist the small.[69] In particular, efficient small scale production depends on: agencies that can help reduce ex ante transaction costs by way of information flows in the search of small firms for contracting partners and production inputs; the government in providing a regulatory framework for reducing ex post transaction costs and; an economic environment of lesser uncertainty in drawing up contracts with other buyers and sellers.

---

[65] Steel (1993).
[66] Clapham (1985).
[67] Staley and Morse (1965), p. 228.
[68] Berry and Mazumdar (1991).
[69] Stewart (1990).

Conclusion

In the above discussion, the relationship between small industries and the institutional framework is analysed using the transaction costs approach. The approach is centred on the firm, with the dynamics pointing to the various levels at which the firm interacts with the institutions, the latter being treated as exogenous and variable. The institutional framework consists of formal government, quasi-government and non-governmental agencies and the informal social codes of conduct and behaviour. Generally speaking, there are economies of scale with respect to the ability to cope with transaction costs. More particularly, it is seen that the form and nature of institutional solutions affect the threshold costs of small firms differentially, thereby having a discriminating impact as far as transaction costs are concerned.

It should be recognised that transaction costs are operational at each level of analysis, and that the direction of causality may vary. As such, the nature and direction of change, if any, may be highly contingent on local, sectoral or national institutions. Whatever the source of such differences, this observation tallies with the remark made in the previous chapter that macro level institutions may display differing degrees of 'effectiveness'. From a normative or policy perspective, then, particular attention ought to be given to the relationship with the government as an agency providing the legal, regulatory and policy framework within which small firms operate. What is more, in addition to the assertion that institutional adjustment at the macro level is likely to be consequential, it should also be emphasised that governmental decisions can affect both the internal organisation of the firm, as well as its linkages with other institutions in the course of drawing up contracts with its transacting partners, through reductions in transaction costs.

This is reflected in the following four chapters containing case studies of four Asian and two African economies, four of which are transition economies in the strict sense of moving away from central planning. Each case study is primarily descriptive and organised around the themes identified in this and the previous chapter. Although the case studies have many things in common, no attempt has been made to impose on them an identical structure. Rather, a loosely defined organising framework has been employed, in each case adapted to local circumstances so as to emphasise the particular institutional environment, both at the macro and the micro level, that individual small scale manufacturing enterprises have had to contend with. In the concluding chapter of this volume, the threads will be brought together and an explicitly comparative framework will be used to the end of drawing lessons not only for Africa from Asia, as it were, but in fact for developing countries in general and other developing transition economies in particular - irrespective of whether they are Asian or African, successful or not.

4 The Asian experience I: China and Taiwan

Bhargavi Ramamurthy

Introduction

While small firms have attracted considerable attention on account of all the benefits they are widely held to bring, the previous chapter of this volume highlighted the fact that the healthy performance of the small scale industrial sector critically depends on a favourable institutional environment. Defining institutions as rules, both formal (such as laws and statutes) and informal (such as norms), that constrain or facilitate certain behaviour or modes of action, the next step is to define the relationship between small firm efficiency and the institutional framework as such. This is usefully done by employing the concept of transaction costs, that is, the costs of operating in a market. Besides the provisions embodied in the legal system, the institutional framework also encompasses, but is not restricted to, public sector agencies and activities that assist or interfere with the actions of private economic agents. In addition, it includes the social norms and standards of behaviour that by and large are specific to individual cultures or historically given situations.[1]

In Chapter Three it was argued that small size itself often confers certain disadvantages not only with respect to indivisibilities and economies of scale in production, but also in terms of transaction costs. To mitigate the resulting higher costs of operating in a market, small firms often devise strategies which, as for composition as well as consequences, are contingent upon the institutional environment. The purpose of the present chapter is to use these insights as an organising and heuristic device and to apply it to the experience of two major Asian economies with a view of illuminating some of the sources of transactional efficiency and inefficiency. Specifically, the focus shall be on policies and institutions that may have had an impact on transaction costs as faced by small scale industries. Above all, by identifying particular areas, indeed the nature of interaction, it tries to clarify the links and reinforcing relationships between small firm efficiency and the institutional framework within which the small firms operate.[2]

---

[1] Eggertsson (1994).
[2] Ramamurthy and Ronnås (1995).

As such it is not the definite story or economic history of the countries concerned. Rather, based on the existing secondary literature an attempt is made to add yet another dimension to the impact of macro policies on small scale industries,[3] while at the same time transcending the emphasis on macro-economic balance and structural adjustment or on industrial policies that have been a primary concern of previous endeavours to derive lessons for Africa from Asia.[4]

The choice of China and Taiwan, and India and Vietnam which are the focus of the subsequent chapter, banks on a particular characteristic of these four economies: they have all experienced a high degree of government intervention. Yet they have distinctively different experiences both as regards to the nature of government intervention and as regards the results. Beyond this common characteristic, China and Vietnam are formerly centrally planned economies currently in transition, and the case of small industries becomes interesting since these countries' admittance of private sector has been recent and the experience of small firms throughout the central plan era offers valuable insights into the critical factors in small enterprise functioning. Particularly, China is of considerable interest to countries with a vast population in rural areas, surplus agricultural labour and a preponderance of dual structures in the economy. This legacy of the socialist past is at variance from the experience of non-socialist emerging economies, and India is an excellent example; also because the bias on heavy industry and import substitution has coexisted with extensive small industry promotion. By a similar token, Taiwan's post-war history usefully sets China's more recent experience in perspective. The inclusion of Taiwan is particularly salient since it shares its culture (and hence its traditional predilection for small scale family firms) with the Mainland. Further, as an East Asian miracle, the catalyst of development has been the small industry, and not least the governing party, the Kuomintang, was structurally similar, if not identical, to the Communist party on the Mainland until the late 1980s.

In describing the dynamics of small firms, economic and non-economic factors are both recognised as constituting the institutional framework that affect transaction costs of small firms. To incorporate both types of factors, a description of the economic history and critical factors in the country's developmental experience precedes the discussion of small firms. These case studies are presented with a fairly detailed economic history to see the linkages that small firms have developed - with government, non-government and other firms - in their attempts to reduce transaction costs. Particular attention is paid to macro-economic policies of the government since they set the overall economic environment which necessitates other linkages to be developed or discarded in reducing transaction costs.

---

[3] Osmani (1995).
[4] E.g., Wallace (1997); and Stein (1995a).

China

The People's Republic of China has attracted considerable attention in the period following its founding, mainly for the intensity with which political decisions have been implemented through successful mass mobilisation and also for the waves of centralisation and decentralisation that have shaken its economy frequently. The economic transformation since 1978 has been another long standing issue of discussion given the pronounced changes in the role of the state and the private sector. Between 1950 and 1990, China increased its real per capita income 600 per cent.[5] Rural reforms in particular have been described as 'phenomenal' and 'spectacular',[6] providing enough motives for investigating the path China has traversed. The issue of small firms, in the private and collective sectors, becomes interesting since pursuit of socialism assigned private sector in general and small firms in particular a marginal role for a long time in the economic history of China, until the reforms.

Political economy of the People's Republic of China

The economic history of China can only be studied in association with the broad changes in its political and economic institutions, beginning with the revolution (of which economic development was the central objective) in 1949 to the reforms of the Deng era in the late 1970s. In order to liberate the productive forces and establish a socialist economy in China, the Communist Party of China (CPC) led the Chinese into a protracted fight against imperialism, feudalism and bureaucrat capitalism in various wars, of which the Third Civil Revolutionary War between 1946 and 1949 resulted in the formation of the People's Republic of China (PRC). The five main sectors making up the new democratic economic system were the socialist state owned economy, the semi-socialist cooperative economy, the private capitalist economy, the individual economy and the national capitalist economy, based on cooperation between the country and individuals.[7]

The birth of the PRC and the three years of restoration: 1949-1952 The PRC was founded on 1 October 1949. Pre-1949 China was scarred by want and suffering.[8] The economic strategy proclaimed 'three years of recovery, then ten years of development' in 1949. The first three years were known as the Rehabilitation period, a period of reorganising and restoring the national economy from the deep financial and economic difficulties it faced under the rule of the Kuomintang government. Agriculture and handicraft industry dominated economic activity and modern industry was hardly present, then. In establishing new production relations, the Government abolished imperialists' economic privileges, confiscated and con-

---

[5] Ministry of Foreign Affairs, Sweden (1992).
[6] Islam (1991), p. 1.
[7] See James (1989), p. 444.
[8] Dietrich (1994), p. 4.

verted bureaucrat capital into a state owned economy. Next on the agenda was breaking the two thousand year old feudal system in China through widespread land reforms, which was completed by 1952. As a result, agricultural production registered a rapid increase. Mutual aid groups and agricultural cooperatives were formed for agricultural labour.[9] In the cities handicraftsmen were organised into workshops to improve technology and efficiency, and industries were given protection. The Shanghai Stock Exchange was sealed to avoid speculation in the financial market. However, there was the problem of price instability due to budgetary deficits. In balancing revenue and expenditure, centralisation of financial and economic management was accomplished under the People's Central Bank (PCB).

In reorganising industry and commerce, relations between state owned and private industry and commerce were regulated. The State now maintained distribution of raw materials as well as purchase orders. Combined with other reinforcing measures, a number of private enterprises began business after the latter half of 1950 as cooperatives. A socialist economy was established and industry began to gain dominance. Objectives were realised in the sense that by 1952 production reached and exceeded pre-war peak levels. Planning was adopted gradually, first experimented in Manchuria, with Soviet advice. The method of central planning adopted was one of 'material balances', which permitted demand forecasting. If supply-demand inequality existed, the plan was adjusted and possibility of foreign aid looked into to fill the gaps. In the early 1950s, the inherited industrial structure was highly skewed towards consumer goods production and the First Five Year Plan (hereafter FFYP) sought to strengthen the capital goods sector by a conscious bias toward heavy industry. The steps the new Government took to combat various economic ills were 'inflation control by a combination of austerity measures, balanced budgets, currency reform, and price controls. By expropriating major industries and the banks, Beijing achieved control over the urban sector. Former capitalists and managers were induced to help get industry and commerce back into operation'.[10]

Socialist transformation and construction: 1953-57 In this period the government acted rapidly to take over what remained of the private sector in industry and commerce, alongside increasing difficulties in controlling the large economy. According to Mao Zedong, socialist transformation of agriculture, handicrafts and capitalist industry and commerce was necessary for a socialist industrialisation of the country. His chief contribution to alleviating economic problems was administrative decentralisation. In July 1955, he organised almost the entire rural peasantry into collectives, impatient with the slow formation of cooperatives in the countryside. The FFYP (1953-58) was oriented towards the development of large scale industry and, as Riskin notes, included a regional focus that implied a

---

[9] By 1952 there were more than 8 million mutual aid groups for agricultural labour and 4,000 primary agricultural cooperatives in China (James 1989, p. 446).
[10] Dietrich (1994), p. 57.

40

relative shift of emphasis towards inland areas.[11] However, the Big Push of heavy industry was undertaken at the expense of agriculture and consumer goods sector and Mao Zedong launched a radically different solution to the persistent poverty problem, called the Great Leap Forward (GLF), in 1958. Meanwhile, the Korean War (1950-53) resulted in a military and economic alliance with the Soviet Union and this translated into China's strength until the two drifted apart over differences in the course China followed during the GLF.

The Great Leap Forward: 1958-60 The GLF constitutes Mao Zedong's attempt to tackle the hitherto unsolved economic problems, including those of the FFYP. The formulation of communes is one of the most important outcomes of this period. In principle, it implied balanced development of agriculture and industry and deliberately promoted and formalised technological dualism in what is known as 'walking on two legs': 'on the one hand the modern sector characterized by a capital intensive and large scale mode of production and on the other hand a labor intensive traditional sector'.[12] It altered the management system of agriculture and industrial enterprises by organising small production groups of ordinary workers into communes which elected their own heads.

The formation of the communes was part of an incentive policy that encouraged collective solidarity and mass responsibility by reducing individual income differentiation. The rural communes consisted of production brigades (actually the old collectives or villages) which were made up of production teams (corresponding to the earlier neighbourhoods). These communes combined economic functions with administrative and political roles and enjoyed complete control over the means of production, not least important of which was the labour force.[13] While agricultural activities dominated, non-agricultural enterprises were found at all three levels of the commune organisation. Urban communes were also set up but were comparatively short-lived. Through the embarkment on the dual economy strategy, implicit in the walking on two legs concept and the decentralisation of economic and administrative power to the communes, the central authorities confined their direct and detailed control over the economy to the 'modern', largely urban, sector and to a limited number of key areas and products.[14]

The scale tipped even further in favour of 'heavy' industry over agriculture as a resolution was adopted in August, 1958, calling for 'taking steel production as the core and achieving a comprehensive leap forward'. In the prevailing euphoria of optimism production targets were set for both agriculture and industry which in retrospect stand out as absurdly unrealistic.[15] Although the policy of complementing large scale modern industry with more labour intensive local industry may have been sound in principle, the focus of the industrialisation drive on heavy in-

---

[11] Riskin (1991), pp. 58-9.
[12] Eckstein (1977), p. 57.
[13] Ronnås (1993), p. 220.
[14] Ibid., p. 15.
[15] Ibid., p. 17.

dustries, such as iron and steel processing, that were not amenable to a small scale and labour intensive mode of production, the total disregard for cost-efficiency and, one might add, quality, turned out to big mistakes.

The exaggerated tempo and the scale of the drive inevitably undermined the sustainability of the rural industrialisation policy. Clearly, most of the non-agricultural units lacked conditions for development or even long term survival. However, before the process of weeding out the unviable activities ran its course, the GLF experiment collapsed, through disasters in agriculture, as abruptly as it had commenced. The neglect of agriculture, in particular the withdrawal of labour from agriculture,[16] combined with unfavourable weather led to a decline in food production in 1959 and 1960. The failure of agriculture had severe repercussions on the whole economy and led to a deep economic crisis between 1960 and 1962. An added external blow was when the Soviet Union recalled all of its 1,400 scientists, engineers, and others in the summer of 1960 due to fundamental political and ideological conflicts that escalated during the GLF. Inoperative market forces and faulty planning resulted in outputs that did not correspond to demands and the GLF led to greater quantity and not quality. When the GLF wreaked havoc on the economy, Mao retreated to the Soviet-style arrangements. For the next fifteen years (from the early 1960s to the mid-1970s), these two approaches - the Soviet and the Maoist - jostled one another at policy-making tables.[17]

Depression, recovery and struggle at the top: 1960-65 The GLF plunged the whole country into hunger, unemployment, despair, and lawlessness.[18] China turned into a grain importing nation. The consumer goods sector and then heavy industry fell into a deep decline in the years 1960 and 1961. A high rate of migration into cities from the rural areas compounded the unemployment problem in the urban areas. The major steps taken were to return these people to the villages and a change in the attitude towards foreign relations. Recovery began in 1962 aided by good weather, changes in commune structure and a higher priority for agricultural development. The slogan 'taking agriculture as the foundation, industry as the leading factor', adopted in this period, reflects the altered priorities. The policy of 'agricultural priority' meant more than cutbacks in heavy industry, capital construction, and development plans to match the available farm surplus; it also implied an increase in investment in agriculture and in those industrial sectors supporting agriculture.[19] Defence, and especially the nuclear industry, appears to have also received high priority during the 1961-65 period, as China adjusted to the deterioration of its relationship with the Soviet Union.[20] A new movement was launched called the Socialist Education Movement, to rekindle the socialist flame in the rural areas in 1963.

---

[16] Jowitt (1989), p. 143.
[17] Dietrich (1994), p. 4.
[18] Ibid., p. 142.
[19] Riskin (1991), p. 152.
[20] Ibid., p. 155.

The decade of the Cultural Revolution: 1966-76 The Cultural Revolution proper lasted from late 1965 to early 1969.[21] This Revolution is described as Mao's reaction to the resistance offered by the Party to the Socialist Education Movement and the bureaucratisation of the Party, with the intention of reversing the trend toward restratification. The Revolution passed through several stages, beginning with a 'cultural' phase, 'in which a series of plays, novels, and essays written in the early 1960s and implicitly critical of party policy and of Mao were subjected to attack',[22] to workers seizing power in factories, until Mao issued a directive ordering the masses to submit in late 1967. The broadened economic mandate for the communes was also reflected in regulations and a certain devolution of power from the central to the local and provincial level as the policy of self-reliance and walking on two legs experienced a renaissance in the wake of the Cultural Revolution.[23] The end of the Cultural Revolution proper did not, however, restore peace and stability.[24] Leadership conflicts within the Party escalated at the same time as there was an expansion of China's diplomatic contacts, mainly to benefit from advanced technology from abroad. Rapid growth in trade occurred and by 1973, an estimated USD 1.3 billion in plant acquisition contracts were signed.[25] These led to balance of payments problems. Combined with imported inflationary pressures from the West, huge deficits were countered by cancelling or postponing imports and striving to increase exports.

Transition and reforms since 1978 When traditional systems of collectivised agriculture, planned industry and commerce, and the pursuit of self-reliance failed to produce satisfactory results, the Chinese government embarked on a major programme of economic reforms in 1978. The economic environment since then has been one of a transition from a centrally planned economy to a market economy. The central issue being resolved is how to reduce the role of government in the economic sphere. Extensive reforms have been undertaken in rural and urban areas, in both agriculture and industrial sectors. In the rural sector, decollectivisation of agriculture, and the introduction of decision making in the rural households, popularised as the household responsibility system (*baogan daohu*),[26] have been the main areas of reform. Curtailment of directives from the centre was also intended to increase independence for the lower echelons of the collectives. The policy of local self-sufficiency was replaced by one encouraging diversification and specialisation. There were considerable increases in the state purchasing prices of farm produce and an improvement in the agricultural terms of trade

---

[21] Ibid., p. 186.
[22] Ibid.
[23] Ronnås (1993), p. 228.
[24] Riskin (1991), p. 188.
[25] Ibid., p. 193.
[26] Under this system, land, draught animals, tools and equipment were distributed to the individual households against an obligation to meet sales quotas, tax payment and contributions to the team for provision of collective services (Ronnås 1993, p. 232).

vis-à-vis industrial products.[27] Favourable results of this programme extended the reforms into the urban industrial sector in 1984. The urban reforms began with the expansion of the decision making powers of enterprises. There has been substantial devolution of power from higher to lower level government[28] and outside the bureaucratic hierarchy, except in key sectors which are still maintained by direct central control. In defining the role of government, the Chinese government hoped 'to use macroeconomic policy tools, including control over the money supply, interest rates, bank reserve requirement, and tax policy as the primary methods of state control'.[29] These were complemented by a policy to open up to the outside world, by improving foreign trade and investment. Special economic zones were developed in improving economic relations with foreign countries, along with an open door policy toward foreign investment and trade geared towards benefiting from imports of technology and international capital, in the modern industrial sector.

China in the 1990s By 1992 the CPC leadership realised that limiting central planning and expanding the role of the market had not alleviated major economic problems like meeting the demand for food, provision of employment, raising state enterprise productivity and curbing the increasing expenditure of the state. So a second round of economic reforms was set in motion by Deng Xiaoping, this time with the goal of building a 'socialist market economy', with the state regulating and controlling the market mechanism. The major issues involve normative standards for evaluating performance, the appropriate mixture of property rights, how economic enterprises should be formed, an appropriate price system, and the economic institutions, laws and policies necessary to regulate the socialist market economy.[30]

Critical factors in development

The experiences, of pre-reform China in particular, reflect strict allegiance to socialism, import substitution and autarky at its extreme. Very high endowments of natural and human resources[31] facilitated the practice of national and local self-reliance through the sheer magnitude of the domestic market. Except for Sino-Soviet relations, which received a jolt in 1960, and a short period (1963-65) when foreign technological assistance was sought, China maintained an economy almost insulated from foreign influences. Central planning handled allocational and distributional decisions and virtually absent market forces did not result in severe

---

[27] Ibid., p. 44.
[28] The devolution of power to the local level was peculiar, since it entailed responsibility to rely on one's own resources without any support from the centre, yet each local or regional units had to supply that centre with inputs, produce and revenue as laid down by the central plan.
[29] Clarke (1992).
[30] Myers (1995).
[31] In 1994 the total population of China was 1,209 millions (United Nations 1995).

inflationary pressures. A critical factor that made this strategy sustain for long periods is the strength of the political parties in ensuring allegiance to the doctrine of socialism, by the people. The CPC found its winning formula in the mobilisation of the rural population, among which its leaders and cadres lived for many years.[32] Rural development has been on the agenda from the beginning because 'no feasible rate of industrialization, however rapid, can quickly incorporate the bulk of the population into the modern non-agricultural economy'.[33] Alexander Eckstein summarised China's main development objectives as follows: 'economic growth . . . combined with a commitment to improve income distribution, assure full employment free of inflation, and promote development with honor through a policy of self-reliance, that is, by minimizing or obviating China's dependence on foreign countries'.[34] This was done by combining elements of traditional, labour intensive methods of cultivation and irrigation, the application of modern inputs - increasingly derived from the gains of the green revolution - and a radical approach to socio-economic institutions and methods of management in rural areas.[35] We must not jump to the conclusion, however, that all of this was done primarily for the benefit of rural dwellers or rural areas as such. Rather, the measures taken were designed to mobilise resources in order to enhance the contribution of rural production to the industrialisation of China.[36] That this frequently implied that the interests of China's peasants came far down on the list of priorities should come as no surprise.

The rural areas have served as the starting grounds for change, a factor that has distinctly played a major role in exploiting the strength of the Chinese countryside. A review of rural industrialisation, which has been one of the oft-quoted successes of Chinese development, points to the importance of successful preconditions. They have been associated with prosperous agriculture and a captive labour force which translated into a strength because of a good rural educational system and the forced retreat of educated youth into the countryside, during the Cultural Revolution, in 1968.

Imperialistic contribution is also a factor to reckon with. Japan took over the north eastern provinces of Manchuria in 1931. After 1931, significant industrialisation occurred only in Manchuria, which was cut off from the rest of China.[37] On the subject of foreign influences, a related aspect is the contribution of Soviet aid. The availability of Soviet loans enabled China to run a trade deficit with the USSR from 1950 to 1955, tapping Soviet savings to supplement Chinese investment at a crucial point in time. Several types of Chinese purchases, including capital goods (plant and equipment), military hardware and shares in Sino-Soviet

---

[32] Riskin (1991), p. 4.
[33] Ibid., pp. 4-5.
[34] Eckstein (1977), p. 4.
[35] Riskin (1991), p. 2.
[36] E.g., Naughton (1992).
[37] Riskin (1991), pp. 16-17.

stock companies previously held by the Soviets, were financed by Soviet credits.[38] The Chinese FFYP described Soviet aided projects as the 'core' of China's construction plans.[39] While the exact amount and composition of Soviet aid is still unclear, 'enough is known to make it apparent that China's tempo of industrialization in the 1950s would have been considerably slower without Soviet help'.[40]

On the eve of liberation, Chinese society was hardly egalitarian with respect to incomes and wealth distribution: the incidence of landlordism varied across regions, and socio-economic conditions hindered investment, innovation and growth.[41] Both for ideological reasons and on grounds of asserting and projecting power, the CPC had to move rapidly and decisively to establish their control over the bureaucracy and economy. As Dietrich notes, they did so with considerable success.[42] The fact that this was achieved in no small part by military means highlights the role, alongside voluntary compliance, of coercion. The sum total, then, was one where

> [t]he political strength of the Party in the countryside, the enthusiasm of a large fraction of poorer peasants for a further redistribution of land and productive assets and the widespread - if short-lived - enthusiasm for the potential collectivization to raise output dramatically brought about full collectivization against surprisingly little resistance.[43]

Land redistribution was not a disaster to the middle peasants which minimized resistance and contributed to its success.

A distinct factor in the Chinese political economy has been a continuous cycle of administrative centralisation and decentralisation: 'a "recurring cycle" was generated, in which "centralization leads to rigidity, rigidity leads to complaints, complaints lead to decentralization, decentralization leads to disorder, and disorder leads back to centralization"'.[44] This cycle was brought about by the rigidity introduced by administrative planning and by the limits of local self-sufficiency. Yet a consistent pattern beyond the cyclical movement between centralisation and decentralisation can be detected. Most policies, irrespective of what end they else were designed for, can be interpreted as a disapproval of the real or imagined effects that markets are likely to have produced with respect both to allocative implications and distributional consequences.

Much the problem of developing economies, the Chinese input markets have been plagued by imperfections. Imperfections in the labour market were largely due to geographical extent, regulations restricting mobility and poor transport in

---

[38] Ibid., p. 74.
[39] Government of China (1956), p. 38, in Riskin (1991), p. 74.
[40] Riskin (1991), p. 76.
[41] Ibid., p. 32.
[42] Dietrich (1994), p. 55.
[43] Riskin (1991), p. 90.
[44] Jiang (1980), p. 55, quoted in Riskin (1991), p. 204.

the hinterland. 'Because of skewed investment patterns in these systems, the infrastructure of transportation and communications, so vital to the establishment of information channels, has long been ignored in all socialist systems, including the Chinese'.[45] Indeed, perhaps because of China's markedly gradual approach to reform, transition has been long drawn out. Yet, administrative institutions always lag behind in keeping up with political decision making. Vestiges of the previous system continue to exist and may either facilitate or hinder the new network of institutions in the post-reform period.

The 'Chinese characteristics' of thrift, Confucian values, adherence to authority and social order and an extraordinary work ethic, have also played their part in sustaining policy reversals, but these have at best complemented other policy decisions. Implementation of land reform, which is held as the 'greatest act of appropriation in human history',[46] stable agricultural production, and high domestic savings have contributed to the success of the developmental strategy. Between 1950 and 1990, the share of savings in GDP has increased from 17 to 35 per cent, while the share of investments has increased from 20 to 34 per cent.[47] The governmental budget has recorded surpluses in most years. However, state investment has been biased towards heavy industry at the cost of social overheads like transport and communication. The extreme emphasis of the concept of local self-sufficiency, combined with labour immobility, have confined the marketing boundaries to local areas. Absence of market determined price signals created pockets of industries utilising local raw materials and inputs so that the handicap of inadequate transport and communication was subdued but it hindered expansion of industries.

A striking feature is the way in which China's development through the decades, until the reforms of 1978, has occurred without excessive reliance on foreign trade. This was possible because of the size of the domestic market and the spurt in oil production during the 1960s and 1970s, which is a major item of developing country imports. Imperfections in factor and product markets have been a common feature, but the industrialisation programme has been almost entirely managed by the state, and has been supported by raising peasant purchasing powers. Chinese socialism departed from the urbanised heavy industry Soviet model, and, even though the heavy bias was explicit, rural reforms and local self-reliance have been the hallmarks of the Chinese developmental experience.

Small firms

Small industrialists and merchants formed part of the 'national bourgeoisie' whose interests were to be protected in the New Democracy ushered in 1949, while enterprises of the high bourgeoisie families were socialised. This 'three-anti' campaign

---

[45] Solinger (1989).
[46] Gray (1990).
[47] Table 1, Ministry of Foreign Affairs, Sweden (1992), p. 52.

47

was to weed out corruption, waste and bureaucratic abuse of power; considered as correlates of bourgeois thinking and activity. Then came the 'five-anti' campaign directed against industrialists, merchants and the middle class, and private industry stagnated. The socialist transformation saw the state take over shares of business capital, either by expropriating or voluntarily requesting enterprises to hand over. Private small and medium scale firms were becoming increasingly dependent on the state because of their state supply contracts, allocation of orders, raw materials and product purchases which were the main instruments of state control in the first stage of state capitalism. In the 'higher form of state capitalism', the Government took direct influence over the firms' production processes.[48] In the 'highest form of state capitalism', owners of private firms were converted to managers of branch companies, formed by combining enterprises in any industrial branch. These developments occurred gradually and by 1956, private economy was virtually non-existent.[49] 'The consolidation phase following the failure of the GLF saw a brief flurry of individual business activity . . . [but] the onslaught of the Cultural Revolution settled the fate of individual business as the "rat tail of capitalism"'.[50] There has been a revival of private business only after the reforms around 1981. Private businesses were legalised in 1988 after a constitutional amendment. Individual

Table 4.1
Development of individual business in China

	Urban areas	Rural areas	Total
	by no. of firms		
1978	140,000 (46.7)	160,000 (53.3)	300,000 (100)
1979	250,000 (44.6)	310,000 (55.4)	560,000 (100)
1980	400,000 (44.6)	497,000 (55.4)	897,000 (100)
1981	867,000 (47.5)	961,100 (52.5)	1,828,900 (100)
1982	1,358,000 (50.3)	1,340,000 (49.7)	2,698,000 (100)
1983	1,821,000 (30.5)	4,159,000 (69.5)	5,980,000 (100)
1984	2,911,000 (29.1)	7,089,000 (70.9)	10,000,000 (100)
1985	2,764,000 (23.7)	8,916,000 (76.3)	11,680,000 (100)
1986	2,910,000 (24.0)	9,200,000 (76.0)	12,110,000 (100)
1987	3,383,000 (24.6)	10,342,300 (75.4)	13,725,000 (100)
1988	3,823,000 (26.3)	10,704,000 (73.7)	14,527,000 (100)
1989	3,694,548 (29.6)	8,774,386 (70.4)	12,471,934 (100)

[48] Krauss (1991), p. 96. Small firms are defined as firms with 4 million yuan fixed assets and profits of up to 400,000 yuan in Wuhan province (ibid., p. 110) which suggests that there have been varying definitions across regions.
[49] At the time of the founding of the People's Republic of China there were 7.24 million independent private craftsmen, merchants and industrialists in the cities and towns. At the end of 1956 only 160,000 small scale businesses remained, and their numbers continued to fall (ibid., pp. 58-9).
[50] Ibid., p. 59.

48

Table 4.1 continued

	by no. of employed		
1978	150,000 (44.9)	184,000 (55.1)	334,000 (100)
1979	320,000 (47.3)	356,000 (52.7)	676,000 (100)
1980	810,000 (48.9)	848,000 (51.1)	1,658,000 (100)
1981	1,056,000 (46.4)	1,218,000 (53.6)	2,274,000 (100)
1982	1,470,000 (45.9)	1,730,000 (54.1)	3,200,000 (100)
1983	2,086,100 (27.9)	5,378,300 (72.1)	7,464,400 (100)
1984	3,390,000 (25.1)	10,120,000 (74.9)	13,510,000 (100)
1985	4,500,000 (24.6)	13,823,000 (75.4)	18,323,000 (100)
1986	4,831,000 (25.1)	14,383,000 (74.9)	19,214,000 (100)
1987	5,690,000 (26.5)	15,793,000 (73.5)	21,483,000 (100)
1988	6,590,000 (28.5)	16,460,000 (71.5)	23,050,000 (100)
1989	5,604,545 (28.8)	13,809,860 (71.2)	19,414,405 (100)

	by turnover in billion yuan (current prices)		
1978	-	-	-
1979	-	-	-
1980	-	-	-
1981	1.13 (53.6)	0.98 (46.4)	2.11 (100)
1982	5.07 (50.3)	5.00 (49.7)	10.07 (100)
1983	7.24 (34.3)	13.86 (65.7)	21.10 (100)
1984	12.27 (26.8)	33.49 (73.2)	45.76 (100)
1985	21.41 (28.5)	53.65 (71.5)	75.06 (100)
1986	27.44 (30.0)	63.98 (70.0)	91.42 (100)
1987	33.60 (32.4)	70.23 (67.6)	103.83 (100)
1988	44.23 (37.1)	74.84 (62.9)	119.07 (100)
1989	54.22 (40.4)	79.70 (59.6)	133.92 (100)

Note: figures in parentheses indicate the rural-urban percentage distribution.
Source: Krauss (1991), Table 3, p. 64.

businesses had been allowed prior to the reforms too. The development of the latter in the post-reform era is shown in Table 4.1. By the end of 1987 China had about 115,000 private firms, 80 per cent of which were in rural areas and a large part in coastal and relatively economically developed regions. Private firms employ on an average 16 people; 50 per cent employ 20-30 workers and less than one per cent employ more than 100 workers.[51] Private enterprise capital endowment averages 50,000 yuan.[52] Private firms are dominated by industry and manufacturing, mining, transportation and construction. Some 80 per cent were active in con-

---

[51] Ibid., p. 97.
[52] At the time the equivalent to one US dollar was approximately 8.3 yuan.

Table 4.2

Sectoral breakdown of industry in China by number of firms (percentage shares in parentheses)

Sector	1985		1986		1987		1988		1989	
Industry, crafts	1,512,000	(12.9)	1,535,000	(12.7)	1,804,000	(13.1)	1,849,358	(12.7)	1,539,681	(12.3)
Transportation	990,000	(8.5)	1,023,000	(8.4)	1,285,000	(9.4)	1,474,210	(10.1)	1,146,671	(9.1)
Commerce	6,225,000	(53.2)	6,428,000	(53.1)	7,290,000	(53.1)	7,721,906	(53.2)	6,830,688	(54.7)
Construction	48,000	(0.4)	47,000	(0.4)	56,000	(0.4)	52,390	(0.4)	26,091	(0.2)
Catering	1,180,000	(10.1)	1,246,000	(10.3)	1,390,000	(10.2)	1,450,903	(10.0)	1,264,049	(10.1)
Services	697,000	(5.9)	728,000	(6.0)	747,000	(5.4)	793,935	(5.5)	705,897	(5.6)
Repairs	824,000	(7.0)	879,000	(7.2)	966,000	(7.0)	988,708	(6.8)	829,474	(6.7)
Other	235,000	(2.0)	225,000	(1.9)	196,000	(1.4)	195,658	(1.3)	129,383	(1.0)
Total	11,711,000	(100.0)	12,111,000	(100.0)	13,734,000	(100.0)	14,527,068	(100.0)	12,471,934	(100.0)

Annual growth rate, per cent

Sector	1985	1986	1987	1988	1989
Industry, crafts	-	1.5	17.5	2.5	-16.7
Transportation	-	3.3	25.6	14.7	-22.2
Commerce	-	3.3	13.4	5.9	-11.5
Construction	-	-2.1	19.1	-6.4	-50.2
Catering	-	5.6	11.6	4.4	-12.9
Services	-	4.4	2.6	6.3	-11.1
Repairs	-	6.7	9.9	2.4	-16.1
Other	-	-4.3	-12.9	-0.2	-33.9

Source: Krauss (1991), Table 6, p. 69.

struction and manufacturing (in the late 1980s).[53] Most entrepreneurs came from village or county firms or were cadres in rural production teams and brigades. Table 4.2 shows the sectoral shares of various activities in individual business. As can be seen, the shares of industry and crafts have been declining since 1987.

Table 4.3
Sectoral breakdown of industry in China,
employment shares (per cent)

Sector	1985	1986	1987	1988	1989
Industry, crafts	16.7	16.9	18.6	17.8	16.8
Transportation	8.8	8.4	8.7	9.2	8.2
Commerce	47.4	47.3	46.8	47.4	49.8
Construction	1.9	1.8	1.9	1.7	0.8
Catering	11.7	12.1	11.9	12.0	12.7
Services	5.4	5.5	4.9	5.0	5.2
Repairs	6.0	6.1	5.8	5.6	5.7
Other	2.1	1.9	1.4	1.3	1.0
Total	100.0	100.0	100.0	100.0	100.0

Source: Krauss (1991), Table 7, p. 70.

Sectoral shares of various activities of individual businesses in employment generation are shown in Table 4.3. Industry and crafts have accounted for substantial employment shares, though their shares are seen to be declining after 1987.

The rationale for small, local industries did not originate in the GLF. It had been spelled out as early as 1951, and received considerable attention in the FFYP itself. However, because of the preoccupation of the political and economic leadership with the establishment of a Soviet-type, centralized system of planning and management, and with the correction of sectoral and regional imbalances that seemed to call for centralized control of the resource allocation mechanisms, little attention was actually paid to local industrialization during the First Plan period. In contrast it was one of the pillars of the Great Leap strategy.[54]

This policy was in part based on ideas originating prior to the launching of the GLF. At an early stage local industry was considered a useful instrument for the mobilisation of resources under circumstances or in sectors where large scale enterprises would not, or could not, operate. Thereby, or so it was thought, overall

---

[53] Krauss (1991), pp. 96-8.
[54] Riskin (1991), p. 118.

production could expand at low cost. Furthermore, local industry would also help supply agriculture and other rural needs, thereby enabling state owned enterprises 'to concentrate on its own expansion'.[55] In other respects, however, the policies of the GLF with respect to local small scale industry did imply a break with the past. Its focus on mass initiative and the concomitant depreciation of technical expertise, and its insistence on local self-reliance resulted in a regional dispersion of productive assets and production. As such it was a major departure from the previous strategy. Instead, local enterprises 'epitomized the social mobilizational and anti-bureaucratic aspects of Mao's "vision", and were intended to provide China's localities with both means and motivation for extraordinary efforts on behalf of industrialization and agricultural modernization'.[56]

Small scale production has survived the onslaughts of the modernisation and heavy industrialisation drive because of the very small base of modern industry and poor transport infrastructure which resulted in fragmentation of markets into a large number of small and poorly integrated markets. This is particularly true of the rural non-agricultural enterprises.

Dispersed industrialisation Dispersed industrialisation is as much an experience of China as of Taiwan. Factors conducive to dispersed industrialisation have been the stress on local self-reliance, good infrastructure and network of towns, high rural education, a dynamic agricultural sector and equitable distribution of income in rural areas.[57] There is also very little rural-urban migration. But unlike Taiwan dispersed industrialisation did not go hand in hand with balanced regional development. Coupled with immobility of capital, especially human capital, disparities are widening with respect to development of market based economic systems.

Regional distribution of industry was lopsided when the PRC was founded. More than 70 per cent of industry, mainly light industry,[58] was concentrated in the eastern coastal areas, which account for less than 12 per cent of the country's territory, and in a small number of cities.[59] Between 1952 and 1985, the number of industrial enterprises in this distribution changed and by the end of 1985, inland areas accounted for 52.5 per cent and coastal areas 47.5 per cent. This has been the result of a deliberate policy initiative to achieve balanced regional development of industry and promote local self-sufficiency.

Rural industrialisation The merits of rural industrialisation lay in its capacity to increase employment in industry; in aiding agriculture through provision of inputs, which raised marginal productivity of the labour force in agriculture; and in ex-

---

[55] Riskin (1971), pp 258-9.
[56] Riskin (1991), p. 118.
[57] Johansson and Ronnås (1995), p. 49.
[58] Light industry refers to the production of consumer goods and hand tools; heavy industry refers to production of intermediate goods or the means of production.
[59] The cities where industry was concentrated were Shanghai, Tianjin, Qingdao, Guangzhou, Wuxi, Shenyang, Anshan and Dalian (James 1989, p. 516).

ploiting differences in relative factor costs between the city and village. Poor transport and the insistence on local self-reliance resulted in the use of locally available resources and savings in transport costs. There was limited interaction with modern industries in terms of inter-firm flows of technicians and equipment in upgrading skills. Their geographic isolation resulted in high costs and primitive technology and constituted investment misallocations. Immobility confined the gains from rural industrialisation to rural areas.

Rural enterprises had their heyday during the GLF since the communes were sufficiently large to form relatively self-contained units capable of operating with little assistance from above. By acting as multi-enterprise conglomerates, communes could pool resources, spread risks and draw benefits from economies of scale as they embarked on the development of new non-farm enterprises.[60] In 1962, there was a ban on establishment of non-agricultural enterprises at the commune and brigade levels, reflecting the priority given to agriculture after the collapse of the GLF. This ban was revoked in 1970 and the pace of rural industrialisation accelerated. This renewed spurt once again correlates with prosperous agriculture and other favourable institutional factors like the captive labour force, liberalised availability of inputs, inability of the planned economy to satisfy local demands and the three tier system of communes.

Rural enterprises comprise both officially sponsored Township and Village Enterprises (TVEs) and various 'below-village' categories, such as cooperatives, partnerships and private and individual firms.[61] TVE is the general term used for rural enterprises at the township level and below. They include both collective and non-collective enterprises, covering enterprises run by townships (the former communes, including towns and districts), villages (the former brigades), villagers' group (the former work teams), jointly owned enterprises, private and individual enterprises. Rural enterprises engage in all types of activities, ranging from agriculture to industry, from construction to services.[62]

The ownership structure of TVEs form a continuum, from collective ownership to individual businesses. Under collective ownership are found township enterprises, village enterprises and villagers' group enterprises. The assets belong to the collective along with decision making and the enterprise contributes a portion of its profits to the township and/or village for local economic development. The second form is the privately owned enterprises consisting of private enterprises and individual businesses. A third form of ownership is the jointly owned enterprises which include entities operated and owned by several households, cooperatives and joint ventures in various forms.

As is clear from Table 4.4, the ownership structure has changed greatly since the initiation of the reforms. There has been a faster rate of growth of non-collective

---

[60] Ronnås (1993), p. 234.
[61] Ody (1992).
[62] Cai Fang et al. (1991), p. 17.

Table 4.4
Ownership structure of township enterprises in China 1978-88
by number of firms, employment and output value

Year	Total		Percentage		
		Township	Village	Joint	Private
No. (1,000)					
1978	1,544.2	21.0	79.0	-	-
1980	1,424.6	23.7	76.3	-	-
1984	6,065.2	6.6	24.1	15.0	54.3
1985	12,224.5	3.4	11.7	9.2	75.7
1986	15,153.1	2.8	8.6	7.2	81.4
1987	17,501.0	2.4	6.6	6.8	84.2
1988	18,881.6	2.2	6.2	6.4	85.2
Employment (1,000)					
1978	28,265.6	44.5	55.5	-	-
1980	29,996.7	46.5	53.5	-	-
1984	52,081.1	36.1	40.4	10.0	13.5
1985	69,790.3	30.3	31.7	11.0	27.0
1986	79,371.4	28.7	28.5	10.5	32.3
1987	88,051.8	27.2	26.4	10.5	35.9
1988	95,454.6	26.1	25.2	10.2	39.5
Output (million yuan)					
1978	49,307	57.0	43.0	-	-
1980	65,690	56.2	43.8	-	-
1984	170,981	47.8	37.9	7.4	6.9
1985	272,839	41.7	33.4	9.0	15.9
1986	354,089	39.9	31.1	8.8	20.2
1987	476,420	38.3	29.6	8.9	23.2
1988	649,566	37.5	29.6	8.6	24.3

Source: Cai Fang et al. (1991), Table 5, p. 20.

enterprises. In spite of the ban on private business during commune formation, traditional skills have greatly influenced the choice of the business lines enterprises engage in.[63] According to Ody, ten years into reform more than 18 million enterprises based in rural areas employed as many as 90 million people, or almost one-fifth of the national labour force. These rural enterprises produced more than one-fifth of the national gross value of output. Although strictly speaking making up only a small proportion of all rural enterprises TVEs, most of them engaged in

---

[63] Ibid., p. 18.

industrial production, accounted for the bulk of employment and output. Furthermore, they made a very significant contribution to China's total industrial production, exports and employment.[64]

The dynamics of small firms Private firms largely began their activity as individual or family firms, or from break-ups of large firms or leasing state and collective firms in later stages, until late 1980s, when proprietorship, partnership and limited liability companies have been founded and owned by private entrepreneurs. These private firms differ in organisational structure from the operation of collectives and communes. In general, the collectives enjoyed better environment owing to their close links with the local government. This improved their access to input and product markets. The private sector firms, however, have borne the brunt of the socialisation pursuits. Collective enterprises contributed to the industrialisation programme, but private firms were almost absent until their resurrection in the late 1980s. The capital for small firms, both fixed and working, was raised by the households starting the firms. Apart from this, the Industry and Commerce Bank and the Agricultural Bank were the main credit institutions. Since these banks insist on security and other information about ability to repay, a private credit market has also established itself. Even though the interest rates are higher, the flexibility they offer as against the bureaucratic credit institutions has made banks an important source of credit, especially in the rural areas.[65] A tightened credit policy since 1985 has added to the problem of industrial credit and China needs an effective credit policy that could operate through the PCB.

Illegality of firms has also been an outcome of the reforms since instruments of control that raise the risks of operating illegally are also found wanting. In fact government authorities have been, if not encouraging, passively aware of this but have not taken strict action since their tax and other small industry policies are not yet rationalised. The dual pricing system (i.e., the coexistence of fixed and market prices) of products and of intermediate goods has resulted in the emergence of small firms who take advantage of this and profit by selling goods, procured from the government, in the free market. While this is largely a problem of traders, genuine manufacturing firms resort to illegal operations due to the licensing policies. A weak legal regulatory framework increases the disadvantages to the firms since the officials can thereby wield their pre-reform powers. Granting of permits is a long winding process ridden with complexities and red tape. It has been recorded that the time required from the date of application of permit to the day the firm begins operation is anywhere between one and a few years.[66]

Labour supply is more a problem of urban than rural small firms. Current regulations place them in a vulnerable position, since workers in collective firms could change over to privately owned firms only if they agreed to pay a portion of their

---

[64] Ody (1992).
[65] Krauss (1991), p. 148.
[66] See ibid., Chapter IV, for identifying transaction costs of enterprise management.

pay to the collective. The rural firms are benefiting from improved productivity in agriculture and the consequent release of surplus labour force into non-agricultural activities. Regulations regarding worker treatment abound, including a stipulation that the owner's earning should not be more than ten times the average wage of his employees. Trade unions are legalised though their links with the CPC are still not clearly specified. The supply of raw materials and finished products has been made easier for the private small firms since the reform process was initiated. Export oriented firms are not placed in any considerably advantageous position since they face the same red tape in the process, even though they enjoy certain other privileges.

Even though dependence on the state is being reduced, as also Chinese commentators point out, 'the relationship between enterprises and government has to change from administrative subordination to those of contracting partners which reflect certain market relationships. Horizontal associations do exist, some "loose" associations which result in a cartel-type organization which may jeopardize competition'.[67] As a result, these commentators suggest, China is in need of reforms aiming to: (i) establish a monetised factor market; (ii) deal with the monopoly position that financial organisations in China hold, for instance through introduction of specialised banks and increased competition; (iii) encourage labour mobility, between occupations as well as between rural and urban areas; (iv) introduce truly autonomous management at state owned enterprises; and (v) establish intermediary organisations, competing internally for assignments of mediating subcontracting arrangements from government to enterprises.

Corruption in tax administration is pervasive since there are a lot of loopholes in the tax system. A high proportion of tax evasion exists since there is arbitrariness in the framing of tax policies which leaves much room for manoeuvre by state officials and also because of the fact that citizens do not have the 'habit of paying taxes'.[68] The weak institutional framework has been complemented by the existence of informal methods of solving tax evasion cases like recourse to mediation or conciliation, without litigation.

Government and collective enterprise relations are also interesting. There is little conflict because the government owns and has considerable interest in developing them, and determining how they stand in competition with other local governmental levels in their claims to central government funds.[69] Further, the influence of interest groups in governance and policy making is absent. Small firms, especially in the rural areas, have exhibited very strong backward linkages with agriculture. A symbiotic relationship was envisioned where the mechanisation of agriculture was the task of rural small enterprises and agriculture in turn was to release surplus labour for non-farm pursuits. Vertical linkages of labour intensive local enterprises with modern large industry, mainly state enterprises, have also been

---

[67] China Economic Structural Reform Research Institute (1988).
[68] Jinyan Li (1991), p. 24.
[69] See Qian and Stiglitz (1996).

56

strong, except for the drive for steel production which was not viable for small scale production.[70] Since 1984 individual businessmen have an organisation of their own, the Association of Independents, which, though under the leadership of the CPC, has been set up to protect the interests of small firms. By 1986, a National Association of Entrepreneurs had also been founded to perform supervisory functions in addition to conveying the needs of small firms to the Government. In spite of this umbrella of protection, 'it is generally admitted that private businesses are on the lookout for a "red cloak of invisibility" which would protect them from attacks'.[71] This is done by registering firms as cooperative, rural or neighbourhood firms.

The private economy has had an inferior legal, economic and political status which is changing since the reforms from an attitude of elimination to one of tolerance.[72] The overall picture one gets of the status of private small firms is that they are still discriminated against and private entrepreneurs are constantly in fear of sudden policy reversals. The high degree of policy uncertainty in turn reflects the short time horizons in the production plans of small firms.

The financial market

The financial market was highly centralised in pre-reform China. Credit and interest rates were not used as economic levers. China had a monobank financial system, with the People's Bank of China (PBC) vested with the monopoly over currency issue, transaction clearing, savings and lending for working capital. Under the old system, banks were passive, administrative units with the major economic decisions being made by the planning ministries under the State Council.[73] The design of the banking system was such that each level of the bank was roughly parallel to a corresponding level of the government hierarchy, and thereby under the control of central and local governments. Bank branches had geographic and administrative jurisdictions within which they had to conduct their duties.

With the reforms, the PBC has taken over the responsibility of being the Central Bank with four specialised banks: the Industrial and Commercial Bank of China, the Agricultural Bank of China, the Bank of China and the People's Construction Bank of China as the mainstay. Other monetary organisations like insurance companies, credit cooperatives, investment companies, trust companies, and lease companies act as subsidiary organisations. The PBC is the only foreign exchange bank. While bank credit predominates, commercial credit, trust and folk credit also exist.

The capital market has been a weak link in the financial sector in China. It has not performed the functions of raising funds for enterprise capital, supply relevant economic information, provide market signals and restrain corporate enterprise

---

[70] Examples of which are provided by, e.g., Ronnås and Sjöberg (1996).
[71] Krauss (1991), pp. 96-7.
[72] Ma Jisen (1988).
[73] Bowles and White (1993), Chapter 3.

managers. Share and bond markets have so far developed only in Shanghai and Shenzhen, but are not effectively integrated with the banking and public finance systems.[74] Enterprises still rely on bank loans for their capital and place earnings in bank deposits rather than buy securities; laws governing the capital markets are still falling into place.

Fiscal policy

With China's choice of a highly centralised economy, its fiscal policy and financial planning gave a major role for the state budget in influencing the nation's economic activity. Next came the cash and credit plans of the banking system and the financial plans of the individual enterprises. The state budget was almost exclusively the means through which the national financial resources were mobilised and allocated to different productive units as capital, based on rate of growth, industrial composition and geographical distribution. It also performed a supervisory role, monitoring the efficiency of state enterprises. While the budget carried out its first responsibility adequately, its performance on the supervision function deteriorated with time.[75] Supervisory functions have decreased after the reforms were initiated in 1978, giving greater financial independence to production units. In the post-reform period, the budget has attempted overall macro-economic control through taxation and governmental expenditure. Receipts from personal income tax are negligible and indirect taxes have been the most important since 1980. Revenue from agricultural tax is low due to political considerations of stimulating agricultural output and poor administration.

The process of socialisation is reflected in both budgetary receipts and expenditure. While the private sector accounted for approximately two-thirds of the government revenue in 1950, this ratio was less than one per cent in 1976.[76] From 1956 to the late 1970s, the major tax revenue was from turnover taxes,[77] to secure a regular transfer of funds from the enterprises to the state. Income taxes were neither necessary nor imposed, except for collectives which had to pay them in addition to turnover taxes. Direct taxes have become significant only in the post-reform period, with the introduction of a new tax system. With the reforms and open door policy, there was need to distinguish taxes for foreign investment from the domestic system. Customs duties were rescheduled and foreign investment income accommodated. With a greater role for private business, taxation now has a role as an economic regulator in China in addition to the revenue raising function it performed in the pre-reform years.

---

[74] Myers (1995).

[75] Hsiao (1978), p. 2.

[76] Ibid., p. 5.

[77] They provided over 80 per cent of the total tax revenue prior to the 1984 tax reform and still provide over 40 per cent of the total (Jinyan Li 1991, p. 32). See World Bank (1990) for a discussion on the tax framework.

A protective tariff policy safeguarded the economy from excessive imports and exports until the open door policy was adopted. While there existed no duty on most exported goods, in 1982 some 34 commodities were subject to duties ranging from 10 to 60 per cent. Import duties were increased on most machine tools, mining equipment and farming implements to protect domestic manufacture after reforms had been initiated. On the other hand, tariffs were reduced for certain types of commodities like natural raw materials for industry which are in short supply in China.

On the expenditure side, expenditure on capital construction has been the greatest, primarily to urban state enterprises. Agriculture has not had a large claim in spite of the dominant rural economy, mainly since communes were meant to be self-financing. Defence spending has been a major component of non-economic budgetary expenditure though its share has been reduced since the reform. The growing current expenditure since the reform was mainly due to increased subsidies to cover losses of state owned enterprises. On the whole the total revenue exceeded total expenditure in the period 1950 to 1985. Deficits were seen in the years of the GLF, in 1967 due to the Cultural Revolution and in the initial years of the reform which continued until 1985.

Industrial policy

China adopted an autarkic industrial policy implying pursuit of economic self-sufficiency, along with a closed economy and a heavy industry bias in the beginning stages of its industrialisation programme in the post-war period. Also part of the industrial policy was the goal of spatial decentralisation. The industrial policy 'reflected both the muting of international competition and the dissipation of economies of scale in pursuit of the regional dispersal goal'.[78]

Paralleling India, steel dominated Chinese Heavy and Chemical Industry (HCI) and the development of alternative materials such as petrochemicals was retarded. Other globally dynamic post-war sectors, such as vehicle production, were also slow to develop.[79] There have been three HCI Big Pushes in post-war China. The first two were planned and comprise the Soviet inspired push of the mid-1950s and the defence driven push launched in the late 1960s. Auty argues that the Third HCI Big Push (1984-88) was not planned, but rather an unintended by-product of the reforms of the Deng era.

The FFYP reflected ambitious plans of industrialisation, mainly in the heavy industry sector, while the consumer goods sector lagged behind. The High Tide in industry and commerce ensued in 1955 and from enormous political pressures, industry and commerce were socialised by the end of 1956. Virtually the entire private sector had been taken over or reorganised into cooperatives.[80] The capi-

---

[78] Auty (1994b), p. 215.
[79] Ibid.
[80] Dietrich (1994), p. 96.

talists now worked as salaried managers and received bonds for their expropriated properties.[81] The First Big Push was executed with Soviet assistance and ended in the GLF. The Second Big Push was part of a strategy of industrial decentralisation associated with the Cultural Revolution. It aimed to make each province self-sufficient, so that a military invasion would need to be total to be effective. The industrial policy during the recovery period focused investment in a small number of sectors regarded as being of high priority for economic or strategic reasons.[82] Authority over resource allocation with regard to industry, commerce, finance, and labour, which had been handed down to localities in 1958, was now recentralised.[83] Management policy, like all other aspects of industrial policy, was guided during the recovery period by the 'Seventy Articles on Industrial Policy'.

Trade policy

Following the founding of the PRC in 1949, a blockade and trade embargo was imposed on China by the United States and its allies and trade has not been an engine of growth ever since, even though the embargo has been lifted. Foreign trade underwent a profound change during the recovery period (1960-65). Foreign trade policy was captive to the dictates of necessity, which exerted three distinct but interrelated forces upon it, according to Riskin: the general post-GLF crises, which led to a sharp decline in overall trade; the break with the Soviet Union; and the food crisis.[84] This resulted in a sharp decline of producer goods' imports in particular. There was a change in the pattern of trade with the shift away from socialist bloc countries after the reforms.[85] Historically, however, trade has been unimportant for various reasons. The United States embargo on China made China's turn to the Soviet Union imperative. A further setback occurred in 1960, with the withdrawal of Soviet technical and financial assistance and this, combined with the policy of self-reliance and the effects of boycotts aginst trade with China, connived to keep total trade at a very low level. Trade relations improved after 1970 but did not become important until the reforms.[86] An exception to this conservatism occurred in 1978-80, when the Ten Year Plan gave rise to a 'great leap outward'.[87]

---

[81] Ibid.

[82] Riskin (1991), p. 152.

[83] Ibid., p. 158.

[84] Ibid., p. 155.

[85] Only about 5 per cent of exports and 9 per cent of imports involved other centrally planned economies and the bulk of the trade is with developed capitalist and Third World countries including Hong Kong. China's largest trading partners have been Japan, Hong Kong and the United States in that order (Riskin 1991, p. 323).

[86] Prior to 1979, there were virtually no foreign owned enterprises operating in China, but by the end of September 1990, about 25,000 foreign funded businesses had been established with a total capital of approximately USD 45 billion (Jinyan Li 1991, p. 99).

[87] Riskin (1991), p. 319.

That oil production came on stream contributed towards a favourable development of trade and helped underwrite extensive purchases of machinery and transport equipment, the main types of goods imported during the first decade of post-Mao reform. With a low debt service ratio to match, China has been able to avoid financial dependence and related pains often associated with the opening up of formerly inward looking economies. In fact, trade balance statistics reveal that surpluses have been larger and more numerous than deficits on the trade account. Deficits incurred with capitalist bloc countries were financed by surpluses from trade with developing countries. Furthermore, shipping, insurances, services and remittances normally run in China's favour. All in all, unlike in many other developing or transition economies, foreign exchange reserves have been kept at a healthy level.[88]

The Chinese experience: implications for transaction costs

The political economy of China since 1949 has been filled with institutional changes, which have sought to encompass political, economic as well as social life of the Chinese, in cultivating the socialist spirit. Needless to say this has had implications as far as the transaction costs of economic agents in general, and small firms in particular, are concerned. It is possible to consider the collective and non-collective enterprises separately in this context since the economic environment these groups have faced has been somewhat different.

The local governments are the legal owners of collective enterprises and to the extent that transaction costs vary with differing relations with the government, the private firms have been placed at a less advantageous position and have experienced higher transaction costs. While it is difficult to attempt a generalisation of this attitude, it can be safely understood that this relationship could have been anything from 'strongly supportive to outright predatory'.[89] The symbiotic relationship between collective enterprises and the local government served well to reduce transaction costs to small firms, mainly benefiting through the local government's control over market access. Non-collective enterprises, however, suffered on two counts: lack of access and higher costs, since they had to pay more for the inputs from the government distribution. Many of these enterprises sought to overcome this problem by registering as red hat firms. Sometimes this was done with the knowledge of the local government officials, 'in the form of an administrative fee to the village or township government'.[90] These red hat firms also owe their existence to the macro-economic uncertainties that prevailed with respect to the operation of the private sector. In an institutionalist perspective this implies a lack of formal institutions of property rights and poorly developed economic legislation which are major factors contributing to high transaction costs of the small firms.

---

[88] Ibid.
[89] Johansson and Ronnås (1995), p. 47.
[90] Ma Jisen (1988).

'Chinese formal institutions, that is, the legal rules and norms', Zhang and Sjöberg note, 'are found to be unstable with a high degree of uncertainty prevailing in the enforcement of existing formal rules. Such a characterisation typically implies high transaction costs'.[91]

The negative impact of arbitrary legislation is reinforced by subjective interpretations of ambiguous legislation by the government officials. The complexity of the situation is increased by the poor legal awareness of the average citizens. 'It is a major problem today', the Prime Minister observed in 1986, 'that too many people ignore the law'.[92] Transaction costs have also been high since limited experience with making efficient contracts raise contract costs on the one hand and the monitoring and enforcement costs on the other. Poor enforcement of contracts manifest in reduced quality of contracted goods.

China also suffers from poor financial accounting since many small firms started out as household enterprises and had a passive existence. This increases the costs of drawing contracts and the possibilities for opportunism. It then becomes interesting to see how the firms have coped in this environment of uncertainty and this leads one to underline the importance of informal institutions in reducing high transaction costs, especially to the private small firm. In China, social norms, conventions, behavioural codes and so forth together with the formal rules, shape modes and patterns of conduct in economic interaction. Two specific forms of informal institutions that Zhang and Sjöberg note have been the influence of informal local policies and the influence of *guanxi*, an informal code of behaviour stressing bonds of personal interrelatedness between contracting partners in economic transactions. Informal social contacts have been major sources of information and the impact of this on transaction costs cannot be stated clearly. On the one hand, while it increases the search costs, it could also decrease ex post transaction costs in the form of monitoring of contracts. The absence of a well-defined system of contract enforcement and the poor familiarity of the local government with the legal system, makes informal local policies an important way of dealing by the local government too.

In fact Zhang and Sjöberg also go further and note 'what passes for a decidedly collectivist spirit and behavior is perhaps better seen as attributes which define the position of a person in relation to others'.[93] While this guanxi was something the CPC tried to eradicate all along its drive towards socialism, in the post-reform period this informal institution has played a major role in reducing the high transaction costs that follow the uncertainty in the transition period. On a related issue, Solinger notes the importance of 'relational contracting' (recurrent exchanges with known partners) in post-Mao China.[94] These patterns of exchanges have served to reduce the threats of opportunism in the contracting partners and overcome the cloud of uncertainty hanging over the economic scenario in general. Firms have

---

[91] Zhang and Sjöberg (1992), p. 42.

[92] Zhao Ziyang (1986), p. 50, quoted in Zhang and Sjöberg (1992), p. 18.

[93] Zhang and Sjöberg (1992), p. 22.

[94] Solinger (1989).

tended to engage in a 'second' or 'grey' economy to overcome breakdowns in the formal supply system that threatened to prevent fulfilment of planned targets.

Thus, a few, if not all, vestiges of the central planning era have helped the firms adjust to a changing economic environment. Another instance of this benefit is that firms came to count on supplies from particular plants with which they were associated during the plan. This relational contracting has gone a long way in reducing the uncertainty around contract and control costs. While these strategies have helped reduce transaction costs, one cannot count on them as efficient, long term adaptations. Temporarily, they can be counted as second best solutions, compensating for inadequate formal contractual exchanges.

High transaction costs follow from the absence of efficient markets for goods and services providing strong incentives to internalise as many transactions as possible in order to reduce these costs. Inefficient input markets have also led to high transaction costs to the small firms. The pursuit of local self-reliance further encouraged the 'micro level import substitution', that is, the attempts of entrepreneurs in a centrally planned system to internalise as many functions within the local unit as possible. The high degree of external insecurity made the enterprises produce as much as possible of the intermediate inputs they needed within the enterprise and lessen the dependence on local authorities for these inputs.[95]

Further the fragmentation of markets resulted in protection and growth of inefficient enterprises through lack of competition, especially external. Limited access to non-local markets also hindered the expansion prospects of small firms, while also resulting in promotion of cost-inefficient small firms. With the introduction of reforms, industries which have hitherto flourished under the garb of protection undoubtedly have to tune up or perish in the face of competition. Protection from foreign competition, protection of rural firms from urban and state enterprises has led to local industries exploiting local increases of purchasing power during periods of agricultural prosperity. However, this has also resulted in breeding inefficient units and perpetuated fragmentation. Immobility of human capital has increased the search costs of small firms, especially in the area of skilled labour. Though rural firms benefited from the forced retreat of skilled labour after the Cultural Revolution, firms in areas without this scarce resource have faced high search costs in addition to the negative impact of insufficient labour skills.

The support of the government has been largely passive as far as private small industry is concerned, even in the period of the GLF. Active support, in the form of credit policies, organisational framework, improved information on technology and other know-how has not been recorded, which have increased the search costs considerably. Private small firms have generally relied on their own resources and the informal credit market. The poorly developed financial market, with the banks' insistence on cumbersome procedures make informal sources more attractive. Uncertainty in the policy environment has not only hindered expansionary efforts by small firms, it has made fine internal hierarchies impossible within the firm;

---

[95] Winiecki (1989), p. 366.

consequently, gains from capital market as a source of investment finance have been largely overlooked. The poorly developed capital market has also contributed to this high degree of dependence on informal credit sources. The government budget has not provided much for improvement of infrastructure, though it has been recording surpluses and the debt service ratio has been quite low. This has helped perpetuate fragmentation of the markets and raised transaction costs to small firms by limiting information about non-local markets. There is a consensus that Chinese formal institutions need to be overhauled, especially the financial market and the foreign trade, in providing a healthy environment for small firms to grow.

Contributory factors for reduced transaction costs, especially to collective enterprises have been the three tier administrative structure since 1970s, a strong local government and strong linkages, both backward and forward with state enterprises.[96] However, horizontal linkages have not been very useful in reducing transaction costs given the dispersed nature of industrialisation. Links with state enterprises have mitigated the problems of lack of information on technology and quality standards, but subcontracting relations have also been perceived as risky since they could be curtailed on short notice. Joint ventures have only been with other prominent business partners. There has also been the problem of harassment of private firms by local government officials and of locally owned units by higher administrative powers adding to the uncertainty and encroachment fear of firms. Krauss records an experience which reflects the harsh environment small firms still continue to face:

> On September 17, 1988, only two and a half months after the regulations had gone into force, the official Xinhua news agency reported that 'exhorbitantly high payments in Shenyang had forced 14,000 private shop owners in the first five months of the year to go out of business. They had to pay 43 types of fees, of which only 15 went to the city administration. The others were irrational duties and fines, enforced with all kinds of excuses.[97]

There is, however, a changing attitude toward the community of private entrepreneurs in general, and the aversion earlier recorded is gradually giving way in Chinese social strata as well as the government. The repeated resurgence of the private economy, in spite of all the suppression in different historical periods, shows that its existence is inevitable and the policy of the CPC and the Government has a direct bearing on the development of private economy.

---

[96] Johansson and Ronnås (1995).
[97] Krauss (1991), p. 158.

Taiwan

As an important member of the 'Tiger Club', an East Asian 'miracle', a high performing Asian economy, and one of the 'Four Dragons',[98] Taiwan, Republic of China[99] warrants a closer look at its spectacular story of rapid economic growth, in the last few decades. Literature on the success of Taiwan is abundant.[100] While different schools of thought have emerged in explaining the rapid growth,[101] there is consensus that it has been spectacular. The spectacle of Taiwan is not as much about its structural transformation as it is about the pace with which it occurred, along with few distortions. Particularly, its outward oriented economic development has occurred without widening inequality in incomes; there has been a balanced growth of both industry and agriculture; dispersed industrialisation[102] aided by agriculture; and successful export orientation.

Economic history

In the four decades following the end of World War II, per capita GNP in Taiwan rose from approximately USD 150 to USD 6,135,[103] with an average 9 per cent growth rate in per capita income in this period. From 1951 to 1991, Taiwan's real GNP increased 28.5 times - an average annual growth of 8.9 per cent - and per capita GNP grew 10.9 times in real terms, reaching USD 8,815 in 1991.[104] Within the rather limited span of less than 25 years, Taiwan has emerged as an industrial economy of considerable size and repute and a leading exporter. From being characterised as a producer of agricultural products and unsophisticated consumer goods, it is today not only an exporter of consumer durables and electronics: it is also characterised by outward foreign direct investment in search of cheap labour and the recipient of illegal immigrants in search of job opportunities and higher wages. 'The transformation from a minor to a major trading nation', Wade has observed, 'has occured within twenty-five years without inflation, fiscal crises, periodic doses of stabilization programs, or high levels of foreign debt'.[105]

The Japanese colonisation: 1895-1945 Taiwan's progress cannot be dissociated from the Japanese colonisation which gave it 'a clear head start in embracing the Japanese model of development'.[106] Given the economic intents of colonisation,[107]

---

[98] The others include South Korea, Singapore and Hong Kong.

[99] Hereafter referred to as Taiwan.

[100] See e.g., Ho (1978); Galenson (1979); Wade (1990); Ranis (1992b); and World Bank (1993).

[101] See Gunnarsson (1993) for a useful summary of the neoclassical vs. dependency theory debate.

[102] See Ho (1980), and (1982); and Ranis (1979).

[103] Thorbecke (1992).

[104] Shea (1994).

[105] Wade (1990), p. 39.

[106] Ministry for Foreign Affairs, Sweden (1992), p. 118. Referred to as the 'flying geese pattern', 'with Japan at the head, followed by the four high-flying newly industrializing economies (NIEs), South

the Japanese strategy included policies directed towards improving productivity in agriculture, and establishing institutions that minimised resistance from the Taiwanese countryside.

Taiwan was developed by the Japanese principally to supply rice, sweet potatoes and sugar.[108] Excluding the small Japanese nucleus of administrators, technicians and entrepreneurs, even toward the end of the period Taiwan remained largely agricultural, with relatively high agricultural productivity, but with industrialisation and modernisation impulses and agents lying as it were, outside its mainstream.[109] '[B]y the end of the colonial period', Thorbecke notes, 'a number of essential features were present which were conducive to a potential take-off in the post war era. These major elements were an appropriate labor-intensive technology relying on modern inputs, a physical infrastructure, particularly in terms of irrigation and drainage, which increased greatly the productivity of this technology, and, finally, a set of rural institutions that helped to disseminate knowledge, provide extension and credit services, and market both inputs and outputs'.[110]

The transition period: 1945 to the early 1950s This period is characterised by the surrender of Japan to the victorious allies in World War II, the resulting retrocession of Taiwan to Nationalist China, and the move of the nationalist government from the mainland into Taiwan. The rapid economic progress achieved in the following decades was possible largely because of this shift in decision makers. Being outsiders, economic expansion was the only way of convincing the native Taiwanese of the Nationalist (Kuomintang) Government's ability in governance. This task was made easier by the still 'Chinese agriculture and its nonagricultural complements'[111] and the absence of interest roots of the new rulers. Thorbecke notes three policy elements that played a crucial role in agricultural development in the transition period.[112] First, the Chinese-American Joint Commission on Rural Reconstruction, established in 1948, and later emerging as the actor which realised the potentials of the Taiwanese agricultural sector with powers similar to a ministry. Second, resources to the above mentioned institution, which to a large extent were financed by U.S foreign aid. This started in 1951 and was initially aimed specifically for the agricultural sector. Third, and according to Thorbecke the most important decision for growth and the equal dispersion of its returns, land reforms were introduced.

Korea, Taiwan, Hong Kong and Singapore . . . with shifting comparative advantage as the countries advance in technolo-gical sophistication' (Shibusawa et al. 1992, p. 1).

[107] From the start, Taiwan was regarded as an agricultural appendage to be developed as a complement to Japan (Amsden 1988).

[108] Little (1981).

[109] Kuznets (1979).

[110] Thorbecke (1992).

[111] Kuznets (1979).

[112] Thorbecke (1992).

Post transition: from import substitution to export orientation This period coin-cided with changes in the production structure - the relative decline of agriculture and the rise of the manufacturing sector, in terms of their shares in GDP and employment.[113] What stands out distinctly in this structural shift is the absence of a widening income inequality. Kuznets suggests that it might be credited, at least in part, to the widening diversification of industrial and other income sources in the total income of the relatively large, average Taiwan household.[114] Explaining this shift leads us to examine the import substitution and export orientation policies of the Nationalist Government in the post transition period.

Taiwan's initial industrial spurt in the 1950s was largely based on primary import substitution.[115] Supported by heavy US aid, it was mainly in consumer non-durables. To promote import substitution, Taiwan employed the usual policy pack-age of tariffs, import controls, and multiple exchange rates. Within a short period of time - from 1948 to 1955 - average tariff rates for all imports more than doubled in nominal terms (rising from 20 to almost 45 per cent).[116] Import quotas were also used as a major instrument of protection. By decreasing the import of consumer goods and stimulating the import of intermediate and capital goods, import sub-stitution altered the import structure but did not reduce the total demand for imports.[117] This high demand caused deficits on the trade account and was finan-ced by US aid. The economy reached a seemingly dead end by late 1950s since the export sector depressed and a rapid rate of industrialisation was difficult to main-tain given the high import demands. The turning point came in 1958, with attempts to rationalise the import substitution policies and end discrimination of the export sector since growth rates in the late 1950s began to decline and the apparent gains of import substitution were exhausted.

The stage of incipient export orientation, the early 1960s to the 1980s, was characterised by rapid growth in per capita incomes, savings, and industrial output. There was a shift in the centre of gravity from agriculture to industry. Ranis contends that the relatively dispersed rural character of Taiwan's industrialisation effort represents a key to its successful growth and export performance.[118]

The shift from import substitution to export promotion was accompanied by the unification of the multiple exchange rates, liberalising imports, tax rebates for in-dustrial exports and fiscal incentives for domestic and foreign investors.[119] Tight credit policies to contain inflationary pressures and devaluation of the Taiwanese dollar in the early 1970s caused slow growth, but economic recovery began in the

---

[113] The share of agriculture and relative industries in GDP fell from over 33 per cent to 13 per cent; that of industry (including transport and communication) rose from 26 to 51 per cent. In terms of em-ployment, the share of the total labor force in agriculture fell from 49 to 31 per cent and that in the industry sector rose from 15 to 35 per cent (Kuznets 1979).

[114] Ibid.

[115] Ranis (1979).

[116] Ho (1978), p. 191.

[117] Ibid., pp. 193-4.

[118] Ranis (1979). Cf. Johansson and Ronnås (1995) for a useful description of rural industrialisation.

[119] Ranis (1979).

late 1970s with easy credit and higher government investment. Export friendly trade and other policies, mainly incentive driven but along with protection of the domestic market comprised the policy framework. Export processing zones (EPZs), export credit, duty free imports for exporters, tax incentives and so forth were the main instruments used. Coupled with exchange rate unification and currency devaluation, the institutional framework gave an open field for private entrepreneurs. In Riedel's[120] classification of incentives - financial (loans/interest reductions, guarantees); fiscal (tax exemption and relief, depreciation of allowance, exemption of customs duties); and factor incentives (training, research and development, sites, buildings facilities - Taiwan had all but the training incentive adopted. The government also switched its strategy of taxing agriculture to one increasingly protective of it. This adjustment in the total environment permitted the economy to shift from being essentially based on domestic raw materials and land to one where production and exports were based on imported raw materials and a comparative advantage in labour.

In the 1980s, price support and stabilisation programmes, government investment in strengthening rural infrastructure and the second stage of land reforms increased protection to the agricultural sector. Import liberalisation accelerated in the 1980s. In 1984, the Ministry of Economic Affairs declared its intention to bring Taiwan's tariff schedule into line with those of the OECD countries within six years.[121] The economy diversified substantially, 'with rice constituting less than 12 per cent of the value of agricultural output in 1986-88 and sugar having become a marginal crop'.[122] Liberalisation and internationalisation, particularly of the financial sector, were the hallmarks of the 1980s. The development programme was designed to 'shift its economy away from reliance on labor-intensive industries towards the development of technology-intensive products and industries'.[123] Consistent export surpluses resulting in huge foreign exchange reserves,[124] domestic savings in excess of domestic investment and an undervalued currency has made efforts towards increasing domestic demand and reduced surpluses and savings necessary. Foreign direct investment, particularly into ASEAN, has been rising consistently in the 1980s and this has helped alleviate problems of excess reserves.

Critical factors in the success

In addition to 'lucky circumstances'[125] and 'fruits of history and of fortune'[126] the timing of responses of the public and private sectors to changing economic environment, both internal and international, deserves mention.

---

[120] Riedel (1988).
[121] Ibid.
[122] Thorbecke (1992).
[123] Smith (1995).
[124] In February 1988, its foreign exchange reserves reached a peak of USD 76 billion (second only to Japan) of which USD16 billion was with the United States (Shibusawa et al. 1992, p. 74).
[125] Little (1979).

A small country in terms of size, with a high density of population to cultivable land and poor endowment in natural resources, economic rationality lay in pursuing a trade dependent industrialisation strategy. 'It could only prosper, and has in fact prospered, by exporting what effectively are labor and capital services. These services, however, have mainly taken the form of adding value to imported raw material rather than being services pure and simple'.[127] Early industrialisation was aided by a dynamic agriculture which was a major source of industrial labour and capital. Agriculture also provided a good market for industrial goods. As labour markets were almost free - with very little government intervention by way of minimum wages, very little action in collective bargaining through trade unionism - inter-sectoral mobility was facilitated. The land reforms of the 1950s played a major role since it resulted in a favourable redistribution of income, modernised agriculture and so productivity and rural incomes grew extending the market for industrial goods. Fiscal measures like 'hidden taxes'[128] caused a net capital outflow from agriculture until the early 1970s. The land reforms were accompanied by organisational changes facilitating technological up-grading, and easy credit to agriculture largely through US aid in the 1950s. Thus agriculture was in a position to withstand the fiscal burdens. Human capital was at a very high level, owing to the large influx of skills during the large scale migration from the mainland in the 1940s and the huge public investment in education by the Kuomintang.

Decentralised industrialisation was possible thanks to a number of factors, including the Japanese policy of locating industry closer to labour and raw materials, a dominant agro-processing sector and a developed rural infrastructure.[129] Ranis notes five factors in this dispersed industrialisation: Taiwan's topography; the physical infrastructure built under Japanese colonialism and later constantly improved; the connection of this network to the main ports; special zones for export processing as well as bonded factories in a dispersed pattern over the island for minimising bureaucratic procedures; and electrificaton of rural areas.[130] The result was a rural sector actively engaged in industrialisation, and the emergence of small and medium undertakings as the most important actors. Meanwhile, this development took place without hampering the agricultural sector.

Further, Taiwan has had an exceptionally stable political system, with 'an absence of insurgencies, military coups, mass demonstrations common in other poor countries, and sharp swings in the direction of policies'.[131] This has imparted certainty to the economic environment and thereby helped private sector investment.

Economic success is also complemented by cultural factors which hold that Confucian ethics with respect to hard work, discipline and thrift have speeded up

---

[126] Levy (1990).
[127] Scott (1979).
[128] Coined by Kuo (1975), this term includes land taxes payable in rice, compulsory purchases, the rice-fertilizer barter system, and land taxes paid in kind.
[129] See Ho (1980), and (1982).
[130] Ranis (1979).
[131] Wade (1990), p. 254.

the growth process. Managing all this has been the strong administration system of Japanese origin and a ruling government committed to economic prosperity.[132] A key role in the developmental policy has been played by political personalities and modernising elite.[133] These non-economic forces can at best be considered as catalysts in the process since a comparison with South Korea would show similar backgrounds but divergent economic growth processes. Korea and Taiwan are generally compared in their success stories since they 'reflect divergent, yet equally efficient, responses to varying economic conditions and associated variations in the costs of market transactions at the outset of outward-oriented industrialization'.[134]

However, one of the most interesting features of Taiwan's economic development has been the role of small and medium firms in the industrialisation process. Industrialisation has occurred with a continuous expansion of small firms, imparting a decentralised character in their development. Their flexibility and responsiveness to changing economic circumstances are the more important points in question.

Small firms and prospects

Small firms in Taiwan defined in terms of employment are establishments with less than 100 workers and in terms of capital invested as those with a paid-up capital equal to, or less than, NTD[135] 40 million. The industrial organisation in the manufacturing sector in Taiwan is clear from Table 4.5. Over 80 per cent of the firms had fewer than 20 employees and over 95 per cent were small firms in 1981.

As Shibusawa and associates point out, small and medium enterprises played a very dominant role in the economy.[136] The main source of industrial growth in the colonial period was the food processing industry,[137] especially sugar refining, rice milling and a few chemical industries, most of them in the small scale sector. In the post-war period, import substitution was accompanied by upgrading technology in these units, but a relative decline in their shares. Textiles and apparels, products of chemical, petroleum, coal, rubber, plastic, metal products, machinery dominated the early post-war period.[138] But during the 1980s, small firms sprung up in higher technology sectors, such as computers, integrated circuit design, machine tools, high quality sports goods, and expensive toys. By 1985, almost two-thirds of Taiwan's manufacturing exports was produced by firms employing less than 300.[139] Not only had Taiwan's exports shifted from 10 per cent non-agricultural in

---

[132] See Little (1979).
[133] Shibusawa et al. (1992), p. 56.
[134] Levy (1990).
[135] New Taiwanese dollars.
[136] Shibusawa et al. (1992), p. 74.
[137] Ho (1978), p. 71.
[138] See ibid. for details.
[139] Wade (1990), p. 70.

Table 4.5

Distribution of manufacturing enterprises in Taiwan by number of employees (percentages)

		1-19	20-99	100-499	500-999	1000+	Total
1961	No.	-	99.2[a]	-	0.8[b]	-	-
	Emp.	-	61.2	-	38.8	-	-
	Prod.	-	35.5	-	64.5	-	-
1966	No.	85.6	11.7	2.3	0.5[b]	-	27,709
	Emp.	21.4	21.4	22.5	34.8	-	589,660
	Prod.	19.3	15.2	19.9	45.6	-	85,085
1971	No.	81.9	13.5	3.8	0.8[b]	-	42,636
	Emp.	15.7	19.9	28.2	36.1	-	1,201,539
	Prod.	11.5	14.8	26.0	47.3	-	242,940
1976	No.	81.0	14.3	4.1	0.3	0.3	69,517
	Emp.	16.4	22.2	30.2	9.7	21.5	1,907,581
	Prod.	10.4	16.9	29.2	11.2	32.3	819,452
1981	No.	82.1	13.8	3.5	0.4	0.2	91,510
	Emp.	17.4	24.1	28.8	10.3	19.6	2,201,470
	Prod.	8.9	17.6	26.0	10.6	36.8	2,067,430

a) firms having 1-499 employees; b) firms having 500+ employees
Source: Wade (1990), p. 67.

Table 4.6
The size structure of Taiwanese manufacturing
by some industrial categories

	Average no. of persons engaged	No. of firms	
Sectors	1986	1966-1970	1986
Food processing	17	1,129	217
Beverages, tobacco	160	13	9
Textiles	37	428	1,039
Clothing	44	112	417
Leather, fur	63	156	618
Wood products	15	505	760
Paper, printing, publishing	12	478	1,093
Chemical materials	67	70	73
Chemical products	25	265	113
Petroleum, chemicals	465	2	1
Plastic products	29	388	1,603
Rubber products	28	88	283
Non-metallic minerals	27	270	402
Basic metals	27	189	213
Fabricated metals	9	722	3,728
Machinery	11	504	1,091
Electrical equipment	61	274	1,010
Transportation equipment	30	209	445
Precision equipment	29	53	169
Miscellaneous	26	261	765

Source: Pack (1992), Table 3.12, p. 104.

the 1950s to 95 per cent by 1989, fully 50 per cent of her exports were now in high technology areas, that is machinery and basic metals, transport equipment, and precision instruments, a marked change from the almost exclusive concentration on labour intensive manufacturing exports in the 1960s and the early 1970s.[140]

The comparative size structure of manufacturing by industrial categories is given in Table 4.6. This table indicates the wide dispersion of the industrial activities. The growth in the number of firms and the shift from food processing to other areas is also very evident.

A spatial analysis of industries shows that they are widely dispersed in nature. Apparently, in Taiwan, considerable industrial growth occurred in or near small

---

[140] Ranis (1979).

72

and medium rural towns.[141] The rural shares of manufacturing establishments in the size categories 50-99 workers, 100-499 workers and 500+ workers were 49, 49 and 46 per cent respectively in 1971. Ho maintains that early agro-industries and good rural infrastructure have caused the dispersed pattern. The location of EPZs in the port cities has also helped in the process.

In Taiwan, small and medium sized industrial enterprises provide employment opportunities in rural areas and have thereby contributed to the narrowing of urban-rural gap.[142] Scitovsky suggests that the small structure of the firm encouraged workers to start their own firms and made it easier to accumulate enough capital through informal channels to finance the establishment of the firms.[143] He also links this phenomenon to the rapid growth in the household savings rate.

The dynamics of small firms All the oft-quoted strengths of small firms seem to have combined well in Taiwan to reduce transaction costs substantially. Their advantages lie in a high degree of flexibility, enabling swift shifts of business activity; a management of labour which is conducive to improvements in levels of productivity; and their potentials to realise economies of scope as well as their key role as subcontractors in the emergence of networks.[144]

Levy notes that the Taiwanese entrepreneurs established independent footwear firms more readily than their Korean counterparts, supported in the initial stages by the Japanese who identified and encouraged reliable and ambitious individuals already employed in footwear factories to start up production facilities of their own.[145] The presence of a large number of export traders and possible subcontracting with international firms explain the greater ease of entry into the small scale sector. When interpreting Taiwanese census data from 1961 to 1966, a certain pattern emerges, giving the impression that small manufacturing units show a rather high death rate. Establishments with less than 100 workers tend to be more mobile, upwards as well as downwards, but small units moving up still contribute substantially to the growth of the largest size category. Though reasons are not offered why, elsewhere undercapitalisation due to limited access to institutional credit is mentioned as one reason for the high mortality rate.[146] Amsden notes that small metal working and machine establishments in Korea and Taiwan have prospered so far not through specialisation, but through versatility and low market costs.[147]

---

[141] Ho (1982).
[142] Myers (1985).
[143] Scitovsky (1985).
[144] Pack (1992).
[145] Levy (1990).
[146] Ho (1980).
[147] Amsden (1977).

73

Credit needs of small scale enterprises are met largely through non-institution-alised sources. Small businesses depend more on the curb market.[148] This is largely because of the risk averse, government dominated banking system insisting heavily upon collateral and post dated checks. As is well known, banks find it more costly to collect and process information on the performance and prospects of small firms than on larger entities. Similarly, difficulties in providing acceptable collateral often prove to be a considerable obstacle to small units, which in turn 'put them at a serious disadvantage in the competition for finance vis-à-vis larger firms. This unequal position is reinforced in some countries where the government is a large player in the banking sector (e.g., Taiwan, Philippines) by the preference of the bureaucracy for dealing with large firms'.[149] The credit needs of the small and medium businesses are met in the formal sector through general banks, medium business banks, credit guarantee fund and the Integrated Assistance Centre (from 1982). The Small Business Administration, part of the Ministry of Economic Affairs, was established in January 1981. In coordination with several other government and private organisations, the SBA has set up programmes to provide advice on finance, management, production technology, and marketing.[150]

Regarding inter-firm linkages, existing literature records the importance of both horizontal and vertical linkages in efficient small scale production, though vertical linkages are stressed upon. The smaller firm structure permitted more detailed supervision, and the avoidance of principal-agent problems, flexibility in product niches, subcontracting and the exploitation of economies of scope, and the tapping of the ability of many innovative skilful entrepreneurs who would have been consigned to employee status in a larger industrial structure.[151] This is somewhat in contrast to Ho who states that while both small scale enterprises and large scale enterprises exhibit dispersed production, the linkages between the large scale and small scale enterprises are not very strong.[152] Amsden argues that 'in metalworking and machinery industries, the division of labor is also restricted by the type of market they face, composed of a large number of small customers with limited resources',[153] given the Taiwanese buyer's 'preference of low prices to high quality'.[154] However, EPZs are said to have specialised in international subcontracting with US firms though they accounted for only 8.6 per cent of Taiwanese exports and 13 per cent of FDI stock in 1975.[155] The role of multinational companies in enabling local firms to overcome information bottlenecks is an interesting experience of Taiwan. Through technological spillovers, both of the market access and productivity type, trading activities and inward investment by MNCs enabled local

---

[148] Wade (1990), p. 161.
[149] Berry and Mazumdar (1991), p. 37.
[150] Yang (1994).
[151] Pack (1992).
[152] Ho (1980).
[153] Amsden (1977).
[154] Ho (1980).
[155] Lin (1989).

firms to emulate practices, adopt new technologies and fostered competitive pressures. Not least could aspiring entrepreneurs as employees accumulate experience and ideas as a base upon which to launch their own ventures.[156] Wade holds that Taiwan's big firms have been 'indirect exporters' by supplying the small exporting firms with inputs such as petrochemicals, textiles and steel.[157]

Horizontal linkages were both competitive and cooperative. Little and associates describe the importance of export associations in restricting entry into the industry and quantity of exports so as to maintain export prices and prevent restrictions being imposed on their imports by certain countries.[158]

As far as direct linkages with the government are concerned, historical reasons have prevented business interest groups from colluding with the ruling party, with its mainland origin. This is also made manifest by the lack of formal channels through which the views of the private sector can be sought; informal contacts frequently take place, however.[159] Bans on trade union activities and passive enforcement of the minimum wage regulations have added to the weak links with the government.

Future prospects Pack states that the overwhelming issue facing firms in Taiwan in the decade of the 1990s is their ability to identify new products that will enable them to maintain an inevitably slower but respectable rate of export growth; with 'the evolving comparative advantage . . . likely to be in market niches that are being abandoned in the developed countries rather than in the newest consumer of producer products'.[160] Amsden fears competition from large firms, not in the area of supplying competitive goods, but by demanding labour at higher prices.[161] The ability to cope with incipient labour shortages is another test of flexibility of the small firm.

The financial market and fiscal policies

The financial market in Taiwan is characterised by a dualism, with a strong illegal curb market coexisting with an undiversified government dominated formal financial institutions.[162] The formal institutions comprise the Central Bank of China, full service domestic banks, foreign banks, medium and small business banks, cooperatives, postal savings, investment companies and insurance companies. Informal market financial transactions include rotating mutual credit, deposits with firms, loans against post-dated cheques, and secured and unsecured borrowing and len-

---

[156] Pack (1992).
[157] Wade (1990), p. 70.
[158] Little et al. (1970), p. 255.
[159] See Wade (1990), p. 284.
[160] Pack (1992).
[161] Amsden (1988). Cf Shibusawa et al. (1992), p. 75.
[162] See Shea (1994); and Lundberg (1979).

ding.[163] The money market consists of three bill finance companies. The capital market includes the bond market and the stock market. Shea notes that 'the traditions of a low proportion of equity funding, a reliance on bank borrowing, and the desire for close management control and little public disclosure have impeded the growth of the stock market'.[164] The authorities have not been very strict with the informal sector, presuming that the latter has played a major role in channelling domestic savings into productive uses. The informal market has been a major source of funding for small firms.[165] Patrick regards the large informal market as a direct consequence of financial repression and credit rationing in organised finance.[166] Ranis sees the dualistic nature as part of the industrialisation strategy: industrialisation throughout the past three decades occurred largely via the rapid expansion of small and medium firms, financed either through internal reinvestment or informal credit arrangements, including the so called *tsouh-wih* family based credit system.[167] This has been possible by the high domestic savings level in Taiwan; gross domestic savings as a percentage of GNP more than doubled over the period from the early 1950s to the late 1980s. Low inflation, a high level of public savings, the need to put aside money for a rainy day - very little by way of social security has been available to the average citizen - and a need to meet the cost of housing and consumer durables from savings rather than credit all play a part in this phenomenal increase, as does a culture where traits such as prudence and thrift are traditionally valued. Nor should the fact that high real deposit rates and tax exemption on interest earned provided additional inducement be overlooked.[168] The main function of Taiwan's financial system has been to channel household savings to finance the investment by private enterprises, and this function was performed reasonably well until the mid-1980s.[169] Financial liberalisation began in the late 1970s and has involved interest rate decontrol, market entry deregulation, and privatisation of major banks as part of a broader liberalisation policy. Government majority ownership (of banks) has, however, persisted into the 1990s in Taiwan, although the government has inaugurated a policy of privatisation and has licensed a number of new banks.[170]

Since the beginning of the 1950s, the government has adopted fiscal policy measures intended to encourage and enforce an increasing ratio of savings and stimulate investment. Government savings accounted for a major share of the national savings, amounting to about one-third of total gross savings in the period 1951-55 and 20 per cent in 1956-60. While defence has been the most important

[163] See Chiu (1992); and Shea (1994).
[164] Shea (1994).
[165] During the period 1864-90, financial institutions provided the business sector with 55 per cent of its total domestic financing. The informal market (as in street market) accounted for 24 per cent, capital markets 14 per cent, and the money market 7 per cent (ibid.).
[166] Patrick (1994).
[167] Ranis (1992a).
[168] Shea (1994).
[169] Ibid.
[170] Park (1994).

expenditure item, social and health budgets have been low but outlays on capital investment, physical and human capital have shown increasing trends. As in most other developing countries, indirect taxes formed the main source of revenue. A much discussed feature of the Taiwanese art of mobilising resources for investment has to do with agriculture. The government, especially in the 1950s, relied heavily on the agricultural sector for its tax revenue, but also encouraged agricultural development.[171] The low effective tax rates have created a stimulating savings and investment climate while at the same time the growth of government expenditures has been kept down to provide government savings.

The industrial policy

Taiwan is said to have adopted a competitive industrial policy which 'creates a positive relationship between structural change and macro policy'.[172] While it is difficult to ascribe definitely the growth process to government or to natural processes, Pack states that government encouragement may have led to a somewhat earlier initiation of production in some products or to slightly lower initial (private) costs, but hardly to the establishment of productive capacity in sectors that would not have been begun at all absent such efforts.[173] Functional industrial policies have been promoted as well, as have a supporting organisational structure built around public service providers and associations. These latter ones were established during the 1950s and 1960s with a view of encouraging product development and improving the level of quality.[174] Incentives and pressure are brought to bear on them through such devices as import controls and tariffs, entry requirements, domestic content requirements, fiscal investment incentives, and concessional credit.[175] In 1982 the Taiwan government also adopted a sectoral policy of identifying and promoting 'strategic' industries as a means of furthering industrial development and restructuring industry.[176] Taiwan's industrial policies affected firms in the small sector only when they tried to enter the international arena. Many support Wade's view on how important industrial policy has been to the country's accomplishments; a policy in which the critical ingredients were the establishment of public enterprises when the private sector struggled with spirit or financing difficulties; strict import regulations; and, at times, support for the private sector to overcome pecuniary obstacles.[177] Although the policy has been in

---

[171] Lundberg (1979).

[172] Auty (1994a). A competitive industrial policy switches its targeted manufacturing sectors as per capita income rises from primary import substitution in stage one to labour intensive manufacturing in stage two, to capital intensive and then to skill intensive manufacturing in stage three (the drive into heavy industry), and finally to research intensive sectors.

[173] Pack (1992).

[174] Wade (1990), p. 111.

[175] Ibid.

[176] According to Smith (1995), strategic industries are those that meet the following criteria: high technology intensity, market potential, high value added and large linkage effects between industries.

[177] Pack (1992).

favour of creating an environment for private firms to grow, without direct firm level assistance, the high level of education has helped small firms to respond to this change through technology transformation and capital accumulation. Moreover, the way in which industrial policies were formulated introduced a large amount of market information and used performance, usually export performance, as a yardstick.[178]

The role of the government

Taiwan's government, throughout the period of transformation, had a unique structure, delinked from potential vested interest groups such as landlords or industrialists. Gunnarsson uses the term 'autonomous' to describe this.[179] The importance of the government's role is indicated by the major decisions made during the 1950s on land reform, on the public and private choices in industrial development, on curbing inflation through the control of money supply and government budgets on regulating foreign exchange and controlling foreign trade, and, most recently, on major public projects that seemed advisable to cushion the shock of the recent world recession.[180] To this may be added the provision of extensive infrastructure and the public investment in development of human capital, in what Wade terms as altering the social structure of investment. However, there are two different opinions regarding the active role of the state in Taiwan's economic development. Wade argues that substantial government intervention has occurred - indeed, industrialisation as led by the government[181] while Little's argument assigns a passive role for government since the economic environment was market conforming.[182] Whatever the contradiction, the important issue is the absence of hindrance from the government in letting private enterprise a fair playing field. But the apparent nonchalance towards small industry has made people in business deny government's assistance to private sector. Wade holds that this 'culture of pessimism' is because of two main factors, one being the fact that most businesspeople are native Taiwanese, 'facing a government that they still tend to identify as mainlander-dominated', and the other that 'many senior industrial policy makers have not altogether concealed their distaste for private business people, in deeds if not in words'.[183]

The Taiwanese experience: implications for transaction costs

Assimilating all the features of the economic environment in a transaction costs framework is a Herculean task. Given the difficulties in measuring transaction

---

[178] Page (1994).
[179] Gunnarsson (1993).
[180] Kuznets (1979).
[181] Wade (1990), p. 301.
[182] Little (1979).
[183] Wade (1990), p. 305.

78

costs empirically, the implications of the economic and institutional environment for transaction costs of a small firm can only be inferred in broad terms, avoiding hasty generalisation.

Levy, in his landmark study of footwear firms in Taiwan and Korea, holds that costs of market transactions have been lower in Taiwan than in Korea.[184] The argument is based on the fact that among the market participants, in terms of sellers and buyers, the high education helped communicate across barriers of language and culture in the international circles. In addition, a large number of export traders, a history of rich commercial experience, and skilful negotiators who migrated from the mainland, along with the government, all contributed to considerable reduction in search and threshold costs in setting up a new firm. Competition among the firms, which is a feature of Taiwanese small firms, reduces the possibilities for opportunism and failed contracts, and to that extent, the risks from information asymmetry. In fact the large number might well have compensated for the absence of a strong legal system to ensure adherence to contracts. Extending this further, it would be hard to ascribe causal relationships between transaction costs and decentralised industrialisation. While it is possible to explain decentralised industrialisation as a consequence of relatively low transaction costs,[185] this would require supportive evidence regarding the access to information and the inter-firm linkages. Since the small scale industries were to a large extent supported by large firms, mainly Japanese trading companies, it could be inferred that information bottlenecks were largely overcome as large companies helped them in various aspects of production. Levy also highlights the role of export traders in easing entry into small scale producers into the export market.[186] These low ex ante transaction costs explain the lesser extent of hierarchical organisation within the firm, including the large ones. Low transaction costs have thus helped the involutionary growth[187] of small firms and the greater tendency toward specialisation. By contrast, Korea offset the high transaction costs by dealing with large orders and a higher hierarchical organisation within the firm and lesser reliance on subcontracting.[188]

The relative aloofness of government from the small scale sector, especially regarding labour regulations and credit provision, explains the thriving curb market. As for the latter, directed credit, and the rationing this implies, clearly also matters. Bordering on legality, these informal credit markets were themselves highly competitive and catered largely to small scale industries. Thus, even though the interest rate was high, easy availability of credit worked to reduce the efforts of the small producer in looking for investment sources. Ex post transaction costs would be quite low given the small volume of orders and the Taiwanese small

---

[184] Levy (1990).
[185] Johansson and Ronnås (1995).
[186] Levy (1990).
[187] Involutionary growth broadly refers to the growth in the number of firms, as opposed to evolutionary growth which refers to the expansion behaviour of a single firm over time.
[188] See Levy (1990).

producer catering to more than one large manufacturer, instead of relying on one. Part of the low transaction costs can also be explained by the 'business culture' of the Taiwanese. However, impersonal trust, 'not already embedded in personal relations' tends to go unsupported by formal institutions, thereby limiting the scope for business requiring trust between partners to a deal; as a result, Wade notes, business people tend to 'start with minor transactions in which little trust is required because little risk is involved and then move towards major transactions'.[189] Somewhat paradoxically, this helps explain why small firms - rather than medium sized ones - thrive under conditions of a weakly developed institutional setting lacking in formal arrangements for ensuring low transaction costs.

A competitive environment, useful linkages with large firms, and the Taiwanese business culture have worked to reduce transaction costs in an economic environment of weak direct governmental assistance to the small scale sector. The government has indirectly assisted the small scale industry through favourable outward oriented policies, infrastructure and its effects on the large scale sector.

---

[189] Wade (1990), pp. 269 and 270, respectively.

5 The Asian experience II: India and Vietnam

Bhargavi Ramamurthy

Introduction

This chapter compares two major Asian countries, both of which share the distinction of being at the lower end of the economic development ladder, but that both have recently taken decisive steps in the direction of better realising their respective potential. India and Vietnam also have other things in common, such as a strong and long held belief in the virtues of planning and the benefits of developing a strong producer goods sector. In both instances this strategy of development has led to disappointment, more so presumably in Vietnam than in India, the latter of which at least can point to a number of successful and advanced ventures within heavy manufacturing as well as to the dynamic development of selected high-tech industries in which the country's not negligible pool of highly qualified, yet relatively inexpensive, labour comes into its own.

Primarily, however, it is the experience of a strongly protective policy of import substitution in both countries, as combined with diverging policies with regard to the small scale manufacturing sector, that warrants their inclusion here. For while Vietnam, formerly a staunch and true adherent of central planning, has long had a significant small scale sector, unlike in India this was out of necessity rather than from choice. Regarded by politicians, planners and ideologues in Vietnam as a regrettable legacy of the past and a result of insufficient funds for the rapid development of a large scale sector, in India the prevailing view was that at least some segments of the small scale sector needed and deserved protection and support.

Setting out with India, the larger of the two, this chapter then proceeds with a description of the relevant policies and institutions in Vietnam. As both countries have experienced a considerable shift in policies over time, an effort to chart these developments in some detail are being made. In the case of India, the story begins at independence half a century ago; in the case of Vietnam, the focus is on the period following the unification of the Democratic Republic of Vietnam and the Republic of Vietnam in 1976. The protracted period of war in what was then still generally known as Indochina, which to most intents and purposes came to an end in 1973, is a convenient point of departure.

India

The 1980s saw a rising concern in India with the poor performance and apparent inertia of the national economy. Although investments remained at a comparatively high level, it did not foster economic growth as expected.[1] The early years following independence in 1947 were propitious, with enviable economic performance and support from the industrialised world, both materially and in the form of sympathy for India's ideas on how to foster development. This was not to last, however, as it became increasingly clear that India had chosen a path of development that led nowhere. Indeed, the world's largest democracy could no longer set an example as it originally had aspired to and, as a result, carried little weight economically. The essence of this deplorable state of affairs, a prominent observer notes, 'lies in her lack-luster growth for a quarter of a century. It lies equally in her consequent inability to remove a significant part of the poverty that afflicts her population'.[2] While Taiwan is often cited as a successful case of small scale industrial development, India stands for inward orientation and comprehensive protection and promotion of small industry by the government. No study on Indian small industry is complete without a historical perspective; within the frame of analysis of the other case studies, what follows is a resume of the developmental story of India with particular reference to small industrial activity.

Economic history[3]

Surprising as it may at first seem, India has an enviable record of relatively low levels of inflation. This is in fact true of almost the whole period since independence in 1947.[4] The annual rate of growth has not deviated significantly from what Raj Krishna terms the 'Hindu rate of growth' of 3.5 per cent, 'despite a strongly rising level of savings and an increasing share of government in both output and investment, despite the "green revolution" and despite the rise and fall of the influence of the Planning Commission'.[5] GNP per capita was USD 350 in 1990[6] but declined to USD 300 in 1993.[7] Structural changes also were slow to materialise and by 1989 the share of agriculture in the GDP was still 30 per cent (down from 44 in 1965) while industry claimed 29 per cent as opposed to 22 two decades and a half earlier.[8] Comparative figures for 1994 show that the sectoral

---

[1] Joshi and Little (1994), p. 319.

[2] Bhagwati (1993), p. 17.

[3] The chronological division that follows, of post-independence India, until 1991, draws heavily upon the scheme elaborated by Joshi and Little (1994).

[4] Joshi and Little (1994), p. 11.

[5] Joshi and Little (1989).

[6] World Bank (1992).

[7] World Bank (1995a).

[8] Joshi and Little (1994), p. 16. Over the same period services increased its share from 34 to 41 per cent. It is also noteworthy that, within industry, manufacturing rose by a paltry two percentage points, from 16 to 18 per cent of GDP.

shares were 30.9, 27.4 and 41.7 for agriculture, industry and services; the share of manufacturing has fallen to 17.3 per cent of GDP.[9] There is a high degree of industrial dualism, with technology intensive software firms coexisting with primitive modes of production, and this is not indicative of a changing comparative advantage. This is despite the fact that the very nature of autarky envisaged for post-independence India defied any notion of India's comparative advantage in labour. India exhibits most characteristics of a typical low income country with close to 70 per cent of the labour force engaged in agriculture.[10] Much of the developmental policies in the post-independence period can only be understood in the light of its colonial experiences.

The British colonisation[11]   The British rule in India can be divided into two epochs: first, the rule of the East India Company from 1757 to 1858, and second, the rule of the British government in India from 1858 to 1947.[12] Apart from tea and spices, India was a major export market for British textile industry and a major supplier of raw cotton and jute to the British industry. Foreign trade was both a mechanism for the transfer of surpluses abroad and an engine for the development of India's home market,[13] but 'the linkages between the home market and the world market were strengthened . . . in a way that was not to India's advantage'.[14] While there was no effort to improve the industrial activity in India, agriculture had to bear the costs of this depressed industrialisation in the form of land revenues and provision of employment opportunities. The British presence in India was relatively smaller, more heavily concentrated in government pursuits.[15] The colonial legacy laid the foundations for the central government and financial institutions, an expansion of the railway network, and an elaborate bureaucracy, but no direct involvement in industry promotion.

1947 to 64   Major events in this period were the creation of the Planning Commission in 1950, the Industrial Policy Resolutions of 1948 and 1956, and the Second Five Year Plan (FYP) 1956-61. The emergence of growing fiscal and balance of payment deficits, at the same time as the second plan started, caused a crisis reaction in the form of imposition of stringent import, foreign exchange, and price controls. These controls outlasted the crisis and became a dominant feature of macro-economic policy thereafter. Joshi and Little trace the 'sentiment' of autarky and a general distrust of the price mechanism to the apparent belief that trade was a process through which colonial relations were imposed upon the country and

---

[9] World Bank (1995a).

[10] Joshi and Little (1994), p. 15.

[11] For a detailed description of industrialization under Colonial Rule, see Rothermund (1993).

[12] Datt and Sundharam (1990), p. 19.

[13] Rothermund (1993), p. 39.

[14] Ibid., p. 42.

[15] About 60,000 of the British were in the army and police and 4,000 in civil government. Only 26,000 British were engaged in private sector activities (Maddison 1990).

the reliance on bureaucracy which 'tends to think in terms of administration by control'.[16] Wars with China (1962) and Pakistan (1965) resulted in increased defence expenditure and a major strain on government funds.

1964/1965 to 1970/1971 Drought in 1965 and suspension of US aid because of the war with Pakistan, together with neglect of agriculture in the Second FYP and little improvement in infrastructure worsened the agricultural situation. Two successive monsoon failures in 1965 and 1966, reduced aid, food importation under US PL 480 aid, fiscal deficits because of war and declining exports were the main macro developments. The government responded by restrictive fiscal policies, rupee devaluation, some import liberalisation and tariff rationalisation, and a long term agricultural development strategy. One reason for the contractionary fiscal policy was 'disillusionment with foreign aid and the desire for "self-reliance"'.[17] Government fiscal restraint meant cuts in expenditure and, combined with suspended aid-flows, public investment declined. While the balance of payments improved after 1966/1967, it was mainly because of declining capital imports following reduced public investment and an agricultural recovery in 1968.

1971/1972 to 1978/1979 The 1970s started well on the macro front but the trend did not continue. A new alignment of exchange rates, bad harvests in 1972/1973, the oil shock of 1973, and aid on the IMF low-conditionality tranches and OPEC caused high inflation and food shortages. Further cuts in government expenditure, a series of tax measures, non-tax fiscal measures, and monetary measures succeeded in bringing inflation under control. However, thanks to huge remittances from migrant labour in the Middle East and the large aid there was no large balance of payments deficit. There was a short reversal in trends during 1977, coinciding with a national emergency (June 1975 to March 1977), but liberalisation did not keep pace. Good rains ensued until 1979 and food stocks accumulated until the second oil price shock and bad harvests dealt another blow. A major criticism is that India was slow to make use of the large reserves of food and foreign exchange.

1979/1980 to 1984/1985 The economic situation worsened in 1979 as a result of drought and rising oil prices. Shortages of petroleum products in addition to infrastructure bottlenecks led to an industrial recession in 1979-81. The policy reaction, however, was different from that to the first oil price shock. This time it was expansionary and the government negotiated a massive loan from the IMF under its Extended Fund Facility. This was supported by serious domestic resource mobilisation efforts in the budget of 1980/1981, but also associated with increasing political populism and a disenchantment with the traditional preference of the bureaucracy for austerity. This 'move away from fiscal conservatism,' Joshi

---

[16] Joshi and Little (1994), p. 12.
[17] Ibid., p. 51.

and Little observe, 'was reflected in growing government subsidies, which increased from 1.7 per cent of GDP in 1973-78 to 2.5 per cent in 1979-84'.[18] Deficits were financed by borrowing, from the IMF and other commercial sources. The expansionary policies combined with modest liberalisation did lead to faster growth in the first half of the 1980s.

1985/1986 to 1991 This period began with a budget reducing direct taxes and with a series of liberalisation measures in trade and industrial policy. The overall liberalisation measures of the Rajiv Gandhi government included industrial deregulation, import deregulation, export incentives, exchange rate depreciation and financial liberalisation. The unsound macro-economic situation, however, of high fiscal and current account deficits also implied that stabilisation measures were necessary and the performance in this direction was not satisfactory. In the wake of threats to the political leadership from Punjab and Sri Lanka, substantive liberalisation was not undertaken. The problem was compounded by poor rains in 1987. In spite of an agricultural recovery during 1988-90, the debt situation worsened and so did the deficit situation. A new government was in power between late 1989 and 1991. The Gulf War in 1990 and depletion of foreign exchange reserves harmed India's credit rating. Political instability and eruption of communal tensions brought down the new government and the crisis became overt. The Congress came back into power in 1991 with a rising inflation and foreign exchange reserves enough for two weeks' import. The new government, however, reacted promptly and announced a programme of macro-economic stabilisation and structural adjustment.

The crisis of 1991 Rising public debt to GNP ratios in the 1980s (to nearly 60 per cent), largely due to the failure of the public sector to generate investible resources and high governmental spending, caused a state of crisis in the Indian public finances. While the Gulf War accentuated the crisis, its origin was 'home made'.[19] It manifest itself through shortage of foreign exchange reserves and eroding confidence in the government. While one view is that the crisis owes its origin to the development strategy itself, there is another[20] which holds that the crisis was due to mismanagement of the economy by the government in the 1980s.

The reforms since 1991 With World Bank insistence came the wave of reform in 1991. The Bank suggested a total revamping of the economy. In the area of industrialisation, it stressed industrial delicensing, public sector restructuring, phasing out of tariffs and protective subsidies to small firms, dereservation of products from the small scale sector and so on. Though incremental reforms were in existence since 1970s, the major step was taken in the policy package of 1991.

---

[18] Ibid., p. 60.
[19] Buiter and Patel (1992).
[20] Vyasulu (1995).

85

Massive industrial delicensing (except for 18 industries), elimination of barriers to entry under the Monopoly and Restrictive Trade Practices (Prevention) Act, rupee devaluation in 1991, elimination of export subsidies (called cash compensatory support), introduction of Exim Scrips (under which 30 per cent of export earnings could be held in foreign currency and traded in a market where the exchange could be used freely for a large range of imports or intermediates and capital goods), partial convertibility of the rupee, automatic licensing for projects involving foreign equity investment up to 51 per cent in 'high-priority' industries, and so forth, comprise the set of reforms.

Critical factors in development

'The experience with a colonial regime of discriminating protection and imperial preferences', Rothermund argues, 'prompted India's planners to adopt a policy of what may be called "indiscriminate" protection. Import substitution was pursued for its own sake, without regard for any economic considerations such as comparative advantage, the economies of scale, efficiency in factor utilization, etc'.[21] Yet the observer of the Indian scene is often left with the impression that, while India's micro-economic policies may have been unsound for the very reasons Rothermund cogently identifies, macro-economic developments were much more reassuring and that they were so precisely because of government intervention at the micro level. As we shall see, informed opinion suggests that this in fact may not have been the case.

The capital needs of the government were to be met through both domestic and foreign sources. While there was an apparent conflict between the Nehru-Mahalanobis and the Gandhian ideology of the pattern of industrialisation, they were not incompatible. The early policy makers, therefore struck a compromise between the two and the blueprint of the declared industrialisation strategy, appearing first under the Industrial Policy Resolution of 1948 and then under its counterpart of 1956, clearly demonstrated that traditional rural industries too had a crucial role to play.[22] The small industry policy targeted three major things: encouragement of production of consumer goods and simple capital goods using small capital; labour absorption; and promotion of regional dispersal of industrial activity. Reservation of products for the small scale sector and classification of backward areas and growth centres, among others, were intended to achieve these policy aims. By the late 1970s, however, realisations were very few and industrial growth, heavily protected from foreign competition, was still tardy. Respectable standards of living became a moving target, 'especially for agricultural workers, small peasants, workers in household industries, etc., as these groups had to bear the main burden of a postponed increase in the level of consumption'.[23]

---

[21] Rothermund (1993), p. 144.
[22] Chadha (1994), p. 13.
[23] de Haan (1980), p. 3, quoted in Chadha (1994), p. 15.

The change in the country's political leadership in 1977 brought with it a change in the emphasis of industrial policy and the new strategy turned the tables in favour of small industry led industrialisation. This, however, did not last long for the national government changed again in 1980, and along with it came a new industrial policy. Joshi and Little conclude that India's system of control 'was not only microeconomically inefficient but also macroeconomically perverse'.[24] They mention three features that stand out in India's macro-economic performance: (i) the relative conservatism with respect to monetary and fiscal policy; (ii) an emphasis on self-reliance with all the distortions that this implies; and (iii) a general distrust of scarcity pricing as a means towards the efficient allocation of resources.[25] With respect to the latter, administrative pricing has been much preferred. Indeed, also where market failure or similar grounds for intervention were not present, administrative fiat appears to have been the method of choice. Extensive bureaucratic controls over production, investment and trade; inward looking trade and foreign investment policies and a substantial public sector, going well beyond the conventional confines of public utilities and infrastructure are said to have stifled efficiency and growth and set limits to what India could get out of its investment.

It is difficult to avoid the impression that planners and civil servants were intent on regulating entry as well as competition, indeed every aspect of investment and trade, not only in order to avoid duplication of effort but above all to retain control over the allocation of resources. They did so in part by employing a wide range of controls, the consistency and transparency of which left much to be desired.[26] 'The large-scale or "organized" sector, in this view, had to be controlled', Bhagwati notes, 'its growth restrained by licensing, in order to create space for the small-scale sector'. As a result, otherwise successful industries, such as textiles, were unduly handicapped.[27] This was based on a static view of the large sector-small sector relationship such that growth of the large scale sector would reduce that of the small scale sector.

Bhagwati has argued, however, that 'planners underestimated the productive role of better health, nutrition, and education and hence underspent on them'.[28] Infrastructure in general had a very low claim on government funds since the budget was always under the strain of subsidies and interest payments. In the period after independence numerous 'interest groups' have sprung up and the institutions needed to mediate between these groups have weakened. Joshi and Little hold that the Congress Party and the civil service were the two institutions that stood above sectional interests at independence.[29] But since, they have degenerated largely due to the self-seeking actions of political leaders themselves and of the bureaucracy. This degeneration translated into fiscal handouts in the form of food and fertiliser

---

[24] Joshi and Little (1994), p. 3.

[25] Bhagwati (1993), pp. 46-7.

[26] Ibid., p. 50.

[27] Ibid., p. 54.

[28] Ibid., p. 36.

[29] See Joshi and Little (1994), p. 69.

subsidies, failure to tax agricultural incomes or wealth, concessions to small industries, overstaffing of the public sector, blatant populism, trend toward higher centre-state transfers, take-overs of sick firms and a failure to wind up loss making public sector enterprises. Strong controls have made rent seeking profitable and generation of 'black incomes' possible and these have therefore been perpetuated by pressure groups profiting in the process. For precisely this reason the liberalisation of controls has not been very fast. Liberalisation in the 1970s consisted mainly of exchange rate flexibility. It is alleged that the liberalisation that occurred during the 1980s was to profit from the support of business. This allegation is based on the fact that most liberalisation occurred in the field of industrial deregulation and softening of restrictions on monopolies. Extending the reservations for small industry at the same time is regarded as another attempt to pacify the small business. During the late 1980s, while industrial deregulation started out fast, it did little to open up the economy to foreign competition. To the extent that imports were liberalised, this was for the most part restricted to intermediate goods and components, thereby in effect increasing the protection of final goods. Whether intended or not, under Rajiv Gandhi the distortive effects of import substitution were accomplished by other means. Thus it is seen that 'ideology and vested interests prevented any significant action in the more difficult areas as trade liberalization, financial liberalization, and reform of the labor market and public sector enterprises'.[30]

Prior to 1991, India saw a gradual erosion of its fiscal conservatism, while at the same time the gradual liberalisation of controls, of which much was made at the time, merely amounted to tinkering with reform of the basic structures of economic governance. On the political front there has been a considerable amount of stability. Except for the periods March 1977 to December 1979 and December 1989 and June 1991 (when the Janata Party and the National Front were in power respectively), the Congress has been in power at the centre, though its hold has not been as powerful since 1991. The three chief players in the economic scenario have been the Ministry of Finance, the Planning Commission and the Reserve Bank of India. Joshi and Little trace India's recent macro-economic problems to the 'proliferation of controls and the breakdown of the fiscal discipline'.[31]

High public investment with the onset of planning was designed to make up for the poor infrastructure inherited from colonial rule. The planners looked up to industry as the key to economic development. In this design, however, agriculture was entirely left to the private sector. While private industry benefited somewhat from the protectionist trade policy, agriculture did not. More so since agriculture, as a matter of policy, was kept out of the tax net. Even the benefits of the green revolution could not be efficiently disseminated to food deficit areas since the transportation network was not geared to handle the task.

---

[30] Ibid., pp. 71-2.
[31] Ibid., p. 349.

An important Indian experience has been the role of foreign capital aid, in financing the plans after 1957 in their pursuit of industrial growth, 'which would have had to be very much reduced, or financed by an intolerable amount of deficit spending, if this aid had not been forthcoming'.[32] The dwindling of foreign aid in subsequent years contributed to the industrial recession which characterised the period after 1965.[33]

The monetary policy

'The correct policy assignment in India', Joshi and Little suggest, 'is to manage the nominal exchange rate to secure external competitiveness while anchoring inflation by domestic monetary and fiscal policies. In this context, India's conservative financial tradition is a valuable asset which it would be unwise to squander'.[34] To do so, Indian politicians and policy makers have a wide range of monetary policy instruments to draw upon, including approaches based on both direct (or quantity) and indirect (or price) means. The direct instruments include reserve ratios and various quantitative controls such as Reserve Bank lending and credit controls. The indirect means primarily imply the administrative setting of interest rates of various sorts, including on Reserve Bank and commercial bank lending and on deposits. Although, as a general rule, these instruments have been available and been made use of over the past three or four decades, emphasis has changed over time. In the 1960s, for instance, indirect measures were favoured, while during the subsequent decade attention shifted to quantitative controls and in particular to the use of reserve ratios.[35]

A high rate of savings was secured by forcing banks to pick up government securities at low real interest rates.[36] The savings rate thus rose from around 5 per cent of GDP in the 1950s to almost 24 per cent by the end of the 1980s.[37] Much of the savings in the post-war period came from the private sector. In spite of the good fortune with the weather the savings rate has fallen; net domestic saving was 14 per cent of GDP in 1990-91, and it was 10 per cent in 1993-94. Consequently investment too declined; net domestic capital formation fell from 17.3 per cent of GDP in 1990-91 to 10.2 per cent in 1993-94.[38] However it is held that strict 'monetary discipline cannot be easily implemented in the Indian context, as the government is pledged to policies of subsidies and price supports, has to resort to deficit spending, and also borrows money in order to make up for the deficits in the revenue account'.[39]

---

[32] Rothermund (1993), p. 137.
[33] Ibid.
[34] Joshi and Little (1994), p. 284.
[35] Ibid., p. 247.
[36] Ibid., p. 257.
[37] Vyasulu (1995).
[38] Ibid.
[39] Rothermund (1993), p. 155.

India relied on domestic rather than on export led growth, which was praised as a marvellous economic remedy by those who were fascinated by the sudden emergence of the newly industrialised countries in East Asia.[40] Based on export pessimism, '[t]he failure to use the exchange rate actively to encourage exports, the inflexibilities introduced by the pervasive controls which must handicap the ability to penetrate competitive foreign markets, the protection and hence attraction of the home market: these policies produced a dismal export performance, while other successful countries expanded their exports rapidly and benefited from greater economic growth'.[41] This export pessimism has been a 'self-fulfilling prophecy in India and India's share of world trade has steadily declined'.[42] The composition and direction of the foreign trade of India has changed since 1950, but its share in world trade has shown a consistent pattern of falling over time. In its first year of independence, India's share stood at 2.4 per cent of world trade; by 1981 it had fallen to 0.41 per cent.[43] This is a consequence of India's inward looking policies as well as the sheer size of the country.[44] Yet, by the early 1980s most exports, or two-thirds, where manufacturer, a proportion which within less than ten years had increased further still, to approximately three-quarters. As for imports, taken together petroleum and fertilizers made up about half of the value, while capital goods and metals also account for a considerable share, or about one-quarter.[45] This is a pattern rather typical of inward looking economies, where import substitution perhaps paradoxically tends to reinforce the dependence on imports, albeit of a different kind than under a more liberal trade regime.

The reason is not far to seek. Starting in the 1950s, India used non-tariff barriers as a means towards infant industry protection. The levels of effective protection rose above 200 per cent, although admittedly with a wide variation around the mean value.[46] Not surprisingly, the impact - and strength - of import controls waxed and waned as the fortunes of the Indian economy changed. Controls were tight during the opening years of Indian development planning, the period known as Mahalanobis Big Push, and again during the late 1960s and early 1970s. Conversely, controls were eased to some extent after the economic crisis of the mid-1960s and again during the period of incipient liberalisation during the closing years of the 1970s. Throughout the period since 1947 controls on imports of

---

[40] Ibid., p. 158.
[41] Bhagwati (1993), p. 57.
[42] Rothermund (1993), p. 158.
[43] In 1950, about 80 per cent of Indian exports consisted of such items as tea and raw materials or semi-finished goods such as leather; by 1990, more than 70 per cent consisted of manufactured goods. The composition of imports changed too. In 1950, more than 60 per cent were finished goods; by 1980, this category had receded to 20 per cent (Rothermund 1993, p. 158). On India's participation in world trade, see Bhagwati (1993), pp. 57-8.
[44] Joshi and Little (1994), p. 17.
[45] Ibid.
[46] Lal (1988).

consumer durables and other consumer goods have remained firmly in place. Rather, it was intermediate and producer goods that were shifted to the so called Open Goods License. Even so, this was by and large restricted to those products where Indian producers could fend for themselves, for the most part being protected by other means.[47]

All in all, the system produced a strong bias against exports. Ironically, but predictably, this trade policy above all discriminated against labour intensive production in which India would seem to have a comparative advantage. A good portion, or about two-fifths of manufacturing, enjoyed rates of protection in excess of 70 per cent in nominal terms. For the most part, those so privileged were to be found among producer goods industries, in particular metallurgy and at the heavy end of manufacturing, and in the production of chemicals. Being more capital and energy intensive, they were also more dependent on imports, than were that part of manufacturing industry that enjoyed relatively low levels of protection. The latter, incidentally, tended to be considerably more labour intensive in nature. In addition, because export incentives as existed rarely compensated for more narrow margins suffered in export markets (as compared to the domestic one), both exports generally and light manufacturing suffered discrimination.

Inward looking as it was, the trade regime effectively impaired India's ability to export. Notably, it put strong obstacles in the way of creating favourable conditions for labour intensive exports. As a result, it had a negative impact on wages and employment, in the end also having an adverse impact on the efforts to alleviate poverty.[48]

Fiscal policy

As can be inferred from the above, fiscal policy has been pursued in a context of high levels of public investment. This investment was to be financed through both public and private sector savings. But the disappointing performance of public sector savings has made recourse to Central Bank borrowings a regular feature. Falling tax revenues and growing current expenditure have added to the inevitability of the last resort. Direct taxes have fallen as a percentage of GDP, this is largely because of rampant tax evasion with the growth of the 'black economy' in the 1980s and an absence of agricultural taxation. The rising current expenditure is accounted for by three components - defence, subsidies and interest payments - with the rise in subsidies largely due to growing political pressure of interest groups.[49]

Indian fiscal policy was known for its conservatism, with strict treasury control and political dominance of the Congress. But the deterioration in public finances began in the late 1970s, and is, as was noted above, possible to trace to the populist policies of the Indira Gandhi government accompanied by the degeneration of

---

[47] This is based on Auty (1994b), p. 189, as is the following paragraph.
[48] Ibid., p. 61.
[49] Joshi and Little (1994), p. 227.

public morality. In addition, the lacklustre performance of state owned enterprises has contributed. Nurtured in an atmosphere of little competition and with few penalties for inefficient performance, public sector manufacturers and service providers increasingly came to rely upon disbursements from the state budget rather than on own revenue.[50] As such, they incidentally came to assume some of the characteristics of state owned enterprises enjoying the comforts that soft budget constraints may bring.

The industrial policy

Not unlike the experience elsewhere, the attempt to attain self-sufficiency in fact led to 'an extremely autarkic industrial policy'.[51] As noted above, the effect of this was to militate against the opportunity to develop export production in areas where India by general consent would appear to have a comparative advantage - and this without necessarily being able to create alternative sources of export strength, which after all is the rationale of the infant industry argument. Not only did unprotected sectors find it difficult to identify international outlets under these circumstances. The outcome of a policy of this kind, Sachs notes, is typically a '[s]luggish growth of labor-intensive employment, postponement of the turning point and amplified income inequality'.[52] By the time that the economic and social costs of the autarkic industrial policy become evident the policy is difficult to modify because the interest groups which benefit from industrial protection have become sufficiently entrenched to block reform.

Apart from imposing a bias against those sectors where the country did enjoy a comparative advantage, and hence inflicting an opportunity cost of some magnitude, India's industrial policy primarily had the effect of promoting the public manufacturing sector. Not only did enterprises in this favoured sector often savour such delights of having a monopoly as high profit margins; their lack of incentive to shape up in the end often necessitated full protection from the onslaught of even mildly competitive challengers at home and abroad.[53] Furthermore, policies such as these often opened up opportunities for rent seeking behaviour, accruing through the abuse of public sector monopolies and the purchase of favours by the private sector in order to circumvent restrictions on factory capacity licensing, imports and price increases.[54]

From the colonial rule India inherited a 'backward economy', poor in human and physical capital. In 1950-51, only 9.6 per cent of the gainfully employed population was engaged in manufacturing which contributed to a mere 11.7 per cent to India's net domestic product.[55] Industrialisation was the first task, and a dynamic

---

[50] Ibid., p. 304.
[51] Auty (1994b), p. 183.
[52] Sachs (1985), quoted in Auty (1994b), p. 18.
[53] Joshi and Little (1994), p. 347.
[54] Auty (1994b), p. 184.
[55] Shirokov (1980), pp. 13-14.

industrial sector was to lead the development of other sectors, including agriculture. The fact that benefits have not trickled down from industry has been the most serious shortcoming of the post-independence development strategy.

Official statements of industrial policies chalked out elaborate plans for industrial development in 1948, 1956, 1977, 1980 and 1991. Heavy public sector industry was given the pride of place in the 1956 policy while the 1977 policy statement prioritised small industry. Corresponding licensing policies and product reservations supported these policies. However, 'the licensing system was reinforced equally by the fact that regional balance in development was necessary for political, pluralistic, and equity reasons in a multi-state system'.[56] This policy, however, did not serve to optimally use economies of scale since 'small capacities often licensed were split further into yet smaller plants to distribute the largesse over different claimants'.[57]

Small firms

Small firms have been on the planners' agenda from the earliest years of planning. In the Gandhian scheme, small industries, especially khadi making[58] were both a 'political and a cultural symbol'.[59] With the advent of planning in 1950 came concrete measures of small enterprise development, in spite of the dominant role assigned to the large capital intensive industries. Even the Second FYP, which corresponds to the Mahalanobis Big Push, protected traditional household industries by way of limiting factory production to investment goods and intermediaries.[60] It was with the visit of the Ford Foundation team in 1954 that a string of administrative units were set up to promote small industries. These include the All India Small Scale Industries Board, to cater to small industry producing modern products, small industry service units for technical assistance and industrial extension under the Central Small Industries Organisation, and a Small Industries Corporation (for marketing, including government purchase, and supplying machinery on hire purchase) and were in operation by the beginning of the second plan period in 1956. The major promotional policies have been the provision of fiscal incentives (in the form of tax exemptions and preferential pricing policies and financial subsidies); quantitative restrictions on the output of large scale firms (reserving products for small industry); and infrastructure, marketing and other industrial extension services,[61] by both central and state governments.

Official statistics in India define small industries in two ways: first, based on employment and, second, on the product and fixed investment. By the first definition, small firms are those which do not have to register with the Government of

---

[56] Bhagwati (1993), p. 56.
[57] Ibid., p. 56.
[58] Khadi refers to coarse handspun cotton cloth.
[59] Little et al. (1987), p. 22.
[60] See Mahalanobis (1963); and Little et al. (1987), p. 23.
[61] See Little et al. (1987).

India and by the second definition, they are firms which are eligible for promotional assistance available from the central and state governments as well as the banks;[62] industrial undertakings in which the investment in fixed assets in plant and machinery, whether held on ownership terms or lease or hire purchase, do not exceed 6 million rupees; or 7.5 million rupees provided the unit undertakes to export at least 30 per cent of the annual production by the end of three years from the date of its commencing production. This sector is generally referred to as the village and small industries sector and has been grouped under different sub-sectors for policy formulation and administering assistance programmes. The sub-sectors are: khadi and village industries, handloom, handicraft, powerloom, sericulture, coir, and small scale industries.[63]

An important experience of India is the case for rural industrialisation. Endowed with a flourishing base of rural handicrafts and industries, the need for rural industrialisation has implications for both employment generation and decentralised industrialisation. But unfortunately, the Lewisian transfer of labour from agriculture to industry has not occurred substantially owing to the poor decentralisation and high technology intensity of the manufacturing industry. The policy for small scale industries was intended to be closely related to rural development, and the responsibility for creating job opportunities was entrusted to small scale and rural industries,[64] a goal yet to be reached.

Rural and small scale industry was looked upon favourably because it was believed to be well placed to create additional jobs and income opportunities despite the limited resources available for investments. Nonetheless, and despite the fact that the encouragement of small scale industry started in earnest already in the early years of independence, progress was often slight. Instead, entrepreneurs and traders in this sector increasingly became a pressure group to be reckoned with. As a result, various concessions (e.g., taxes) were granted, as were exclusive access to selected products and sectors. As Joshi and Little wryly note, '[t]hese groups also made large strides during the Janata regime when reservations for small-scale industry were greatly expanded'.[65] Ironically, alluding to anti-monopoly sentiments the small firm sector - which employs two-thirds of the industrial workforce and produce two-fifths of India's manufacturing output - often succeeded in protecting their turf from the infringement by large manufacturers. This, of course, had the desired effect of off-setting narrow margins due to high overheads and low levels of capacity utilisation.[66]

Organisational framework for small industry promotion Except the small scale sector, each of the sub-sectors is 'looked after' by a specific commission at the central level and boards at the state level, with the boards in charge of imple-

[62] Desai and Taneja (1990).
[63] Sandesara (1988).
[64] Inoue (1992), p. 67.
[65] Joshi and Little (1994), p. 68.
[66] Auty (1994b), p. 203.

menting the policy decisions of the commission. For the sub-sector small industries (not covered under any of the above boards and commissions), the apex advisory body at the national level is the All India Small Scale Industries Board. The principal institution assisting small industries is the National Small Industries Corporation (NSIC). The SSI Board is a policy formulating body, also rendering assistance to State Governments and providing a range of extension services through the network of service institutes, branch institutes, extension centres and testing centres. The NSIC assists entrepreneurs through provision of imported machinery, technology transfer and know-how, and training for both workers and entrepreneurs.

At the state level, the Directorate of Industries, the Small Industries Development Corporation and State Financial Corporations are the major organisations for small industry promotion. The Directorate of Industries is the executive agency for the small industries sector including regulatory and developmental activities. The structure is fairly decentralised at the district, sub-division and block levels, which are the broad administrative divisions of the various organisations of the government. The SIDC caters to supply of machinery, raw materials, marketing assistance, and promotion of entrepreneurship. SFCs provide long and medium term loans for the fixed capital requirements of small industries. At the district level, the District Industries Centre is in charge of providing all types of services and support.

Apart from these organisations, the Small Industry Extension Training Institute, the National Institute for Entrepreneurship and Small Business Development, State Trading Corporation of India, at the national level; the State Infrastructural Development Corporations, Technical Consultancy Organizations and Industrial Training Institutes at the state level operate in small industry promotion, covering practically all requirements of small industries. To cater to financial requirements, there are the Industrial Development Bank of India, The State Bank of India, other nationalised banks and commercial banks. Small scale industry, along with agriculture, transport and export oriented enterprises is a priority sector and the Reserve Bank of India has instructed the banks to extend soft loans to small industry.

While a few studies have shown that assisted small units have performed fairly well, others show that a large number of units have not taken advantage of the incentives offered.[67] The reasons cited often are lack of information, too many formalities, procedures and red tape. The various organisations have a very low level of coordination among themselves and pursuit of 'targets' have often come in the way of assisting the right kind of industries at the right time. This has crystallised into a rigidity that has promoted another rentier class of small industry with 'ghost' units[68] and a substantial frittering away of scare assistance offered. Rao concludes that though the institutional infrastructure is gigantic in nature, its poten-

[67] Sandesara (1988).
[68] See Sandesara (1980).

tial in minimising the problems pertaining to raw materials, market and credit has not proved successful in the sphere of small, rural household activities.[69] Modern small industry has grown but not rural industry. The facilities offered are taken away by the urban, semi-urban and influential sections of society, for whom the programmes are not targeted. Though some satisfactory results are achieved in terms of number of units grounded they are not accompanied by acceptable outcomes either in generating employment or incomes compared to the effort made. The modern small industry is becoming capital intensive and is mostly concentrated in urban and semi-urban areas and the village industry is not getting modernised.[70]

Tyabji usefully summarises the policy intents of small industry promotion thus: 'protecting the small capitalist sector from the large scale sector with the hope, never clearly stated except in terms of "modernization", that all the pre-capitalist structures would either evolve to factory production, or die in an unobtrusive manner, without causing political repercussions'.[71]

Table 5.1
Distribution of industrial labour force in India
by size of firm industrywise 1971 (per cent)

Industry	1 - 9 workers	10 - 99 workers	> 99 workers	All firms
Food products	44.3	18.6	37.1	100.0
Drinks, tobacco	22.9	54.1	23.0	100.0
Cotton textiles	17.9	23.5	58.6	100.0
Garments	69.1	19.7	11.2	100.0
Cement, tiles, etc.	11.3	41.4	47.6	100.0
Metal products	46.4	27.7	25.9	100.0
Machinery	20.7	22.6	56.7	100.0
Electricals	48.0	18.1	33.9	100.0
Other manufacturing	33.3	23.9	42.7	100.0
All manufacturing	33.6	26.2	40.2	100.0

Source: Desai and Taneja (1990), Table 2.4, p. 172.

The size distribution by industrial categories is shown in Table 5.1. 'The common expectation', Desai and Taneja observe, 'that small-scale industry would be found more in rural than in urban areas is borne out only in respect of a few industries'.[72] In fact, the locational pattern found suggests that an old-fashioned or immature industrial structure where producers overwhelmingly depend on sources

---

[69] Rao (1985).
[70] Ibid.
[71] Tyabji (1989), p. 147.
[72] Desai and Taneja (1990).

of raw materials and intermediate goods to the exclusion of market considerations has been preserved. Thus, rural industry is predominantly in food products, tobacco and non-metalliferrous minerals, whereas textiles, metals and plastics production seems drawn to sizeable concentrations of unskilled or semi-skilled labour, predominantly in urban areas.

Table 5.2
Profile of small manufacturing enterprises in India

Year	No. of units [a] (thousands)	Production [b] (Rs. Million)	Employment [c] (thousands)	Export [d] (Rs. Million)
1973-74	416	72,000	3,970	3,930
1974-75	498	92,000	4,040	5,410
1975-76	546	110,000	4,590	5,320
1976-77	592	124,000	4,980	7,660
1977-78	670	143,000	5,400	8,540
1978-79	734	157,900	6,380	10,690
1979-80	805	216,350	6,700	12,260
1980-81	874	280,600	7,100	16,430
1981-82	962	326,000	7,500	20,710
1982-83	1,059	350,000	7,900	20,970
1983-84	1,158	416,200	8,420	21,590
1984-85	1,242	505,200	9,000	25,410
1985-86	1,353	611,000	9,600	27,850
1986-87	1,476	722,500	10,140	36,480
1987-88	1,592	857,000	10,700	-
1988-89	1,712	-	11,300	-
1989-90	1,827	-	11,960	41,400

Sources: a) Yojana, 1-15 March 1988, p. 6; Ministry of Finance, India (1989), pp. 52-3; and RBI (1990).
b) Yojana, 1-15 March 1988, p. 26; and Ministry of Finance, India (1989), pp. 52-3.
c) Yojana, 1-15 March 1988, p. 26; and RBI (1990).
d) Yojana, 1-15 March 1988, pp. 11 and 26; and RBI (1990).

The overall performance of small industry in the decade of the 1970s and 1980s is given in Table 5.2. Although there have been changes in definitions in the period concerned with reference to a particular scale category, the table still gives ample evidence of the small scale sector performance. The share of small scale industries has been rising and was 22 per cent in 1983.[73]

Table 5.3
Distribution of small and tiny units in India by size of investment

Invest. in plant and machinery (Rs. 1,000)	Percentage distrib. of SSIs in 1972	Employment (per cent)	Output (per cent)	Percentage distrib. of SSIs in 1982
< 25	73.13	47.4	29.5	74.19
26 - 50	10.73	12.7	12.4	11.29
51 - 100	7.39	12.2	14.1	8.52
101 - 300	6.26	16.4	22.9	4.30
301 - 600	1.78	7.5	12.9	1.21
600+	0.71	3.8	8.2	0.49
Total	100.00	100.0	100.0	100.00

Source: Rao (1985), Table 3-12, p. 188.

The small sector itself is heterogeneous with respect to employment and output, and Table 5.3 shows that while the share of the smallest category (with investment up to Rs. 25,000) has risen, that of the largest category has fallen between 1972 and 1982. The capital intensity in the small scale sector has increased, due to various institutions offering credit like commercial banks, state level financial corporations and so on.[74]

Dynamics of small firms Describing the small industrialists of Chopur in North India, McCrory notes that '[they] have every earmark of the successful entrepreneur, *except success*', highlighting growth constraints on the small firm.[75] On the basis of his analysis of sick units among modern small units, Sandesara states: 'The statistics on closure . . . show an alarming picture. The numbers are large as such (over 3 lakh[76]), as also in the context of working units (52 per cent). Nearly half of this large number of closed units are found closed within five years of production'.[77] Enterprise mortality rates can presumably be explained by recourse to small size and locational disadvantages. The survey reported in Table 5.3 notes that major causes for closure include lack of finance (35 per cent of all respondents) and marketing problems (14 per cent). This is perhaps only to be expected; while entry into the small scale sector, and in particular its modern

---

[73] Ibid.
[74] Rao (1985).
[75] McCrory (1956), quoted in Staley and Morse (1965), p. 233; emphasis in the original.
[76] Lakh is a unit of account. One lakh is equivalent to 100,000.
[77] Sandesara (1992).

segment, may be easy survival is typically far more difficult.[78] Production and marketing engaged much of managerial effort in the small and medium firms and absorbed the bulk of scarce managerial time.[79] Problems with credit are in part a by-product of the major concerns with markets and supplies; the problems are less with the cost of credit, or even its absolute availability, than with its inflexibility, and especially with bank credit not being available when required, and occasionally even withdrawn when most necessary.[80] It is, however, important to distinguishing financial difficulties arising out of poor access and availability of finances from those that arise due to bad managerial abilities. While lack of funds constitute external organisational constraints, bad financial management reflects internal constraints.

The assistance programmes tend to make entry easier in an area even when there may be too many firms.[81] It is also noted that a number of small units had started without assistance. This has important bearings with the pull and push factors of non-farm sector in general. Especially in the case of rural industrialisation, small units might spring up as 'distress industries' driven out of restrictive opportunities in a traditional agriculture.[82] Small modern industries, however, are more a response to pull factors in industry since they are necessarily associated with a reasonable amount of technical know-how, investment and so on. India's experience is that while entry into small modern industry is smoothened by the gigantic organisational structure, it is extremely difficult to close down a unit or even expand, since expansion means loss of a lot of assistance to the unit. Labour legislation, especially in the organised sector, and trade unionism are major problems of the larger of the small enterprises. Flexibility is inhibited in the labour market by minimum wages, both for the organised and unorganised sector. But apart from this, very little regulation exists outside the organised sector. Laws concerning layoffs and conditions of employment make exit difficult, even for a small industry. While credit needs of the small firms are met by specific institutions and banks, their insistence on collateral and bad financial management of the small firm often result in firms seeking non-institutional sources of investment. However, 76 per cent of the firms in a study by Desai and Taneja borrowed from banks, 28 per cent from official institutions and 18 per cent from other institutions.[83]

Studies on relationships between small and large firms show that subcontracting is conspicuous by its near-absence, in India. Papola and Mathur state that 'linkages or subcontracting appeared to be an outcome of the policy bias disfavoring largeness'.[84] Kashyap notes that the benefits of government fiscal and financial subsidy to the small scale sub-sector have ultimately flowed to the large scale sector due to

---

[78] Kashyap (1993).
[79] Desai and Taneja (1990).
[80] Ibid.
[81] Sandesara (1988).
[82] See Chadha (1993a), and (1993b) for a detailed review of the Indian non-farm sector.
[83] Desai and Taneja (1990).
[84] Papola and Mathur (1979).

the peculiar kind of dependence Indian small firms have on the large ones.[85] There has not been any evidence of technology transfer from the big firms. The reasons for this poor subcontracting often cited are that 'small firms fail to meet the orders in time and are often not in a position to provide the desired quantities of goods according to specifications'.[86] There are horizontal linkages in the form of industry associations at the district and state level, but the benefits have not flown to small units in substantial measure. Rather they have become the platforms for voicing the needs of a rising group of urban based modern small scale industrialists, in mainly consolidating their position with the government. The government is an important outlet for firms in metal products, machinery and electricals,[87] but its poor payment record reduces the dynamism of the small firms. Desai and Taneja also note that the more successful firms take the least advantage of the government's measures to secure a market for small firms - government purchases, marketing assistance, or reservation. They underline the need for improved distribution channels, in the form of more and financially better endowed wholesalers, more shops for more specialised goods, trade fairs and magazines. Furthermore, industry consistently receives preferential treatment where trade receives no support or is even discriminated against. This is as true of credits and tax concessions as of the allocation of land. As a consequence, Desai and Taneja plausibly suggest, '[a] reversal of this broad-front discrimination may actually help small industry more than the measures taken by the government to aid it directly'.[88] Put differently, India would be well advised to support its small scale industries sector by promoting rather than protecting it, by consciously encouraging specialisation and the development of complementarities between small firms and between small entities and larger enterprises. Its applicability in India is very well summarised by Kashyap thus:

> [The Indian industrial policy] is based on the unshaken belief that the goals of poverty removal, employment generation, dispersal of industries, and diffused incomes could all be achieved or approached by arranging the scales of production rather than product choices. Therefore, India has an institutional umbrella that envelops all small-scale firms (though it is sometimes felt that those who really need help are left out) and is generally non-discriminatory between output types. The available evidence unfortunately suggests that the policy has not been based on correct premises and the assistance arrangements have been wasteful, ineffective, and even counterproductive.[89]

---

[85] Kashyap (1988), p. 677.
[86] Ibid, p. 678.
[87] Desai and Taneja (1990).
[88] Ibid.
[89] Kashyap (1988), p. 674.

The framework Levy provides in his analysis of footwear firms in Taiwan and Korea may be used purposefully in the implications for transaction costs in India, particularly the small scale sector.[90] With reference to the size of the market and transaction costs, Levy holds that the larger the number of potential transacting parties, the less vulnerable is a market participant to non-competitive tactics, and the lower will be the costs of market transactions. The Indian small scale sector, large in both number and extent might have helped in reducing transaction costs. But the dispersed nature of the sector, the heterogeneity, and poor infrastructure (physical and human) increase the search costs substantially in the pre-contract or contact costs. Low levels of education and absence of access to information about government assistance, technology and market may well combine to raise the transaction costs. This might not be the case with a firm catering to a small local market, but to a growing small firm in an area of high domestic and international competition, substantial gains from education and export promotion have been overlooked. Ex ante transaction costs rise steeply in the absence of such a competitive economic environment. With enormous pressure groups acting on policy making, transaction costs for the small firm as a collective entity and as an individual entity will be quite high. The corrupt bureaucracy and the red tape further raise the ex ante transaction costs.

Obtaining permits, licences and other approvals consume a lot of the entrepreneur's resources, both financial and other. India is one of the countries where administrative delays are great.[91] Obtaining an import licence, for instance, create delays to an average of five to seven months in India.[92] Further it is held that the lengthy and cumbersome procedures are highly discriminatory against the small firm.[93] While this has negative effects on transaction costs, it is pointed out that it also discourages entrepreneurship in countries where this is a scarce and valuable resource.[94] The government, in envisaging a role for itself in post-independent India, has attempted to achieve various socio-economic objectives which have been conflicting at times. Small industry promotion was also used to encourage diversification of the entrepreneurial base by recruiting from among the members of various castes, classes and professions which have hitherto contributed poorly to the entrepreneurial resource.[95] But without a complementary social infrastructure support, mainly education and health and nutrition, this policy would not fit in well with the overall aims of economic growth. In the framework of transaction costs, it makes entry easy but survival difficult. As mentioned earlier, perpetuation of the institutional rigidity by rentier classes has worked against particularly the

---

[90] Levy (1990).
[91] Little et al. (1970), p. 211.
[92] Bhagwati and Desai (1970), Table 18.1.
[93] Little et al. (1970), p. 211.
[94] Ibid.
[95] Sandesara (1988).

smaller of the small firms. The necessity of bribing government officials in obtaining favours raise the ex ante transaction costs to a large extent.

The overall protectionist policy has created a strong institutional framework, but this raised the transaction costs for the small firm since the gains from escaping controls were quite high. Further, dispersed industrialisation along with low linkages with large scale sector is likely to have caused higher transaction costs to the Indian small firm since there has been an absence of technology transfer and other information from the larger, resourceful firms, thereby raising the search costs of the small firm, both in its efforts toward finding outlets for its products and in upgrading technology. International participation has been very little owing to the economic environment and this lack of competition may have led to a certain passivity among the small firms, curbing their efforts toward seeking distant markets. It could be expected that protection would lead to a greater degree of inter-firm competition, but the experience of India shows very low inter-firm linkages in this regard. Reservation of products reduced competition from the large sector, but this very absence of competition may have led to the much-cited inefficiency of the small scale sector. In this sense, low inter-firm linkages have not led to the benefits of agglomeration economies, in Levy's framework, in reducing transaction costs. Levy also notes that buyers and manufacturers can offset high costs of market transactions by dealing with orders for large volume, but this implies that the production hierarchy in the firm is fairly well organised, with little scope for subcontracting.[96] But as is noted in the characteristics of Indian small firms, there is a predominance of the smallest of the small firms, and this restricts the scope for fine internal hierarchies. Problems of skilled labour and lack of knowledge of proper financial accounting are some of the factors that inhibit such attempts. It can thus be inferred that the small firms face high transaction costs in India.

Monitoring and enforcement of contracts is another weak point in the institutional framework for small industries. The non-payment of bills is cited as an important problem of small industries. But this is a problem partly because of the fact that firms very often exist on the border of legality, and so cannot use the legal framework to offset these problems. The small firms do not possess the resources necessary for confronting failed contracts through legal channels. Other non-governmental organisations do have a role to play in this regard and this stresses the need for strong horizontal linkages.

While the liberalisation could go a long way in reducing transaction costs in administrative matters, and fostering domestic and international competition, a lot depends on the strength of the private sector itself in responding to the changed situation. Having grown in an environment of protection, transaction costs may be high in the transition period, but should diminish with greater linkages, domestic and international.

---

[96] Levy (1990).

Vietnam

The developmental story of the Socialist Republic of Vietnam is one of an unsuccessful attempt in central planning followed by a structural economic reform, which has occurred without impeding national growth rates. Its distinctive experience lies in the fact that its industrial sector remained relatively small throughout the period of central planning (1961-89), though there were substantial achievements of a wide range of industries and development of an industrially skilled workforce.[97] Wars, natural and economic disasters have taken their toll of prosperity, but the relative stability in its post-reform era shows promising signs for the future, as far as the economy in general and small industry in particular are concerned.

Economic history

During the two decades that followed the Geneva Accords (July 1954), the economics of North and South Vietnam evolved in quite different directions: the former was based on an attempt to construct socialism while the latter was set on the capitalist path of development.[98] The Democratic Republic of Vietnam adopted a Soviet-style developmental strategy aimed at socio-economic development through autarkic, centrally planned, heavy industry oriented industrialisation. This economic model of the North was extended to the South after the reunification in 1976, the birth of the Socialist Republic of Vietnam, when it was confidently predicted that the transition period from being essentially an economy of small scale production directly to socialism would be completed in twenty years.[99]

Reunification and 'socialist transformation': 1976-81 Following unification, a painful process of integration and adaptation followed. The South was to be transformed as had the North been before it. This proved less straightforward than Hanoi probably anticipated. As Beresford puts it, 'the political and economic system that had stood up well to the test of war, was much less suited to meet the demands of peace time development'.[100] In fact, while the North had to bear much of the direct costs of integration, it also imposed an opportunity cost of a considerable magnitude upon the South. Further, the bias in favour of heavy industry was carried out at the expense of the other sectors. Replacement of the market mechanism by central planning in the South, and the abolishment of prices as a resource allocation mechanism caused a highly inefficient resource-use pattern and resulted in a stagnated economy. The first five years after the unification with the South saw a 10 per cent decline in the per capita national income. In spite of the differing developmental strategies, both economies were heavily dependent on

---

[97] Beresford (1995).
[98] Vo Nhan Tri (1990), p. 58.
[99] Ibid., p. 73.
[100] Ronnås and Sjöberg (1991), p. 3.

foreign aid, experienced excess of consumption over production and ran a trade balance deficit.[101]

The socialist transformation of the South comprised of the appropriation of the private sector assets by the government, nationalising industrial firms, transport companies and banks, the introduction of a new currency, readjustment of land holdings, and organisation of mutual aid groups for agricultural production. A major economic development in this period is the Second Five Year Plan (FYP), covering the period of 1976-80, and in retrospect described as an exercise in attempting 'over-optimistic' targets. Agricultural and light industry development were to be aided by heavy industry, which was the main focus of attention. The socialist transformation of the South had to be completed in this period. Agriculture was subject to a forced collectivisation drive and quota procurement price fixation in the South. However, because of the low prices fixed, agricultural production fell in less than two years. Neglect of light industry in favour of heavy industry also caused a shortage of consumer goods, which also affected inter-sectoral linkages. A number of policies were underlined in 1979 in response to this crisis and their importance lies in the tolerant attitude towards private sector in general and light industry in particular, though their implementation registered a time lag.

Initial reforms: 1980-86 The 'DRV model'[102] came under severe strain during the late 1970s when bad harvests, in combination with the occupation of Kampuchea and the political and economic isolation of Vietnam from most of the outside world, triggered a serious crisis as the capacity of the state to supply the economic system with inputs, and the people with food, declined drastically.[103] As a reaction to this, Vietnam's political economy has been subject to reforms from the period of the early 1980s, though 'the goals have changed substantially' since then.[104] In the initial period, the reform was aimed at creating a modified socialist development strategy that achieved growth, efficiency and equity ideals.[105] Economic integration with the North was a failure on all fronts and led to economic stagnation. There was no industrial take-off in spite of the high accent on industrialisation. External factors, such as the withdrawal of assistance from China and most Western countries as a result of the occupation of Cambodia, aggravated the situation and in 1979-80 the country plunged into an economic crisis.[106] The first set of economic reforms was undertaken in 1982 as a reaction to this crisis. The reforms legitimised the previously prohibited economic activities outside the plan, in providing greater scope for the non-planned economy. The first five years

---

[101] Ibid., p. 59.
[102] This term has been used by Fforde and de Vylder (1988) to indicate the development model of North Vietnam. Also see de Vylder (1993).
[103] Fforde and de Vylder (1988), p. 9.
[104] Gates and Truong (1993).
[105] Ibid.
[106] Johansson and Ronnås (1995), p. 53.

of this period witnessed spontaneous grass roots change and ad hoc official reforms that sought to restore economic growth through various incentives and decentralisation measures, to strengthen the state sector by increasing its efficiency, and to utilise resources outside the state sector more effectively.[107] While these had favourable effects on efficiency in the economy, it also set in motion a cumulative process that made the official economy increasingly dependent on the parallel economy[108] and inadvertently undermined the already weak centrally planned economy. No delimitation of the centrally planned sector was undertaken and the reforms were thereby unsuccessful. By late 1986, a deterioration of the state's fiscal and financial positions and a hyperinflation of around 500 per cent were attributed to this unviable model of the reform and the Communist Party abandoned its support. The Sixth Party Congress in 1986 changed the process by adopting more fundamental changes, popularised as *doi moi*, or renovation. However, the preoccupation with hyperinflation caused serious reforms to emerge only in 1989.

The reforms since 1989 The goal of the initial reforms was altered in 1989 when the government 'abandoned any pretense of preserving a socialist development strategy, opting instead for a developing mixed economy'.[109] This reflects the interplay of internal economic and political forces like the unviability of Vietnam's traditional socialist model, economic stagnation, and the questions of political consensus about and sustainability of reform and the ongoing changes in the international political economy like the collapse of the Soviet Union and Eastern European countries, the demise of the Council for Mutual Economic Assistance (CMEA) and of the Warsaw Pact.[110]

As far as the sequencing of reforms is concerned, they began in agriculture, with a land law in 1987 and a resolution in 1988 towards decollectivisation of agriculture and changes in the regulations relating to procurement of agricultural produce by the state, in favour of the producers. These had beneficial effects and in two years, Vietnam turned into the world's third largest rice exporter from being a net importer of food. This was followed by reforms in the state enterprise sector towards increasing their autonomy and financial responsibility and making them more market oriented. Legitimacy of the private sector was also ensured by ruling out discriminatory behaviour towards private sector firms. In 1989, comprehensive macro-economic reforms were undertaken, including a massive 90 per cent devaluation and the introduction of market based exchange rate, which wiped out the black market for foreign exchange; price liberalisation and a deregulation of

---

[107] Gates and Truong (1993).
[108] Johansson and Ronnås (1995), p. 53.
[109] Gates and Truong (1993). The five economic sectors presently recognised as the major constituents with equal legal status are: the state, collective (agricultural and small industry), household and individual, private capitalist and the state capitalist (joint ventures between state and private enterprises and between state enterprises and foreign capitalists) sectors.
[110] Gates and Truong (1993).

foreign and domestic trade. Measures to combat inflation included a credit squeeze, introduction of positive real exchange rates and better fiscal discipline. These measures were greatly successful and inflation was brought down to near zero from over 300 per cent in 1988. Liberalised trade increased the supply of both domestic and imported goods and further reinforced the reform measures. These efforts have been facilitated by a boom in oil production, which has boosted the state sector manufacturing activity in addition to casting favourable impacts on foreign trade through a shift in trade away from the so called ruble zone.[111] Domestic markets were liberalised through removal of direct government controls over state owned enterprises (SOEs), full liberalisation of most domestic prices and gradual abolishment of subsidies. External trade liberalisation included legally admitting foreign investment, removal of state monopoly, removal of state administration of import and export prices and sharp devaluation towards unified exchange rates. A major achievement of these reforms has been the accompanying growth of average per capita incomes, at the rate of 3 to 4 per cent per annum.

Future prospects   For future development, the major constraint is the rural sector,[112] which has not been integrated with the more resourceful mainstream urban sector in the development path. Agriculture employs nearly 70 per cent of the population but generates only 30 per cent of the GDP. Export earnings from agriculture are insufficient to meet the import requirements for its own transformation and for the economy in general. While industrialisation is an urgent necessity, lessons from the past should not be forgotten. Promotion of EPZs and improved linkages between sectors can go a long way in spreading the benefits of opening up. This can be done through large scale improvements in infrastructure, which invites thoughts on the future role of the state sector, in providing supportive services for the industrialisation programme. In this regard, the role of the overseas Vietnamese community in bringing about economic change is recognised as crucial.[113] Utilising the labour intensive skills can alleviate problems of unemployment and low productivity.

Critical factors in development

Vietnam boasts of rich natural resources, especially coal and oil deposits, though the per capita availability is not very high, and it is this abundance that can translate into an economic strength and sustain high growth rates in the near future, if carefully managed. A labour intensive economy, the average Vietnamese is more educated than his counterpart in other low income countries. Benefits from this high literacy has not helped in improving private sector performance, reflecting external constraints, but they clearly point to the availability of an important

---

[111] Johansson and Ronnås (1995), p. 59.
[112] Dinh (1993).
[113] Ibid.

resource. Socio-cultural homogeneity has played an important role in the struggle for social and economic development. The physical proximity to the Pacific market holds great potential in the era of opening up that has been initiated. Vietnam, however, suffers from grave economic problems: shortage of food for its growing population, and huge external deficits. The former has been largely the result of the neglect of agriculture, except for the slight recovery during early 1980s when a reform within agricultural cooperatives was undertaken, while the latter owes itself largely to poor export performance and high foreign debt. Vietnam has also been under the threat of high rates of inflation, reaching hyperinflation figures in mid-1985.

Regional disparities between the northern and southern regions exist and owe as much to history as to natural resources and development strategies. Thus, commercial agriculture and economic modernism was to some extent the preserve of the South. In the North, by contrast, development was slow and industrial development for the most part confined to the parts of the Red River delta.[114] The imposition of the socialist model on the South, which had a fairly well developed system of commodity exchange, dealt a severe blow to the Socialist Republic, since it was hastily done and encountered a lot of resistance.

Even though Vietnam pursued a closed door policy as far as trade was concerned, external influences have played a major role in shaping its developmental experience. The major factors in this area (after reunification) are the assistance of Soviet Union and the relations with China. Soviet assistance, apart from military, in the form of economic aid was the 'mainstay of Vietnam's development plan'.[115] China was also a major source of grants, until 1978, when they were stopped.[116] With the refusal of USA to assist in its economic rehabilitation, Vietnam turned to CMEA countries, particularly USSR, for economic assistance, and signed the 'Friendship and Cooperation Treaty' in 1978. Soon after this, Vietnam attacked Cambodia, which instigated China's attack of Vietnam. Tensions had already heightened with China after Vietnam's move toward eliminating the bourgeoisie in the late 1970s, since it was the Chinese merchant population that owned large amounts of businesses. The attack of Cambodia was also largely responsible for massive aid suspension from many Western countries.[117] In fact these reactions contributed in part to the non-realisation of the goals of the Second FYP, which had banked upon a massive amount of foreign aid.[118] Vietnam's military indulgences have had huge claims on the state budget and thereby caused inadequate investments in other sectors.

---

[114] Ibid.

[115] Vo Nhan Tri (1990), p. 98.

[116] Before 1976, all of China's aid, in the form of grants, amounted to USD 300 million a year (Vo Nhan Tri 1990, p. 98).

[117] It had received aid from Sweden, France, Denmark, Norway, Finland, Japan, Australia and Canada (Vo Nhan Tri 1990, p. 101).

[118] Vo Nhan Tri notes that the goals of the Second FYP were set too high because of the overconfidence of Hanoi leaders regarding their military victory and they expected a massive amount of foreign aid (Vo Nhan Tri 1990, p. 76).

A large part of Vietnam's population is rural but agriculture has not been able to absorb the growing labour force and rural industrialisation has not been actively pursued. Local governments never attained independence to the degree prevalent in China in terms of political, administrative as well as economic powers, with the result that they did not actively engage in the industrialisation programme in the rural areas. This is because Vietnam did not witness politically induced fragmentation (as in China) of the economy into local self-reliant units and rural reform was never undertaken in a big way. The fragmentation that did exist was due to poor communications and inefficient distribution channels.[119]

Vietnam's infrastructure, in terms of road and rail networks, energy, transport and communication, 'is highly inadequate to encourage trade and external private investment'.[120] Labour markets have been far from perfect and administrative regulations have hindered the free mobility of labour, though the degree of immobility is not as high as in China. Despite the generally improved social and economic climate, the political system is as yet largely unreformed. Crucial indicators of the present state of affairs are the tensions and difficulties still attached to foreign contacts, the uneasiness with which the Party and government authorities alike treat even the term private entrepreneurship and the lack freedom of expression and organisation within the country.

Even though inadequacies abound, the Vietnamese economy has not experienced significant income losses in its transition period. This has been attributed to the flexibility in the economy (flexible relative prices and mobile factors of production).[121] The growth of agricultural production since the early 1980s and above all the expansion of the service sector since 1988 cushioned the consequences of the temporary decline of the industry sector in 1989/90. Further, the SOEs have also been very successful owing to the higher investment in the past and the channelling of FDI towards the state sector.[122]

In the second half of the 1980s, the Soviet Union embarked on a programme of far-reaching reforms. As Vietnam's main ally and ideological mentor, the development in the Soviet Union obviously had a strong bearing on the situation in Vietnam. Linked to this was the recognition that under the new regime, Moscow could not be expected to continue much longer to provide massive assistance to underpin an unreformed and inefficient Vietnamese economy.[123] Further, the very rapid development of its neighbours in South East Asia, notably Thailand, provided strong incentives for undertaking pragmatic policy decisions. The lifting of the US embargo in February 1994 and the resumption of aid by donor agencies form a major source of financial assistance in the reform process. The dissolution of CMEA trading relations made the search for new markets and improvements in

---

[119] Johansson and Ronnås (1995), p. 54.
[120] Dinh (1993).
[121] Diehl (1994) p. 27.
[122] Ibid., p. 28. The growth rates of the state sector have almost always exceeded those of the private sector.
[123] Ronnås and Sjöberg (1991), p. 7.

business dealings imperative,[124] and in this context the resourcefulness of its neighbours, particularly Japan, is noteworthy.

Other factors that have implications for the development of Vietnam are the strong social institutions. Important legacies of Vietnam's traditional society have been a belief in the valuable and important role, both managerial and ethical, to be played by a centralised state bureaucracy in national life; a mass historical experience and commitment to collective organisation in local villages that covered a wide range of functions, emotional, spiritual and economic; and an individualism, bound up with loyalty to family, that asserted the individual's existence and, under certain circumstances, rights to push against the pressures exerted by collectives and other powers such as the state.[125]

Small firms

Small scale enterprises were the mainstay of the light industry dominated South Vietnam before reunification. However, with the imposition of the developmental model of the North in 1976, they were categorised as 'non compradore bourgeoisie' which, along with the big business compradore bourgeoisie, had to be eliminated as part of the socialisation process. Transforming the economy from one being dominated by small scale industries to one of large scale, predominantly producer goods manufacturing - the essence of moving from a developing to a socialist economy - was to be 'largely completed within about twenty years',[126] in the process by-passing any capitalist stage of development.

Initially, all non-state industry was identified with small scale industry, but at present small industry in effect includes cooperatives, private business, individual business, the family economies of cooperative members and state employees, and the joint state-private companies.[127] Most private enterprises are small or medium.[128] Small enterprises are defined as units employing between 5 and 50 employees, with capital investment between VND[129] 100 and 300 million. The official policy towards small industry has been 'supportive',[130] and certain measures taken in 1979 regarding allocation of a proportion of the state's supply of goods and imports, freedom to borrow foreign exchange, freedom to engage in trade with non-local markets and price negotiation were helpful to small firms. However, these were inadequate, lacking proper implementation and the small scale sector was constrained until mid 1980s, including the 'internal customs barriers'.[131]

---

[124] Andersen (1994), p. 2.
[125] Fforde and de Vylder (1988), p. 23.
[126] As quoted by Vo Nhan Tri (1990), p. 63.
[127] Fforde and de Vylder (1988), p. 108.
[128] In part, the explanation for the large share of SMEs is that Vietnam continues to apply what may be termed 'the socialist definition' of enterprise size; in other words, some medium sized enterprises in Vietnam would be categorised as large in other economies. (World Bank 1995b, p. 26).
[129] One US dollar was equivalent to approximately 11,000 Vietnamese dong in June 1995.
[130] Fforde and de Vylder (1988), p. 108.
[131] Ibid., p. 119.

A resolution on small scale and private sector activities, adopted in 1988, formally put the private sector on an equal footing with the state sector in as much as discriminatory behaviour against the former was outlawed. As such, it marked a change of heart as prior decisions implying liberalisation had typically been introduced in response to an unyielding reality. In short, private sector initiatives had up to this point been reduced to filling in those gaps that state sector enterprises left behind.[132] Pre-1985 state policies had reduced the role of the legally abolished private sector to that of 'filling in the gaps' of a shortage and crisis prone economy.[133]

The reforms have resulted in better performance of the private sector. Apart from a minor decline for private enterprises in 1990 private sector manufacturing has registered uninterrupted and rapid growth since the reforms, especially the household sector. Available data suggest that there has been both involutionary and evolutionary growth in the industrial enterprises, the former being more predominant, mainly due to fragmentation of the cooperative sector, and the reduction of the number of SOEs. The latter is in line with a more labour intensive manufacturing, characteristic of a labour abundant economy.

However, the small scale industry as a whole has declined since 1985, when it accounted for about a quarter of gross industrial output, to almost half of that by 1989. The small scale industrial sector, for the most part made up by small industrial and handicraft cooperatives, also faced an uncertain future as it was in no position to compete under the more liberal rules that were part of the reforms.[134] Though impressive, the growth of the private sector has not been as robust as the growth of the state sector; this trend can be observed in particular in industry, where sub-sectors which are the preserve of state enterprises have been growing very rapidly.[135] While private enterprises seem to have grown, the expansion of foreign trade and investment has not directly involved the private sector. The domestic partner in the vast majority of foreign financed joint ventures is in fact a state enterprise, and most import and export activity is still concentrated in those sectors where SOEs account for the largest share in output.[136] However, the private sector has been important in absorbing labour released from the state enterprises.

Vietnam's experience is quite distinct as for the size structure of SOEs. Most are small, in terms of both employment and investment criteria, as Table 5.4 shows. This does not describe the private firms which use even less assets and employ even fewer workers than SOEs, while are defined as small. It can be reasonably assumed that private sector small firms are at the lower end of the spectrum of small industries and state small firms at the other end. Carrying this assumption a little further, it could also be observed that the state small firms might have been operating under a better environment given their access to resources of the state.

---

[132] Johansson and Ronnås (1995), p. 56.
[133] Gates and Truong (1993).
[134] Ibid.
[135] World Bank (1995b), pp. 22-3.
[136] Ibid., p. 21.

Table 5.4
Size distribution of state enterprises in Vietnam by asset size 1992

Productive assets (million VND)	No. of SOEs	Total gross	Output (million VND, 1989 prices) Average per SOE	No. of workers Total	Average per SOE
Total	2,268	12,778,912	5,634.44	667,551	294
<500	792	256,316	323.63	42,740	54
500 - 1,000	394	252,411	640.64	47,539	121
1,000 - 3,000	571	1,059,843	1,856.12	121,149	212
3,000 - 5,000	181	672,902	3,717.69	63,955	353
5,000 - 10,000	151	1,076,837	7,131.37	70,530	467
10,000+	179	9,460,603	52,852.53	321,638	1,797

Source: World Bank (1995b), Table 4.4, p. 98.

The private sector industry is dominated by light, consumer goods manufacturing, even after the restructuring in the reforms. Reorientation of industry has occured within, rather than across, the broad categories of manufacturing branches.[137] The composition of small and medium enterprises is given in Table 5.5. Ap-

Table 5.5
Sub-sector composition of SMEs in Vietnam

Sub-sector	Percentage distrib.
Wood products	26.6
Textiles, garments	22.2
Food processing	17.0
Porcelain, ceramics, etc.	1.4
Paper products	0.8
Leather products	0.5
Other	31.5

Source: World Bank (1995b), Table 2.4, p. 27.

proximately 50 per cent of the manufacturing sector output has been produced by non-state enterprises (handicraft cooperatives and private enterprises) which are

---

[137] Johansson and Ronnås (1995), p. 61.

Table 5.6
Gross industrial production in Vietnam 1989-93 (constant 1989 prices)

	1989	1990	1991	1992	1993
Tot. gross production (million VND)	13,583,199	14,011,073	15,470,579	18,116,895	20,300,000
of which:					
State	9,012,824	9,475,790	10,598,947	12,778,912	14,482,000
Non-state	4,570,375	4,535,283	4,871,632	5,337,983	5,818,000
of which:					
Cooperative	1,612,312	1,279,348	746,772	514,794	502,700
Private enterprise	140,185	136,541	228,441	513,305	628,500
Private household	2,817,878	3,119,394	3,896,419	4,309,884	4,686,800
Tot. gross production (% composition)	100.0	100.0	100.0	100.0	100.0
of which:					
State	66.4	67.6	68.5	70.5	71.3
Non-state	33.6	32.4	31.5	29.5	28.7
of which:					
Cooperative	35.3	28.2	15.3	9.6	8.6
Private enterprise	3.0	3.0	4.7	9.6	10.8
Private household	61.7	68.8	80.0	80.7	80.6

Table 5.6 continued

Tot. gross production (% growth rate p. a.) of which:	3.2	10.4	17.1	12.1
State	5.1	11.9	20.6	13.3
Non-state of which:	-0.8	7.4	9.6	9.0
Cooperative	-20.7	-41.6	-31.1	-2.3
Private enterprise	-2.6	67.3	124.7	22.4
Private household	10.7	24.9	10.6	8.7

Source: World Bank (1995b), Table 2.6, p. 30.

mostly small scale firms with less than 50 workers employed.[138] Food processing, textiles and clothing, engineering (machines, electrical equipment, and other metal products) and construction materials are the largest of Vietnam's manufacturing industries, accounting for 44, 12, 10 and 9 per cent of gross manufacturing output in 1991.[139] A distinct experience of Vietnam is the admittance of economic activities beyond the official plan since the early eighties, which has aided in the transition period. Trends in industrial output and the share of private enterprises is given in Table 5.6. The difference between private households and private enterprises is that the households are small businesses employing family members only, while enterprises employ outside labour.

The overall development has historically been different between Northern and Southern Vietnam. Small scale production played a major role in the industrialisation of the South even before the reunification. Factors conducive to this development have been the lower population pressure on land and favourable climatic conditions. The lower population pressure on land strengthened agricultural production and generated pull factors in non-farm activities by expanding the market for non-farm products. The reforms have given rise to a change in the industrial structure, with the cooperatives declining in number. Since cooperatives were more a feature of the North, it has been affected more than the South in terms of the shift to private manufacturing. Thus the differential impact reflects the industrial structure of the pre-reform era, aided by other factors like a better road network in the South. Governmental regulations of the private sector have probably been stricter in the North whereas private entrepreneurship in the South had been encouraged in the early 1980s.[140]

The picture of rural industrialisation one obtains is of 'proto-industries interspersed with a significant minority of enterprises operating in a competitive environment'. The existence of the former is accredited to inefficiencies associated with the previous economic order and incomplete restructuring of the rural economic environment. However the latter have links with the urban markets, and are hindered by inadequate sales channels. Regional variations are also noted, with a majority of enterprises in the north being 'distress' industries, judging from the very low labour productivity and incomes.[141] One of the explanations for this regional variation is the comparatively high population pressure on land in the north which generates more push factors out of agriculture. However, for various reasons, overall transformation of the rural manufacturing sector has not occurred to the degree the Chinese achieved. Among the major ones are: the different role of local governments; absence of a politically induced fragmentation of the economy into local self-reliant areas; and comparatively higher factor mobility and the lower effects of decollectivisation of agriculture. All these have combined to hinder a demand led rural industrialisation in Vietnam. Further, compared to their

---

[138] Diehl (1994), p. 14.
[139] Ibid., p. 15.
[140] Ibid., p. 26.
[141] Johansson and Ronnås (1995), p. 69.

urban counterparts, rural industries are at a disadvantageous position owing to their smaller size, poor access to capital, poor backward and forward linkages, and a remoteness from competitive markets.

While these constitute external factors, internal factors (to the firm) like managerial and labour skills, and technological capability also have their share of hindering growth prospects for the rural firm. In the sequencing of reforms, too, unlike in China, the rural sector did not get a head start and this might be an important aspect for explaining the hard times ahead for the rural sector in general. While this pertains to rural firms, the private sector as a whole suffers from the uncertainty characteristic of the transition period. Gates and Truong note that privatisation of SOEs is faced with the problems of financial intermediation, in terms of finding buyers for state enterprises, limited implementation of legislation on private enterprises at lower levels, lack of a legal framework protecting and regulating private production.[142] A more politico-ideological issue is the uncertainty in defining the proper role, weight, concepts and links of private and social ownership in society. In fact the absence of a regulatory framework is a constraint inhibiting the transformation process as a whole. This has major implications for attracting foreign investment as well as overcoming domestic economic problems.

Dynamics of small firms The description above, of the small firm in Vietnam, shows that it has been operating under circumstances not really encouraging. Though a degree of tolerance, at times even acceptance, can be found throughout the central plan era, the motivation of entrepreneurs for starting a private firm has arisen more 'from the need to create employment and income for themselves and their family members'[143] than for sound commercial reasons. This tendency has been particularly strong in the post-reform era when large amounts of labour were released from the state enterprises. Factors affecting poor motivation have been varied: entry regulations, poor information about markets, technology and production process, weak physical and financial infrastructure and lack of exposure to the international arena. The 'subsistence' scale in terms of employing household labour and earning minimal incomes without expansion efforts is also because of uncertainty in the legal and regulatory framework, in the land use rights and restrictions on foreign trade. In this sense, a small firm's relations with the government have not been very useful.

Entry regulations pose as obstacles by being complicated, time consuming and expensive. There is also considerable room for subjective interpretations by government officials, which gives way to corruption. In addition, the system absorbs substantial administrative resources and yet is largely redundant, as most licensing requirements do not serve public policy objectives.[144] This creates a disincentive for registering and the firm conducts operations without an official existence.

---

[142] Gates and Truong (1993).
[143] Kurths (1995).
[144] World Bank (1995b).

As far as decisions within the firm are concerned, the capital needs of the small firms are met largely through own resources and interest free loans from friends and relatives, accounting for as much as 90 per cent of the investments.[145] The limited reliance on external capital reflects an absolute lack of access to external capital rather than a high price of capital.[146] The presence of push factors in establishing enterprises, rather than pull factors, like new opportunities, has resulted in the sources of capital being more informal than formal. Complementing this has been a weak financial system and formal credit has an insignificant role, especially long term loans. This situation has two implications: the very fact that these enterprises are being established points to some perceived gain, and shortage of capital is one of the major factors hindering realisation of this gain. The reforms presumably generate a demand for small scale units (since the reduced power of state enterprises creates a gap in meeting demand), which have a greater local reach, and combined with a supportive network, they can go a long way in efficiently compensating for the withdrawal of the state. The lack of this supportive network, however, curbs the efficiency of the units and dilutes their importance by shortening their time horizons and production plans, apart from hindering expansion potential. In Vietnam, these hurdles are the poor infrastructure, especially energy, and lack of distribution and marketing channels, which limits the market to local areas. Lack of information about product demands in non-local areas has created fragmented markets. This problem has been felt more in the rural areas. Another dimension of the reform led expansion of the small scale units is the relative decline of the manufacturing sector, which Vietnam experienced between 1986 and 1992. The rise in private sector activity has been greatest in the services sector, which has done well to absorb the gains in urban purchasing power.

Poor linkages with larger, state enterprises have been characteristic of the rural small firm, while the urban small firm has benefited from subcontracting arrangements with state enterprises, especially true of the South. Horizontal linkages have not been evident in assisting the small firms, in either urban or rural areas.

Financial market and monetary policy

Until 1988, Vietnam had a single banking system. The State Bank assumed the responsibilities of both the central and commercial banks.[147] It was a vertical hierarchy concentrating all services to the state sector; sectors other than the SOEs were crowded out from investment funds.[148] Channelling private and household savings into either private or public investment was not very effectively encour-

---

[145] Johansson and Ronnås (1995), p. 67.
[146] Diehl (1994), p. 23; and Ronnås (1992), p. 109.
[147] Le Dang Doanh (1994), p. 13; and Dinh (1993).
[148] Gates and Truong (1992), p. 17.

116

aged.[149] Capital markets existed and continue to exist on a rudimentary, informal basis. Industrial units, especially in the private sector, have not depended on the formal financial system,[150] let alone capital market, in undertaking investments, which relegates the issue of the role of formal capital markets to insignificance.

The financial system, which had remained almost unchanged since 1950s, was subject to reform for the first time in 1988. The efforts since then have been to 're-structure the entire system by re-organizing the state central bank and creating functioning commercial banks, specialized credit institutions and complementary capital markets'.[151] In mid-1988, four new specialised banks - the Bank for Foreign Trade, the Bank for Agricultural Development, the Bank for Industry and Commerce, and the Bank for Construction and Investment - were established and assumed the various commercial banking responsibilities of the State Bank of Vietnam.[152] The banking system, however, suffers from lack of control over the debts of the state enterprises, and these have hindered the commercial operations of the banks. A fundamental problem of the reform of finance has been the inability of the formal financial sector to mobilise domestic savings, and household savings have usually taken the form of hoarding, reflecting in part the lack of trust in banks.[153] This attitude has an important bearing in the success of the monetary policies in general. Monetary policy has also been unable to ensure a low inflation environment with the result that 'it has simultaneously reduced profitability and encouraged enterprises to make short-term investments rather than replacing their ageing and low productivity capital stock'.[154]

Fiscal policy

Fiscal policies in pre-reform Vietnam were weak, mainly relying on state enterprises and foreign aid for financing domestic investment plans. Weak fiscal policies, showing itself in budget deficits financed through the banking system, were one of the main sources of inflation in the late 1980s.[155] The government recorded negative savings and excessive reliance on bank financing that fuelled inflation, with current expenditures exceeding revenue for the most part.[156] The collapse of the trade with CMEA in 1991 resulted in lowered revenue, which, along with lowered foreign assistance motivated extensive reforms in the fiscal system.

Revenue from non-state, especially private sector, has been small, reflecting both the relative economic insignificance of and the nature of the tax system for

---

[149] Vietnam's domestic savings ratio was about 8 per cent in 1990, while the ratio of Gross Domestic Investment/Gross Domestic Product in East Asian countries such as South Korea and Thailand amounted to about 30 per cent in that same year (Gates and Truong 1992, p. 18).

[150] Ronnås (1992), p. 106.

[151] Gates and Truong (1992), p. 16.

[152] Ibid.

[153] Beresford (1995).

[154] Ibid.

[155] Andersen (1994), p. 27.

[156] See Dollar (1994) for a concise overview of the Vietnamese public finances.

small businesses. 'In contrast to most countries', the World Bank contends, 'enterprise income of small households in Vietnam is subject to profit tax rather than income tax. Because household enterprises typically keep rather rudimentary books, profit tax is levied on a presumptive basis, at a rate of 1-3 per cent of turnover, depending on the sector in which the enterprise operates'.[157] Another problem is that years of smuggling and corruption have established patterns of tax evasion that are hard to reverse.[158] It was only during the reform programme that import and export duties, turnover tax, excise duties, personal income tax, enterprise profits tax and land and housing taxes were introduced. Agriculture is also taxed, and its share in government revenues has been rising in recent years, largely due to improved collection performance.

While the state sector still accounts for the major domestic source of revenue,[159] it utilises most part of the government expenditure too. Subsidies to loss making state enterprises have been stopped since 1990, while the share devoted to social sectors, including health and education, has been raised. Medicine, electricity and housing are still subsidised but all other prices are determined by the market.[160] Capital expenditures were axed in the early years of the reform process and the pre-reform levels were attained only in 1993. Privatisation and its consequent falling revenues from state enterprises, and the poor tax base of the non-state sector have serious implications for overall development plans of the state and the lowered investment in physical and human infrastructure. Appropriate support policies for private sector are expected to yield good results in terms of improved indirect tax revenue and efficiency from increased competition.

Industrial policy

The industrialisation strategy adopted by Vietnam was based on the Soviet model which 'presumed a rather autarkic economy and the political and economic feasibility of "squeezing the peasantry" in order to maximise the agricultural surplus available for investment in industry, especially capital goods industry'.[161] The complements of this industrial policy were dependence on internal resources, ignoring comparative advantage in trade, and the belief in heavy industry as the 'leading sector' in the country's long term development. The heavy industry bias resulted in relatively few resources being allocated to other sectors, like agriculture, exports and so forth. This strategy was most evident in the Second FYP which gave highest priority to the nationalisation of heavy industry and huge investments with Soviet assistance. Favourable results, however, did not accrue owing to certain fundamental rigidities in the economic background of the Southern part and lack of supportive infrastructure. Rates of return fell on capital investment

---

[157] World Bank (1995b), p. 71.
[158] Dinh (1993).
[159] State enterprises contributed 71 per cent of total domestic revenue in 1993 (Andersen 1994, p. 30).
[160] Cao (1993), p. 463.
[161] Beresford (1989), p. 169.

since much of the installed capacity was not used. This criticism resulted in altered priorities in the Third FYP (1981-85) which abandoned the 'leading sector' maxim and concentrated efforts on agriculture, the processing of agricultural produce and other light industry, which was apparently more realistic. This policy shift was based on the linkage effects of light industry, which would stimulate development in the long run, though in the short run, its multiplier effects would not be very high. The Fourth FYP (1986-90) underlined the importance of foreign trade in improving the process of industrialisation and sought to strengthen the environment for exports, along with development of heavy industry and infrastructure. It is now apparent that the heavy industry bias has not been given up entirely, though Vietnam with great reluctance gave up the 'leading sector' belief. Official policy toward small industry was almost non-existent, except for small industries being considered as the production centres of consumer goods, which received attention in all plans.

The industrial environment also discouraged competition among SOEs, between the private sector and the SOEs, as well as between local and foreign producers.[162] The local private sector still suffers from discriminatory practices which deprive it of access to capital and foreign exchange.[163] Since the reforms, incentives to export have been important stimuli in improving quality standards but much of the manufacturing sector still remains protected under the garb of duties and tariffs. In fact, indications are that Vietnam is intent on enlisting FDI towards the end of continuing its original policy of import substitution.[164]

Foreign trade and payments policy

Vietnam in the pre-reform era had no clearly stated policy on foreign trade. It followed an inward oriented centrally managed development strategy whereby trade was utilised as a mechanism to expedite the industrialisation process in the long term and to stabilise the internal economic situation in the short term.[165] Trade was primarily bilateral with CMEA member countries, and the exchange rate structure encouraged a surplus of imports over exports made possible by Soviet foreign economic policies. The pursuit of a grossly inefficient and capital intensive strategy cemented the country's economic development on abroad. By the early 1980s, no less than two-fifths of the state budget originated from external aid and the balance of foreign trade was heavily in red. As a result, the economy became ever more dependent 'on countries, which, for ideological or other reasons, were willing to support the cost of the country's dogmatic approach to development'.[166]

In 1990, the CMEA trade protocols were dissolved, which adversely affected the light industrial exports. Coupled with withdrawal of credits from the Soviet Union,

---

[162] Beresford (1995).
[163] Ibid.
[164] Kokko and Zejan (1996), Part II.
[165] Gates and Truong (1992), p. 18.
[166] Ronnås and Sjöberg (1991), p. 5.

this was a major shock to the balance of payments. But the growing export markets of Asia and the boost in oil production and marine products helped Vietnam overcome what might otherwise have proved a disastrous situation. Some products with relatively low quality standards and high degree of protection from foreign competition and the barter trade with CMEA states had to face strong competition,[167] and this is indicative of what is to follow for most protected industries in the near future. All manufacturing branches enjoy significant import protection which is designed to promote higher processing levels by tariff escalation.[168] However, favourable prospects for the future of balance of payments include rising FDI from Hong Kong, Taiwan, Singapore and South Korea, remittances from overseas Vietnamese, and the resumption of lending by credit agencies in 1994.

The major reforms in the foreign trade sector have been the establishment of a new tariff schedule in 1989, trade liberalisation (through quota reduction on imports and exports), fiscal reforms such as lowered export taxes and import duties, and elimination of requirement that local or provincial SOE's trade should be only through the intermediary of the state's foreign trading corporations. EPZs are still in the process of being experimented upon and might not make much headway in the near future given the poor infrastructure. Vietnam now has a *laissez-faire* exchange rate policy, which has resulted in establishment of equalised incentives for producing for both domestic and export markets, but have also led to volatility of the Vietnamese dong.[169] Much of the improvements in exports are seen in rice, crude oil, coal and marine products, and manufactured goods still account for a very small share.

The Vietnamese experience: implications for transaction costs

It was established in Chapter Three of this volume that small firms have certain disadvantages due to their size, and higher transaction costs is one of them. Arising from a relative inability to internalise transactions in the face of risk and uncertainty, small scale enterprises are to a greater extent left to the vagaries of imperfect markets and government failure than are larger entities. Developed technical and marketing support systems in the form of small industry extension services, and horizontal and vertical linkages are ways of reducing these disadvantages as are other means whereby the transactional triad of 'contact, contract and control'[170] can be held in check. Vietnam has scored very poorly in terms of governmental assistance to the small industry and linkages with other firms and state enterprises. The economic environment of neglect of small industry has thereby not assisted small firms and raised transaction costs.

The public budget has made inadequate investments in physical infrastructure, and this has resulted in a fragmentation, with rural areas cut off from urban areas;

---

[167] Diehl (1994), p. 17, and (1995).
[168] Diehl (1994), p. 19.
[169] Gates and Truong (1992), p. 20.
[170] Nooteboom et al. (1992), p. 141.

in fact, one may surmise that here, as in other centrally planned economies, rural areas were planned to remain rural and at most auxiliary to the socialist sector of predominantly urban stock. Be this as it may, the resulting regional disparities have worked to raise ex ante transaction costs, by making information about non-local markets costly. While the state enterprises benefited from FDI, the private sector has been thriving largely on domestic resources. Poor financial markets and credit availability have shortened the time horizons of production and to that extent increased the information asymmetry on the part of the buyers from small firms. Contractual partners have no way of monitoring credibility of small firms and this increases possibilities of opportunism on the part of either partner.

Moreover, the numerous entry restrictions act as a disincentive for registration and many firms lose out on official existence too. This naturally rules out whatever little benefits they would have otherwise received. For instance, the banking system requires the small firms to support an application for credit with a lot of official documents. This requirement complements the poor record maintenance of the small firm and discounts any sort of assistance from an external agency. The small firm's owner has to act independently in arranging for finance, purchase orders, raw materials and other items, with the result that transaction costs are substantially higher than if the firm had a legally 'registered' existence. The informal character also hides the small firm from the view of actors in foreign and other non-local markets. Lack of accountability raises suspicions from the contracting partner and hence increases both search costs as well as contract monitoring and enforcement costs.

The initiation of the reforms has resulted in a spurt in the private sector activity and this adds to the uncertainty to a small firm's contracting partner. Mutual distrust in the absence of a sound legal framework is a sure cause of high ex ante and ex post transaction costs. It is seen that a large part of the small firm spurt has been motivated by loss of employment in the state sector. While there are instances of the new small businessmen having experience in a particular area of activity, most of the new entrants into the industrial arena have to face high transaction costs in the form of search costs incurred in finding markets and inputs. Vietnam has a favourable factor in terms of the high level of education, and this can alleviate some of the problems during the transition, in terms of coping with uncertainty. A high level of entrepreneurial literacy could be positively correlated with the ability to innovate and survive in a competitive world.

Imperfections in the input markets increase transaction costs substantially by raising search costs for inputs. Though labour does not suffer from immobility, poor infrastructure and information about markets does result in an 'induced immobility'. The attitude towards private sector in general has been quite accommodative and this has served to reduce policy uncertainty for the small firm. It is also observed that a majority of state enterprises were themselves small. However, the small firms in the state sector had relatively lower transaction costs than the private sector firms since the former had better access to resources. The credit needs of state sector firms were taken care of automatically by the state budget.

While there are no specific reasons found in the literature for explaining the small size of state enterprises, they were definitely better placed than their private sector counterparts since they even had access to foreign markets. This exposure lowered transaction costs relative to the private firm restricted to local markets.

The poor state of infrastructure adds to the delays in production and make contract monitoring and enforcement an expensive affair. While perhaps self-evident, investors and entrepreneurs alike continue to complain that '[b]reakdown in telephones, power and telex services increase costs and reduce efficiency for businesses. Telephone service is limited in the few big cities. The country's water and energy distribution systems cannot meet private sector demands and ports and railroads need major improvement'.[171]

More important still, Vietnam's legal framework, like that of China, is heavily imbued with socialist ideology and influenced by the doctrine of socialist legality, implying a high degree of instrumentalism in legislation. Predictably, this causes problems in such areas as private ownership of property.[172] It is also stated that the private sector is constrained by the lack of an independent judiciary, other uncertainties in property law that limit development of financial markets and the inherent bias of the system in favour of the state sector.[173] A strong legal framework is required for ensuring a good investment climate in the long run. It can be inferred that vaguely defined property rights have been complemented by a weak formal institutional framework in terms of contract enforcement and monitoring.

Small firms have sought to overcome inadequacies such as those listed immediately above by restricting their areas of operation.[174] In reducing the uncertainties characteristic of the transition period, linkages with other firms have not helped much and the firms have been surviving in a relative isolation. Favourable developments, like the exposure to foreign markets, put the small firms at a disadvantage, not unexpectedly, in the short run, but should help in tuning up the small industry as a whole in the long run. The government has an important role in not only developing linkages but also indirectly in the form of investments in improving infrastructure and eliminating the geographic disadvantages of the rural small firm.

From the above it is clear that, while successfully moving away from the worst excesses of the pre-reform system, Vietnam as much as China has had difficulties in doing away with all the vestiges of its centrally planned past. As we shall see in the concluding chapter, where themes common to our case studies and existing institutional differences are spelled out, Asia's most important socialist polities are not alone in maintaining barriers to successful development of the formal small scale industrial sector. The scale and sheer weight of that institutional legacy, however, set them clearly apart from India and Taiwan, in this respect being more similar to Ethiopia and Tanzania, the subject of the two final case studies. In short, the transition from central planning creates a set of pressures quite of its own.

---

[171] Dinh (1993).
[172] Pham Van Thuyet (1995).
[173] Ibid.
[174] Compare the analysis by Fafchamps (1994).

6 Ethiopia

Maud Hemlin

Introduction

As will become evident, life has been troublesome for the Ethiopian population in general, even more so for those interested in undertaking some kind of economic activity, and in particular for the group that has preferred to do so in private regime. Ethiopia is a country which, until recently, has shown many of the features prevailing in a so called shortage economy, that is, a gravely insufficient supply permanently hampering all sectors of the economy.[1] Symptoms of this kind are, in their most serious and chronic forms, typical for economies in which a socialist system has been implemented. Taking as departure point that such symptoms are actually discernible in Ethiopia, this chapter sets out to discuss the implications.

In no way is the ambition to give a highly detailed picture of the developments within Ethiopia from past to present; more a fairly general résumé of the history of the country, providing the skeleton to clothe with the material central to this publication: the transaction cost perspective. The aim is thus to provide a basic factual background against which individual judgements can be made and factors which increase transaction costs identified, and to give an indication of how the problems of lowering transaction costs for entrepreneurs are dealt with. In other words, a complete picture is not given - more a way of thinking, a particular way of looking at the developments and interpreting the results.

Scope and organisation of the chapter

'The key to an understanding of the socialist system', Kornai writes, 'is to examine the *structure of power*, which receives little or no attention in many comparative studies of economic systems. In my opinion, the characteristics of the power structure are precisely the source from which the chief regularities of the system can be deduced'.[2] This is also the point of departure for this chapter, a presentation of the Ethiopian political setting in which structural as well as ideological features are described. This should provide the reader with a sense of the insecurity that has

---

[1] Kornai (1992), p. 233.

[2] Ibid., p. 33; emphasis in the original.

been prevailing in Ethiopia; external wars, civil wars, terror and the socialist regime have all contributed to an environment in which almost any activity has involved risks. The implications of this in terms of transaction costs will also be assessed specifically.

As one of the fundamental prerequisites for socialism is the replacement of private property with public ownership, an examination is called for regarding the decisions made affecting the Ethiopian economy in general and the judicial implications thereof in particular, in terms of ownership and disposal rights. This can be found in the economic history section, where the effects and results for the business climate will be examined, in general as well as from a transaction cost perspective.

It is thus with the above in mind that the situation for small scale industries should be examined, investigating the policies directed especially towards the SSI sector, but to some extent also drawing implications hereon from other policy decisions. To complete the study, the SSI undertakings have been screened from the transaction cost perspective too.

The political setting

Through a combination of charisma, patrimony and feudalism, Haile Selassie maintained his imperial authority. . . . Almost all in the executive office or Imperial Palace had to consistently court his favour by daily appearing at the palace, fawning over him, and doing his bidding. One might lose power and authority by not showing proper fealty or by appearing too independent.

Peter Schwab[3]

While we expect our organization's discipline and control body to increase its competence so as to guard the purity of members and remove obstacles, all members and bodies should give their full co-operation to this body in order to correct mistakes without delay and implement resolutions, because the task is a complex one. . . . In particular, since failing to implement the organization's aims faithfully is a sign of weak ideological indoctrination, it is important that it be corrected.

Mengistu Haile Mariam[4]

The late imperial era

Although almost 17 years passed following the death of Emperor Menelik before the crowning of Tafari Mekonnen, the latter nevertheless managed to undertake a number of, for Ethiopia, modernising projects even before he was given the title Haile Selassie I. Membership in the League of Nations was applied for and approved in 1923.[5] In 1931 he granted Ethiopia its first constitution, which called for

---

[3] Schwab (1985), p. 11.
[4] Mengistu Haile Mariam (1983), p. 9.
[5] Turner (1993), p. 34.

the establishment of a Chamber of Deputies and a Senate. The executive body consisted of a Crown Council led by the Emperor and a Council of Ministers. The powerful church was made less influential administratively, for instance by limiting its authority to levy taxes, and by defining different ministries' specific duties another influential group, the nobility, lost some of its provincial power.

After the six year war with Italy, triggered by the invasion by Mussolini's forces from Eritrea in 1935, Haile Selassie turned to the US amongst others for financial assistance to help with war damage restoration. He ratified the Charter of the United Nations, and in 1955 he proclaimed the revision of the 1931 constitution. Trade unions were recognised in 1962, but only for privately employed staff in plants or agricultural units employing more than ten people.[6] These organisations were furthermore not allowed to cover different industrial sectors. In response to protests from the unions, students and the military the Emperor made some attempts at reform in the late 1960s. A new Prime Minister was appointed and given the task of writing a new constitution and soldiers were granted higher wages twice in a couple of months. This, however, proved to be insufficient.

With new tax proposals, land distribution and rising inflation, public discontent grew, also amongst the military where many came from peasant stock. Revolts and mutinies broke out within the army, and factionalism too. In early June 1974, a group of junior officers, with the purpose of providing more organised imperial opposition, requested the armed forces to send three representatives per unit[7] to the capital. Thus, being able to claim that they represented the whole military, the Coordinating Committee of the Armed Forces, Police and Territorial Army was born at the end of June, made up of about 100 men,[8] all lower military rank, with Mengistu Haile Mariam and Aman Andom elected chairman and vice chairman respectively. This body launched its first policy statement in July, under the slogan Ethiopia First,[9] in which no particular socialist features surfaced, but rather promises to deal with the draught affected areas, to bring old officials to trial and to make better use of tourism as a source of national income.[10] The Committee manoeuvred in order to gain influence in government, but when the new constitution, approved by Parliament in August, proved a disappointment they instead encouraged public dissent. Thus, after having deprived the Emperor of power, arrested influential imperial officials and taken control of important institutions, the Committee formally assumed power on 12 September,[11] and three days later reformed itself to the Provisional Military Administrative Council (PMAC),[12] also

---

[6] Mulatu Wubneh and Yohannis Abate (1988), pp. 40–41.

[7] I.e. from the army, the police etc.

[8] The exact number remains debatable, see Negussay Ayele (1990), pp. 14 and 27 (footnote 4).

[9] *Ityopya tikdem*, Clapham (1990a), p. 40.

[10] Andargachew Tiruneh (1993), p. 66; Negussay Ayele (1990), p. 15; and Girma Kebbede (1992), p. 8 (footnote 3).

[11] Clapham (1990a), p. 40.

[12] Turner (1993), p. 54.

known as the *Derg*.[13] Aman Andom was appointed chairman while Majors Mengistu and Atnafu Abate were made 1st and 2nd vice chairmen.

The Derg and Mengistu Haile Mariam

The general impression was that military rule was to be temporary until a new constitution had been approved by the people's representatives. But with rather vague goals, plans and distribution of power within the PMAC, internal conflicts soon arose. For instance, Aman Andom, himself Eritrean, spoke in favour of negotiations, rather than the military solutions preferred by other leading members of the Derg, in the conflict with Eritrea which dated back to the 1940s.[14] For this he was killed on 23 November 1974, a fate that also overtook some 60 other political prisoners of importance that same evening. General Teferi Bante assumed Aman's position.

Ethiopian socialism was mentioned for the first time in the Derg's ten point programme of 20 December. The transition to socialism was then further outlined in the Declaration on Economic Policy of Socialist Ethiopia (DEP) in February 1975 and the Programme of the National Democratic Revolution (PNDR) in April 1976. Addis Ababa University as well as all senior secondary schools were closed and the students were to travel the country explaining the revolution to the people, an excellent way of avoiding concentrations of oppositional students in the cities.[15] In addition, Revolution and Development Committees for 'coordination and implementation of rural policies' were established, again, officially only as a temporary measure until local self-administration laws had been issued, but still two years later expected to 'detain and prosecute those who engage in "anti-revolutionary" or "anti-unity" acts . . .'[16] The Derg also replaced the Confederation of Ethiopian Labour Unions with the government controlled All-Ethiopia Trade Union, abandoning protection of workers' rights and ideas of proletarian revolution for the goal of improved productivity instead. The regime wanted to transform the labour movement to something of a 'state agency'.[17] It was by now obvious to everyone how unwise it was to criticise Derg policies for their lack of democracy.

Ethiopian Marxist intellectuals abroad returned to join the revolution, but ended up divided into separate camps, the two most important being the Ethiopian People's Revolutionary Party (EPRP) and MEISON.[18] The former counted the Derg among its enemies and demanded a civilian government immediately, while the latter attempted to direct the revolution from inside through Derg cooperation,[19] and spoke of a yet immature sense of class consciousness. An era of terror

---

[13] Amharic, means council or committee.
[14] Turner (1993), p. 41.
[15] Ghelawdewos Araia (1995), p. 86.
[16] Brietzke (1981), p. 284.
[17] Markakis, John and Nega Ayele (1986), p. 186.
[18] Amharic acronym for All-Ethiopia Socialist Movement.
[19] Negussay Ayele (1990), p. 20.

evolved from these insurmountable differences in position of the civilian left. The EPRP actions, Negussay Ayele writes, included 'killing whole families, hanging children in school yards, gunning down husbands waiting in cars for their wives and fathers dropping their kids off at school, assassinating young members of a family and dumping the bodies in front of the house, so as to shock and brutalize the rest of the family'.[20]

In response, the PMAC eagerly gave weapons to whoever they thought could provide EPRP resistance, some weapons actually ending up in enemy hands. Such unintended effects urged the PMAC to withdraw from external cooperation and later a complete break with MEISON. In 1988 Dawit Wolde Giorgis, who had held a number of influential positions under the Mengistu regime, but who defected to the United States in 1986, wrote: 'He [Mengistu] deliberately gave arms and freedom of action to ruthless people, encouraging them to kill whomever they pleased. . . . People are constantly reminded that terror is always lurking in the wings, that at any moment they or their loved ones could be dragged out of bed and shot. No one sleeps securely in Ethiopia.'[21] After having killed Teferi Bante in February and the successor, Atnafu Abate, in November 1977 Mengistu could assume complete power.

The Soviet Union began supporting Ethiopia in 1977, abandoning its former protégé Somalia in the Ogaden war in favour of a more important and dominating partner, population and politics-wise.[22] It was thus much due to Soviet demands for a civilian vanguard party that the Commission to Organise a Party of the Workers of Ethiopia (COPWE) came about in December 1979,[23] however, including neither workers nor peasants on its Central Committee.[24] On the tenth anniversary of the revolution the Workers' Party of Ethiopia (WPE) was born, supposedly an official communist party, built on the Soviet model but in reality merely a reintroduction of COPWE. Furthermore, a ten year plan was approved, according to which 115,000 people were to be resettled from drought struck areas within a decade, 'a drop in the bucket' of what was even most urgently needed according to Dawit Wolde Giorgis, then head of the Relief and Rehabilitation Commission.[25] The disaster had, in fact, already been reality since 1982[26] but was kept secret so as not to disturb the anniversary festivities. Accused of spending millions on the celebrations and neglecting famine Mengistu later did a U-turn and ordered 1.5 million people to move south (from Tigray, Welo, Gonder and Northern Shewa to Kefa, Welega and Ilubabor). Censorship was made even stricter after 1984, with a

---

[20] Ibid., p. 22.
[21] Dawit Wolde Giorgis (1990), pp. 56-7.
[22] Mulatu Wubneh and Yohannis Abate (1988), pp. 182-3.
[23] Girma Kebbede (1992), p. 4.
[24] Clapham (1990a), p. 73.
[25] Dawit Wolde Giorgis (1990), p. 64.
[26] Mulatu Wubneh and Yohannis Abate (1988), p. xiii.

wide net of informers, reporting on everyone and everything to Ethiopian security organisations, but also the Soviet Embassy was informed.[27]

Due to farmers' unwillingness to join cooperatives, villagisation projects, that is, turning scattered hamlets into concentrated, centralised villages, had been undertaken since the 1970s and became a campaign focus in 1985, although modernisation and improving and increasing infrastructure rather than collectivisation was the stated aim.[28] In 1977 villagisation programmes had been launched in the Bale region to move people away from the area affected by the Ethiopia-Somali conflict. These programmes were extended to Hararge for the same reason in December 1984 and finally by July 1985 covered the entire country.[29] By mid-1988 approximately 12 million people had been resettled through these projects, putting enormous pressure on the environment as well as the people, and calling for adjustment to large scale farming.[30] Critics spoke of army control and Marxist-Leninist indoctrination.[31] While the regime was to uproot some 33 million people to modernise and combat famine, 50 per cent of the annual budget was being spent on warfare.

A draft constitution, based on Marxist principles, was presented for discussion in the 'kebeles' (urban dwellers' organisations) and peasant associations (PAs) in June 1986. Of the 500,000 revisions suggested, just 95 ended up in the amended version,[32] and 'more in the style', according to Negussay Ayele, 'than in the substance of the document'.[33] The final draft, which promised general elections to the National Assembly, was approved in February by 81 per cent of entitled voters; however, the whole procedure has been called into question.[34] At urban and rural associations' meetings in May candidates were nominated, and elections followed in June. The new assembly started work in September, with one-third farmers', one-fourth civil servants' and one-eighth each of armed forces' and workers' representatives. The People's Democratic Republic of Ethiopia had thus been inaugurated with Mengistu as President.

In 1989 the Ethiopian People's Revolutionary Democratic Front (EPRDF) was formed out of Marxist Amhara and Tigray rebel groups, later also Oromo, with calls for a people's government. In May, senior officers with similar demands - an end to the civil war, a new Addis Ababa government with representatives of the opposition and the reintroduction of democracy and freedom of speech, attempted a coup. The upheaval, which was supported even by the Eritrean People's Liberation Front (EPLF) who promised cease-fire in the civil war, was literally crushed by government forces, at the cost of several human lives.

---

[27] Cohen (1987), pp. 15ff.
[28] Clapham (1990a), p. 175.
[29] Alemayehu Lirenso (1990), p. 136.
[30] Alemneh Dejene (1990), pp. 179-80.
[31] Deming and Wilkinson (1986), p. 32.
[32] Keller (1993), p. 215.
[33] Negussay Ayele (1990), p. 25.
[34] Ghelawdewos Araia (1995), p. 100; and Dawit Wolde Giorgis (1990), pp. 68ff.

In September 1989 representatives of the Ethiopian government met with delegates from the separatist EPLF in Atlanta, Georgia. Both sides were somewhat tired after 28 years of war and the US was tempting with improved West-Ethiopian relations while the Soviets indicated better need domestically for their scarce (Soviet) financial resources. However, negotiations later broke down. By the end of that year Ethiopia voted to condemn the Iraqi invasion of Kuwait in the UN Security Council, thereby gaining some leverage. In his Central Committee speech in March 1990 Mengistu stated that he welcomed the participation in the political process of the rebels in the north and claimed he wanted a society open to different religions and ideologies, however, he completely rejected a multi-party system.

The Transitional Government and the EPRDF

In May 1991 Mengistu fled Ethiopia. By then he had watched the fall of several socialist governments around the world, the WPE army capitulating in Eritrea and the EPLF transformed into Eritrea's Provisional Government, the ending of Soviet aid, and even the defection of a number of government officials to the West. Taking the helm were Tesfaye Dinka and Tesfaye Gebre-Kidan, former Prime Minister and Vice President respectively, who urged the rebels to lay down their weapons while promising all opposition groups representation in the planned transitional government. As peace negotiations started in London, headed by the US deputy Foreign Minister Herman Cohen, Tesfaye Dinka claimed that the army no longer was under government control. Cohen then encouraged Meles Zenawi, the EPRDF leader, to let his troops march into Addis Ababa in order to stabilise the situation, something that made Tesfaye walk out of the negotiations, leaving the EPRDF, the EPLF and the OLF, the Oromo Liberation Front. The disturbances did not automatically cease with the rebel take-over though.

In July a national conference with approximately 30 political and regional groups was held in the capital. The charter agreed on there guaranteed human rights, multi-party democracy and respect for ethnic interests through the establishment of 12 ethnic based, widely empowered, administrative regions and two multi-ethnic chartered cities, Addis Ababa and Harar. 600 'weredas' (districts) were to serve as basic administrative units. A transitional government, the TGE, with Meles Zenawi as President was appointed with 32 of the 87 seats going to the EPRDF. According to Ethiopia's Economic Policy during the Transition Period, TEP, published in November after public screening and debate since August, villagisation and resettlement programmes were to be abandoned.

Laws coming into force from January 1992 onwards outlined the rights and obligations of the lower level administrations, while foreign affairs, economic policy, the printing of currency and suchlike were tasks kept exclusively in the domain of central government. When taking over the EPRDF had sacked the entire police force, temporarily replacing it with Peace and Stability Committees (PSCs), thus aggravating the already serious judicial situation resulting from the imprisonment and dismissal of judges 'inherited' from the WPE. PSCs were later replaced with a professional police force.[35] Regional elections, initially set for October 1991 but postponed until spring 1992,[36] were finally held in June, as were wereda elections. Similar elections for local governing committees had taken place in April. Claiming harassment and cheating by the EPRDF, also confirmed by international observers, the OLF boycotted the elections and left the TGE.[37] There had by then been several armed clashes between the two at various places in Ethiopia. Other groups, such as Isa, Afar and the EPRP, were also on bad terms with the EPRDF. Several human rights incidents were later reported in 1993, in connection with protest demonstrations against the EPRDF and the question of Eritrea's status. In 1993 the Eritreans voted for independence. This was granted in May.

In June 1994 a constituent assembly was elected, seven-eighths of the seats going to the EPRDF.[38] Though more than half of the candidates were independent the main opposition parties were not represented, again boycotting elections and complaining injustice.[39] In December the new constitution of the Federal Democratic Republic of Ethiopia was ratified, from then on with nine ethnically and linguistically based member states (formally proclaimed in August 1995). Now regions where two-thirds of the regional legislative council were in favour of secession, supported by a majority in the referenda organised by the federal government, would be granted independence.[40] Also, in that same month the gigantic court proceedings against some 3,000 Mengistu regime accomplices were initiated.[41]

In the federal and regional elections in May 1995, the EPRDF won more than 90 per cent of the seats, although the major opposition parties did not participate, claiming unfairness during the campaign and irregularities in the voting procedures.[42] Although press freedom is said to have been implemented since 1992, several newspapers critical of the new regime have been banned and staff members sent to jail.

Implications for transaction costs

It is difficult to imagine a state of full information, a world of costless information

Thráinn Eggertsson[43]

Even in democratic societies where the state conducts its debates in the open, where the press is free and where the people elects those who form the rules of the

---

[35] Baker and Arnesen (1992), p. 14.
[36] Ibid., p. 13.
[37] Bartholet (1992), p. 19.
[38] Hansson (1995b), p. 7.
[39] The Economist, 4 June 1994, p. 50; and Makau wa Mutua (1994), pp. 23ff.
[40] Hansson (1995b), p. 9.
[41] The Economist, 17 December 1994, p. 39.
[42] Svenska Dagbladet, 9 May 1995, p. 7; also supported by Amnesty reports according to Upsala Nya Tidning, 10 May 1995, p. 2.
[43] Eggertsson (1990), p. 15.

system, the future cannot be perfectly predicted. Imagine then, how much further away from Eggertsson's ideal is a country where none of the aforementioned circumstances exist, where information means power and when power is concentrated mainly in the hands of one, or very few, citizens.

When information, amongst the general public, is incomplete the mere process of trying to acquire information, without any surety of success, demands a certain personal contribution of time, money or effort or combinations thereof. When such contributions can be ascribed to the purpose of exchanging and enforcing property rights[44] the term transaction costs is used.[45]

Thus, incomplete knowledge gives rise to a feeling of insecurity, a concept that has many aspects. If the political history of Ethiopia is used as a basis for analysis, one could start with the short-sightedness, the lack of continuity of polices and the reactions of the people to this situation. Already Haile Selassie had redistributed land from southern farmers to men serving in the Emperor's forces, thus securing their loyalty. During the military and Mengistu era people were expected to move from whatever land they were tilling in the north in resettlement and villagisation programmes. Irrespective of the real aim of such projects, they were rather unenthusiastically looked upon by the farmers. Some 50,000 fled to Somalia,[46] many were threatened with weapons,[47] human rights were disregarded,[48] and the actual production figures were completely subordinated to government set quotas.[49] Under such conditions there was no, and could not be any, long term links to the land. Many people were uprooted from whatever system of contacts and linkages they had established, and all incentives to reinvest, increase output for storage or for higher revenues from sales were lost. As Eggertsson puts it, '[w]hen exclusive ownership rights by individual farmers are restricted and long-term leases not allowed, the farmers are unlikely to allocate resources to various potentially lucrative investment projects because their rights to yields accruing in future periods are uncertain'.[50]

Wars and upheavals could have effects similar to those already mentioned. Wars, or disputes of any kind for that matter, involve at least two sides, trying with or without violence to persuade the environment of the superiority of their views. Who will emerge as winner cannot be known in advance, hence making people reluctant to undertake long term projects until a victor and his/her future 'system' can be distinguished. In Ethiopia political solutions were sought long before Haile Selassie's days. Then came the war with Italy, an attempted coup and the struggle for independence in some regions. The first years of military rule where characterised by internal power struggles within the Derg. Once that was settled, the

[44] For various meanings of this concept, see ibid., pp. 34ff.
[45] For differentiation between information and transaction costs, see ibid., p. 15.
[46] Deming and Wilkinson (1986), p. 32.
[47] Cohen (1987), p. 16.
[48] Girma Kebbede (1992), p. 23.
[49] Baker and Arnesen (1992), pp. 6-7.
[50] Eggertsson (1990), p. 127.

winner turned to the task of taming the population through terror, later replaced by party control. The overthrow of Mengistu was very violent, and still today there are some ethnic groups aspiring to independence, at times in armed struggle. As Eggertsson puts it, 'the distribution of political power within a country and the institutional structure of its rule-making institutions are critical factors in economic development'.[51]

A high degree of transparency in the work of state agencies is another aspect of eliminating insecurity. Political parties in democratic societies present their agendas before elections and the process from intention to implementation can thereby be tracked. However, in the case of Ethiopia, not only has the decision making process been secret, but also the people involved in the process were to a large extent unknown. The Emperor had absolute power in a number of matters. He appointed staff to influential positions; for instance, judges and members of governing institutions,[52] thus making way for what today is termed DUP activities (Directly Unproductive Profit seeking activities) amongst the nobility, that is, working hard to win the approval of the Emperor rather than establishing an influential position by providing the population in the province with a favourable economic environment and thus furthering growth. While certain civil rights and liberties were set out in the constitution, for instance, freedom of religion and speech, these were all subordinated to public order and the general welfare needs.[53] Under military rule the names of Derg members were kept secret.[54] This inner circle was then narrowed even further in dubious ways[55] and '[a]fter 1978', according to Dawit Wolde Giorgis, 'the PMAC did not meet once and yet all decisions were made in its name . . .'[56] Before the formation of COPWE, something akin to employment interviews were conducted as Mengistu handpicked his team.[57] All other political parties were banned and formal organised opposition made impossible.[58] Once the WPE had been launched, decisions of its Political Bureau were taken in secret,[59] the procedures as such also being veiled in secrecy.[60] Elections of members for the National Assembly through urban and rural association nominations were rigged in advance.[61] Likewise, the current regime has been accused of indirectly shutting out the opposition from elections.

Consistency is also important in helping to reduce insecurity. Promises made by regimes should be kept in order to gain people's confidence. 'The state', Eggertsson writes, 'by using its political power and the courts, assists private individuals

---

[51] Ibid., p. 248; emphasis in original.
[52] Mulatu Wubneh and Yohannis Abate (1988), pp. 19-20.
[53] Ghelawdewos Araia (1995), p. 41.
[54] Clapham (1990a), p. 66; and Negussay Ayele (1990), p. 27 (footnote 4).
[55] Ghelawdewos Araia (1995), p. 97.
[56] Dawit Wolde Giorgis (1990), p. 61.
[57] Clapham (1990a), p. 70.
[58] Ghelawdewos Araia (1995), p. 98.
[59] Keller (1993), p. 213.
[60] Clapham (1990a), p. 83.
[61] Ibid., p. 95; and Ghelawdewos Araia (1995), p. 101.

in enforcing legitimate contracts and thus lowers the costs of exchange, particularly when the state uses its power to enforce contracts in a *systematic and predictable manner*'.[62] Mengistu started villagisation projects before having set standards and norms for the programme, thus forcing some people to move again. Once the Ministry of Agriculture had circulated its 'Villagisation Guidelines', in which criteria were set for geographical location, size, population and so forth, some of the newly established villages had to be moved as these did not meet the criteria.[63] Similarly, postponement of elections under the post-Mengistu regime might have dented its credibility. In November 1991, Meles Zenawi himself answered 'No, nothing.' to a question posed by a Swedish reporter when the latter asked if there was anything that could postpone the free elections that were to be held within two years.[64] However, elections are complex procedures and preparations are rather time consuming. After criticism was voiced regarding the 1992 elections, people were educated about voting and all EPRDF members had to take a six week course in topics such as the rule of law.[65] Mr Zenawi also witnessed how debates in the Council of Representatives were rather lengthy procedures, but favoured the ambition of consensus as this would facilitate implementation and enforcement of laws resulting therefrom.[66]

Other procedures that have put the government's reputation at stake have been the delays of trials of former Mengistu allies, some being imprisoned for three years without charge.[67] Again the task is gigantic and the means limited. This was a matter of such importance to the Ethiopians, thus, proud of dealing with it themselves, UN observers were not invited.[68] However, as pointed out by Baker and Arnesen, the dismissal of all judges that had served under the WPE regime did create rips in the judicial net.[69] The question is, which is worse? Former 'WPE judges' or no judges at all?

Political insecurity, as we have seen, results from a population ignorant of the decision making processes and the appointments to influential positions, as well as being unable to influence these procedures and from experiences of having been lied to. Moving decision making as close as possible to the people is one way of getting round this problem. Such a solution was at work during the 19th century,[70] and is now being tried again by the EPRDF through the establishment of a federal system. A high degree of autonomy for individual regions might prevent internal ethnic disputes as well as make it is easier for state agencies to enforce laws when these resemble what is generally perceived among the population as 'right' and

---

[62] Eggertsson (1990), p. 46; emphasis in the original.
[63] Alemayehu Lirenso (1990), p. 139.
[64] Norrman (1991), p. 11.
[65] The Economist, 4 June 1994, p. 50.
[66] The Economist, 14 December 1991, p. 56.
[67] The Economist, 17 December 1994, p. 40.
[68] The Economist, 30 July 1994, p. 38.
[69] Baker and Arnesen (1992), p. 14.
[70] Mulatu Wubneh and Yohannis Abate (1988), p. 13.

'fair', that is, corresponding to already existing social norms.[71] In a country such as Ethiopia, where the cultural and ethnic flora is rich and varied, the number of local customs is bound to be great and the problems associated with constructing a legal system adapted to such customs nationwide are bound to be even greater.

However, there is also a risk of Ethiopia disintegrating since the matter of independence has two sides to it. On the one hand, the mere institutionalisation of a way out of the federation might actually encourage some regions to stay in as they know that with a guaranteed way out, they would not have to struggle as hard as before to find the door, so to speak. On the other hand, those resisting the break-up of the Ethiopian state now see this risk becoming a legal right. And, as pointed out by Hansson, as any secession must be the result of democratic procedures and as opposition groups have already claimed being treated unfairly, and even with hostility, by the government, there is risk of further upheavals. 'In fact, as long as the mere risk for this to happen is emphasised by opposition groups, it can be expected to hamper the expansion of economic activities. The reason is that this risk increases the uncertainty about the future political and business environment and thus increases the transaction costs of various economic activities'.[72] Since the overthrow of Mengistu, the Oromos have been talking about setting up a state of their own.[73]

The recent economic history of Ethiopia

In the sixteenth century, Ethiopia was not far behind Europe in terms of development.

Paul Brietzke[74]

The degree of economic centralisation was, prior to the 20th century, even less than that of political centralisation. A vital explanation may have been the strong influence the southern landlords enjoyed. Here, all land belonged to the Emperor and he in turn allocated it to soldiers as remuneration,[75] thus placing some 70 per cent of the southern peasantry under landlords who were either rewarded northern soldiers and warlords, traditional southern feudal lords, or under the church. These rights were more extensive than those of the *gult* system in the north, whereby the right to collect taxes and use the peasants as labour followed automatically. In the north there was also the *rist* system which, along with the obligation to pay rent, gave the peasants 'inherital and inalienable rights of descent, which entitled them to a share in the collectively held land', rights which could also be claimed by a

---

[71] Eggertsson (1990), p. 35.
[72] Hansson (1995b), p. 10.
[73] The Economist, 1 June 1991, p. 45.
[74] Brietzke (1981), p. 262.
[75] Turner (1993), p. 31.

peasant if he moved to another village where his ancestors had once resided.[76] This concept should not, however, be mistaken for private ownership.

The late imperial era

The years of Italian influence contributed more to the centralisation of administration than to economic development. Some 6,000 km of roads were built to facilitate communications, but as Mulatu Wubneh and Yohannis Abate write: 'With only a very small proportion of the population engaged in the money economy, trade was largely characterized by barter; wage labor was limited; economic units were largely self-sufficient; foreign trade was negligible; and the market for manufactured goods was extremely small'.[77] Property rights 'in the western sense' were gradually introduced, but the northern and southern systems evolved along different paths. The northern rist system remained, however, challenged by growing population density, thus feeding rivalry and hostility, aggravated by demands for dues, taxes and tithes by the feudal class. In the south landlord-tenant relations assumed rather informal structures, most contracts being oral and obeying no formal legal norms regarding fees or validity but rather showing a degree of political and social servility.[78]

Meanwhile, Haile Selassie made payment of land taxes equal to ownership of land and what no one paid for was automatically considered state property. As tax collectors had the land for which they were accountable registered in their own name they thus became land owners in state registers.[79] In a proclamation in 1942 the Emperor introduced a new system for the calculation of land taxes with their collection being undertaken by salaried civil servants appointed by the Ministry of Finance. However, it was the local elite, beyond imperial control, that graded the land according to its quality, thereby influencing taxes.[80] Peasants then sold some of their output to middle-men in the towns who, through the small amounts sold by each peasant and the tax burden borne by these peasants, acquired oligopolistic positions.

Prior to 1974 the Ethiopian investment climate was considered among the most favourable in the world with tax holidays and duties favouring export.[81] Because of the risks involved in heavy dependence on one single raw material kind of export good, and the discouraging effect this had on industrialisation, Haile Selassie gradually altered the legislation in favour of import substitution, still, however, with heavy emphasis on a mixed economic system.[82]

---

[76] Pausewang (1990a), p. 40.
[77] Mulatu Wubneh and Yohannis Abate (1988), p. 79.
[78] Taye Mengistae (1990), p. 31.
[79] Pausewang (1990a), p. 44.
[80] Harbeson (1990), p. 79.
[81] Eshetu Chole (1987), p. 15.
[82] Ibid., pp. 9-10.

The First Five Year Plan (1957-61) was devoted to development of a base for further industrialisation (i.e. physical infrastructure) and in the agricultural sector this meant large scale modern farming for the purpose of supplying inputs.[83] The aim of the Second Plan (1962-67) was to provide further infrastructural investments and the development of a mining industry. Cash crops for export were the foci for agriculture in both these plans. The third (1968-73) later extended to 1974, emphasised income distribution, hence peasant agriculture and education. Alongside these plans targets were set for economic growth, employment and diversification of the Ethiopian economy.[84] In an investment policy statement from 1966 to promote industrialisation, prerequisites for tax and import and export duty relief were clearly stated.[85] Licences, temporary or permanent, for manufacturing enterprises became obligatory by a proclamation in 1971. After fulfilment of 'specific requirements, including meeting of industrial standards', applications had to be approved by the Ministry of Commerce and Industry .

But plan targets were unrealistic, based on erroneous data, and perhaps more an attempt to create an illusion of constitutional reform. The interest and competence within the lower levels of the bureaucracy, for example the landlords, to implement these plans is also debatable. Furthermore, the fundamental problems, such as a growing population on already overpopulated scarce arable land, remained unsolved. Thus the remaining peasants were squeezed by taxes due to landlords and a shortage of funds to use for improved farming equipment. By the Third Plan the emphasis on industrialisation was lessened following international pressure from, amongst others, the World Bank. Foreign aid programmes were implemented, stressing the importance of raising smallholder real income but also directed towards fertilizers, improved grains and assistance with credits and marketing. However, these projects proved to be expensive as mechanisation made some small farmers superfluous, because high downpayments were required for fertilizers and because land prices and rents, which in part had to be paid in cash, soared.[86]

The Derg and Mengistu Haile Mariam

In the Derg's ten point programme, under the motto 'Ethiopia First', self-sufficiency at all levels was emphasised.[87] Now all assets were to be owned by the state, and as such belong to the entire Ethiopian people. Ownership of land was to be reserved only for those who worked it and several agricultural product prices were to be regulated by the government.[88] Industry was to be managed by the state, however, allowing for some private entrepreneurs deemed useful to the public (but

[83] Dejene Aredo (1990), p. 49.
[84] Mulatu Wubneh and Yohannis Abate (1988), pp. 79-80.
[85] Teshome Mulat (1994), p. 13.
[86] Mulatu Wubneh (1990), p. 200.
[87] Lefort (1983), p. 84.
[88] Befekadu Degefe and Tesfaye Tafesse (1990), p. 116.

only until further notice). In January 1975 a programme of nationalisation of banks, financial institutions and urban land was initiated, followed up in February when several enterprises went the same way. Then, in the DEP, state ownership and control of natural resources and key sectors of the economy was announced as the only way of avoiding the exploitation of the Ethiopian people.[89] As a result, during these two months some 200 business entities were nationalised without compensation. The future private sector role was further defined in March, leaving it with small scale business and industry, trade and road transport.[90]

All rural land was nationalised without compensation and plantations and the few large commercial establishments that existed were made state farms. Agricultural wage labour, except for the old and infirm, was prohibited, as was ownership of plots larger than ten hectares per household.[91] The newly established PAs were to have the overriding responsibility for distributing land and credit in accordance with stated policies, establish villagisation programmes and marketing associations and build schools and health clinics with state support. PAs were organised on several levels, initially with rather vague directives, prompting a proclamation of a clearer definition of task in December.[92] From then on PAs had to register with the Land Reform Ministry, thereby obtaining legal personality and thus authority to issue and implement internal regulations. The actual results of land redistribution are somewhat uncertain and very varied[93]. The reforms were in any case less popular in the north, where tenancy was more limited than in the south but in cases where landlords protested they were removed and executed.[94] Usufructuary rights were now based on residence with a fixed amount of land allocated to each PA to be split amongst its inhabitants. Illegal forms of tenancy did survive the reforms, as did land fragmentation and degradation as well as shortages of plough oxen, livestock and land in general.[95]

In July all urban land and all but one of a family's houses (which was to be the residence) were nationalised.[96] At the time 95 per cent of Addis Ababa land was owned by 5 per cent of the population.[97] Rents were lowered and were to be paid to the government through the kebeles. These kebeles, each comprising some thousands of inhabitants, were, in addition to collecting rents (rents up to USD 50 per month[98]), initially responsible for providing basic needs, education and health and arranging court cases involving sums under USD 250, in practice, however, at times imposing death penalties. In 1981 Paul Brietzke wrote: 'Procedural rules are so vague and incomplete that they could hardly be held to create a judicial pro-

---

[89] Hansson (1995a), p. 22.
[90] Ibid., p. 25.
[91] Harbeson (1990), p. 84.
[92] Brietzke (1981), pp. 283-4.
[93] Dessalegn Rahmato (1984), pp. 52ff.
[94] Schwab (1985), p. 27.
[95] Dessalegn Rahmato (1990), p. 101.
[96] Hansson (1995a), p. 25.
[97] Brietzke (1981), p. 279.
[98] Ibid., p 287.

cess'.[99] Kebeles were organised at national as well as sub-national levels, and were gradually given increased powers. By late 1976 they were collecting local taxes, registration duties and acting as defence squads during the terror years. They were tools of the central administration, organising allocation of food as well as military conscription.[100]

In December 1975 the issuing of business licences was made a responsibility of the Ministry of Commerce and Industry, although only one licence per person was permitted and no licences were issued to people who already had permanent employment. No new share companies or partnerships with more than five partners could be created.[101] Enterprises must not exceed ETB[102] 500,000 in investment capital, and special licences were required for international trade.[103] In April 1976 the Programme for the National Development Revolution identified Marxism-Leninism as the future lodestar, and this was, until the goal had been reached, to supply the basic tenets of the ideology. Agriculture became more strictly regulated with the establishment of the Agricultural Marketing Corporation (AMC) a government agency to which state farms were to sell their output, but which also set quotas for PAs and cooperatives to deliver, at fixed village prices.[104] Even private wholesale dealers were required to sell 50 per cent of what they had bought directly to the AMC.

Main directives were issued in June 1979 for the formation of producer cooperatives, intended as a defence against the revival of rural capitalism.[105] While at the highest level complete collectivisation commune-style was practised, at lower levels it was possible for farmers to reserve about half a hectare for private use. A minimum of 30 dwellers was set in order to be registered. In turn, registration was a prerequisite to acquiring credits and closing deals with state farms, but to get such a registration could take up to two years. Service cooperatives were also instituted to sell inputs to, give credit to, and educate the peasantry; all in a socialist spirit.[106] A Ministry of Industry, divided into 12 corporations, was established, thus calling for decisions regarding state farms to pass through the government, the ministry, the corporation and the enterprise itself. Furthermore, directives were sometimes conflicting, aggravated by shortages and interfering of the Party representatives.[107]

A Joint Venture Proclamation was launched in 1983, allowing for relief from taxes and foreign trade duties as well as from taxes on dividends, repatriation of

---

[99] Ibid., p. 288.
[100] Clapham (1990b), p. 226.
[101] Brietzke (1981), p. 288.
[102] Ethiopian birr.
[103] Mulatu Wubneh (1990), p. 210.
[104] Mulatu Wubneh and Yohannis Abate (1988), p. 100.
[105] Dessalegn Rahmato (1990), p. 102.
[106] Mulatu Wubneh (1990), p. 205.
[107] Ibid., p. 210.

capital and protective tax measures but permitting only 49 per cent foreign owner-ship at the most.[108]

A Central Planning Commission had been established in 1977, thus introducing a high level of central planning, but already by September the following year this was replaced by the Central Planning Supreme Council, CPSC. Thereby, Ethiopia's economic problems had supposedly been properly dealt with as had the lack of inter-ministerial coordination. The CPCS had initially used yearly plans to deal with unemployment and various shortages, but as several programmes covered more than one year the need for a long term approach had become clear and the Council had to formulate and focus development plans. In June 1984 the CPCS was replaced by the Office of the National Committee for Central Planning, NCCP, led by the head of state and accompanied by an executive 'daily work' committee and an extensive, vertically hierarchical, set of territorial planning agencies supervising and implementing policy down to district level.[109] Now, ten year plans could be implemented, aimed at improving productive capacity, increasing the industrial share of national output, ensuring balanced economic development between regions and establishing a foundation for socialism, technically and materially.[110] The plans had growth targets, for the entire economy as well as its parts, for investments, prices, work opportunities, infrastructure and so on. Investment costs were to be fairly evenly distributed between domestic and foreign sources. A year later the upper private investment limit was raised to ETB 1,000,000.

By 1986 the lack of urban housing was becoming a major problem as the previous nationalisation campaign had discouraged private constructing, while the state sector was unable to meet the demand. In January attempts were made at establishing standards for housing space,[111] and house owners were later given the right to let spare room, however, at rents set by the Ministry of Urban Development and Housing. The economy as a whole was in rather bad shape, not only as a result of the enormous absolute and alternative costs of war. The population was growing fast and the ideology had made private investment in all sectors virtually impossible. Interest rates, for instance, were 6 per cent and 8 per cent for public but 8 per cent and 9 per cent for private enterprises in agriculture and industry respectively from June onwards.[112] While cooperatives had to supply 15 per cent of an investment project and borrow the rest, the figure was 30 per cent for private undertakings.

The Sokolov report, submitted by Soviet advisers to the NCCP in 1985, recommended the government to direct more attention and resources towards the small farmers' sector regarding tools, inputs, legislation and others. Some revi-

---

[108] Mulatu Wubneh (1994), p. 262.
[109] Mulatu Wubneh (1990), p. 201.
[110] Provisional Military Administrative Council, Ten Year Perspective Plan 1984/85-1993/94, Addis Ababa 1984, extracted from Mulatu Wubneh (1990), pp. 202-3.
[111] Mulatu Wubneh and Yohannis Abate (1988), p. 106.
[112] Itana Ayana (1994), p. 243.

sions to agricultural marketing policies were declared in December 1987, including higher producer prices and freer agro trade, but deeper obstacles, such as collectivisation schemes, remained. The tone had drastically changed by the time of Mengistu's visit to Moscow in July 1988. President Gorbachev now called for economic and political liberalisation in Ethiopia and a non-violent end to ethnic conflicts or Soviet support would cease.[113] Hence, at the November WPE Central Committee Plenum Mengistu presented new resolutions, inviting private initiatives into industry and service, yet still stressing collectivisation, self-sufficiency and state planning even in private undertakings. The aim was to make the private sector contribute to the creation of a socialist society.[114] In July 1989 he reformed foreign economic participation through the Joint Venture Proclamation, allowing unlimited private investment, remittances for private investors and exemptions from import duties for certain goods. More sectors were now opened up for private investments, but each project still had to be approved by the Ministry.[115]

By March 1990 Mengistu was promoting a mixed economy in which public enterprises were to become competitive, private investment encouraged and usufructuary land rights extended indefinitely. Cooperativisation was to be voluntary and former hampering restrictions on the private sector were to be removed regarding quotas and sectors.[116] Some areas remained under the jurisdiction of the state (defence, postal services and telecommunications, radio and television broadcasting) while others called for the consent of the Council of Ministers (banking, tobacco processing).[117] Rather generous tax exemptions were also provided, differentiated according to company size. Duty free imports for company start-ups and expansion schemes and so on became available for all private actors.[118] These reforms were welcomed among implementers as well as private actors, but as implementation was somewhat slow many foreign donors assumed a wait-and-see attitude, pointing to the continuing war and areas lacking reform. As a result, opposition to the programme grew within the government, hampering developments still further.[119]

The Transitional Government and the EPRDF

When Mengistu fled the country in May 1991 a Transitional Government took over, and issued a draft for a new Ethiopian economic policy which, after consultations with a variety of economic and political organisations, was approved by the Council of Representatives in November.[120] The role of the State was now

---

[113] Andargachew Tiruneh (1993), p. 358.
[114] Eshetu Chole and Makonnen Manyazewal (1992), pp. 34-5.
[115] UNIDO (1991), p. 109.
[116] Eshetu Chole and Makonnen Manyazewal (1992), pp. 36-7.
[117] UNIDO (1991), p. 109.
[118] UNIDO (1991), pp. 110-11.
[119] Hansson (1995a), pp. 98ff.
[120] For a thorough description, see ibid., pp. 102ff.

declared to be one of creating favourable economic conditions for the development of the country, enacting laws and regulations and promoting private initiatives. Local administrative agencies, if they so wished, had more freedom to participate in policy implementation and a solid national basis for growth was to be provided through a sound macro-economic environment, tempting and inviting also foreign actors. The sale of agricultural products on the free market, introduced by Mengistu, was to be continued, but the heavy bias of investment towards state farms would now be redirected to rural infrastructure, advisory agents and productivity improving inputs. Within industry and services all sectors were to be open to private competition, perhaps with joint or total state ownership in certain key national establishments but domestic investors would be favoured over foreign ones. Private initiatives were to dominate transport and distribution but air, sea and rail sectors would remain state controlled due to insufficient private sector capacity.

Those entities that remained state owned were to focus on profitability and capacity utilisation. Up to one-third of the votes on the boards of state or state/private firms were to be given to the workers. Banking and insurance was to remain state owned and controlled, although with greater freedom within certain guidelines. Trade would, on the whole, be liberalised but state control would remain over 'areas that cut across sectors' regarding foreign trade. Non-tariff barriers were to be replaced with tariff barriers and paperwork was to be reduced. Virtually all prices were liberalised, interest rates adjusted to positive real levels and the tax system revised to allow marginal rates of 50 per cent (previously 89 per cent). Foreign currency earned from exports was to be handed over to the state, repaid in birr, and then used where needed most. The state budget was to be balanced, but not until the damages caused by war had been seen to, including demobilisation of former soldiers. Cuts would be possible though, through future smaller military outlays.

In September 1992 the TGE presented their Policy Framework Paper for the period 1992-95, a product of IMF and IBRD.[121] Tariffs on trade were to be reformed, that is, import duties were to be lowered (from 230 to 80 per cent[122]) and removed for exports, except coffee. The state budget was to be consolidated through a stronger tax administration, fewer subsidies, the allocation of all external grants through the budget and the public sale of government bonds. In order for government borrowing not to crowd out private borrowing, ceilings were set for the former within the banking system. The market was, as the banking system developed, to replace administratively set interest rates except for a minimum deposit and a maximum lending rate, the state only intervening indirectly.

The birr was devalued with effect from 1 October 1992, and from May 1993 the exchange rate was set through currency auctions. Public enterprises were principally deprived of their soft budget constraints and were, starting February 1994,

---

[121] The description is based on Ibrahim Abdullahi Zeidy (1994), pp. 153ff.
[122] Hansson (1995a), p. 115.

to be privatised. Assigning enterprises to ministries has been somewhat difficult as responsibilities between different government departments have sometimes been unclear and, at times, even conflicting.[123] Privatisation has also been difficult, with former public enterprises being difficult to put a value on. Land ownership was also dealt with in the constitutional assembly in 1994, the result of which was the following: 'Land is a common property of the nations, nationalities and peoples of Ethiopia and shall not be subject to sale or to other means of transfer'.[124] Peasants enjoy life-long user rights but the government can, in the public interest, expropriate private property.

Implications for transaction costs

The adherents of the official ideology are imbued with the Messianic belief that socialism is destined to save mankind. The conviction that the socialist system is superior to the capitalist is one of the most important ingredients in the ideology.

János Kornai[125]

Running like a thread through the above presentation is the sense of insecurity prevailing under the imperial as well as the military/communist rule. What separates one regime from the other is the form and magnitude this insecurity assumed.

In order for economic agents to participate in any kind of transaction, a clear definition, institutionalisation and ex post control of property rights is a basic prerequisite. 'The enforcement of property rights', Eggertsson writes, 'involves excluding others from the use of scarce resources'.[126] This is usually facilitated by the state, through a judicial framework involving laws, courts and various forms of sanctions for those who refuse to conform to this framework. This may not be enough however. 'When appropriate social norms are missing', Eggertsson continues, 'individuals may establish structures of property rights that rival those of the state, particularly in activities where the enforcement of state rules is relatively costly'.[127] In Ethiopia, the relation and interaction between social norms and a judicial framework is of particular interest as it was the actions taken by the state which, to a large extent, influenced social norms to the degree that farmers, for instance, refrained form participating in transactions, thereby losing the potential economic benefits this may have brought, and limiting production first and foremost to feeding the family.

During the imperial era, property rights were either incomplete (as in the north where land was transferable only through heritage) or very unevenly distributed (as in the south where the bulk of the peasants were tenants). The Mengistu land reforms did initially, to a limited extent, correct the inequality problem. However,

---

[123] See for instance Teshome Mulat (1994), p. 22.
[124] The Constitution of The Federal Democratic Republic of Ethiopia 1994, Article 40:3, quoted from Hansson (1995b), p. 11.
[125] Kornai (1992), p. 50-51.
[126] Eggertsson (1990), p. 35.
[127] Ibid., p. 36.

with the institutionalisation of PAs, each allocated a non-alterable area of land, the problem resurfaced. Immigration implied redistribution, each time with less available for everyone. In either case people were not entitled to dispose freely of the fruits of their labours and so were discouraged from further yield improving investments. The land did not fully belong to them and could either be taken from them (in the south) or exchanged for another plot (in the north) and the investment would in either case be lost.

As with the villagisation and resettlement programmes, mentioned in the previous section, it is the lack of continuity that is striking, but here absent from economic, rather than political, policies. In a capitalistic system, far-sightedness has to be combined with flexibility. In socialist systems frequent change has to be avoided at all costs, because of the devastating effects it has on the intricate planning procedures.[128] Ethiopia, which for six years limped along with yearly plans, had neither.

While redistribution was a matter dealt with locally, the nationalisation campaigns swept the whole country, and not only farmers. Those who had engaged in various industrial activities were suddenly deprived of their assets, and all forms of property rights that accompanied these. The effects of this could be compared what Eggertsson terms 'predatory public finance'. He writes: 'The way in which the state conducts its finances affects the definition and stability of exclusive rights. Predatory public finance creates de facto incomplete exclusive rights, and wealth-maximizing individuals respond to uncertain property rights by making various adjustments to minimize the risk of appropriation. These adjustments tend to lower the level of investment activity and change its nature'.[129] He gives examples of such adjustments as alterations of technology, changing the durability of the investments, using other inputs or changing the type of output. The net result of fewer new or reinvestments from the longer perspective is likely to have a detrimental effect on production quality, an effect that rational producers are eager to hide. In terms of the different steps in a transaction as defined by Eggertsson,[130] this will, in particular, raise transaction costs in the search for information and finding 'the true position' of the counterpart.

The Ethiopia of the Mengistu era can only be described as a shortage economy. People were poor, resources were scarce and whatever existed in the form of assets was reserved for state purposes in the first instance. Under Haile Selassie resources had instead been directed to encouragement of foreign investments. With demand for inputs exceeding supply, a phenomenon particularly prevalent in socialist countries, the search for inputs will be more time consuming and require more in terms of efforts on the part of the economic agent as well. Quality is likely to be lower, quantity will definitely be lower, but prices will not necessarily hold any kind of vital information. In Ethiopia oligopolists had, under Haile Selassie,

---

[128] For an overview of the efforts involved in the planning procedures in socialist systems, see Kornai (1992), pp. 110ff.

[129] Eggertsson (1990), p. 341.

[130] Ibid., p. 15.

been able to influence prices a great deal. Under Mengistu many prices were fixed by the government, through rent controls, the AMC, and restrictions on, or manipulation of, foreign trade. Prices are extremely important carriers of information in an economic system. They provide useful facts about quantity, quality, competition and so on, but only if they are allowed to do so. Changes in relative prices breed opportunism, also in transactions between private agents, and imperfect information, which in itself raises transaction costs, will lead to even more imperfect information.

Pausewang contends that in a country like Ethiopia, with a seriously underdeveloped transport network, an agency like the AMC, implementing a national, unified price level, might be necessary.[131] His critique is instead directed to the inflexibility of this agency and the high administration costs it brought, which instead of stabilising prices raised them for everyone. State agriculture had been launched in order to deal with food shortages, supply domestic industry with inputs, produce for the export market and to create jobs. These farms were allocated resources quite disproportionate to their importance to total agriculture,[132] and even though their net contribution after taking subsidies into consideration was positive and did, through focusing on export crops, generate badly needed foreign exchange, one cannot escape the fact that their production costs were very high.

Several business relations have also been characterised by a great degree of arbitrariness. Contracts between landlords and tenants under Haile Selassie is one such example, calculation of taxes based on land quality is another. The Mengistu regime did not draw up contracts, but instead interpreted the legal provisions as it pleased, exemplified by its performance in the hides and skins market, open also for private agents. The Leather and Shoe Corporation, a parastatal competing with private firms for export markets, was one example that had to be 'rescued', firstly by revoking export licences to private traders, and then by being given complete monopoly power in domestic as well as international trade.[133] Kornai writes: 'Not infrequently the bureaucracy, particularly certain groups and branches within it, actually infringes on the laws that exist on paper'.[134] With many participants there will be many infringements. He goes on to observe that 'the influence of the bureaucracy spreads to such traditionally private spheres as culture, religion, the life of the family . . . the choice of career and employment. Nor have I even mentioned that every economic transaction qualifies as a matter of concern to the party and the state'.[135] Thus, *one* coherent system, *one* set of game rules will never occur, and in such a situation enforcement of contracts will be extremely costly.

Thus, while it is usually the case that the state can intervene when transaction costs are too high for transferring resources over the market, it is likely, in the case of Ethiopia, to have been the other way around. The state raised transaction costs

---

[131] Pausewang (1990b), p. 217.
[132] For figures see Mulatu Wubneh (1990), pp. 205-6.
[133] Befekadu Degefe and Tesfaye Tafesse (1990), p. 113.
[134] Kornai (1992), p. 47.
[135] Ibid., p. 46.

144

by the actions it took, in other words, expropriation and market limitation, to the extent that people sought other solutions, such as withdrawal into the informal economy. Entry for private entrepreneurs was limited partly through a capital investment ceiling (perhaps more relevant to growth plans, or as a symbol of the power of the regime), partly because of a complicated, but essential, licensing procedure. Many sectors were furthermore completely closed to private initiatives and no one knew how to define 'of use to the public', the temporary prerequisite for the continued existence of some private industry. Neither could anyone explain how 'reserved for tillers' could suddenly be replaced by nationalisation.

Infrastructure may lower transportation as well as transaction costs, but as this is seriously deficient in Ethiopia, people will opt for local transactions as costs at all of Eggertsson's stages in such a process will be lower. This does not mean that better opportunities are not available elsewhere in the country, this is probably the case, but that they are either unknown to the entrepreneur, difficult to evaluate or involve too high a risk for him to dare try them. Another hindrance to development of wider business linkages is when such dealings have to take place across different judicial systems. If provincial rules differ entrepreneurs will face great difficulties and costs in finding out about business partners who come under other, locally administered, judicial systems and also in evaluating cross-border contracts and their enforcement. Something similar was discernible when kebele courts were given wide ranging authorities. One might question whether a country like Ethiopia has sufficient juridical knowledge. This same line of reasoning could well apply in the contemporary situation of self-governing regions when it comes to clearing the legal hurdles set by the judicial systems in the country. And it is important to remember that should contracts be made more specific in nature, stating all details, they will automatically be much more expensive to draw up, monitor and enforce.

Mengistu did, during his last shaky moments as ruler, make some attempts at reform, the sincerity of which is highly questionable. This was also obvious to domestic as well as foreign entrepreneurs, for instance when he spoke of the importance of the SSIs for capital accumulation and the new Joint Venture Proclamation, yet still stressing that central planning should be improved, strengthened and extended.[136] However, due to the ongoing civil war and the lack of confidence in the regime, built up over several years regarding the Ethiopian government, these attempts at reform were mistrusted by the international community, private as well as official, and so had little effect on, for instance, the flow of foreign aid. Furthermore, there were gaps in the reforms compared to the structural adjustment programmes prescribed by the IMF and the IBRD, such as realignment of the birr and the expenditure side of the government budget.

The price of the currency - the exchange rate - is extremely important in all countries. And the exchange rate is, through money supply and exchange rate expectations and so forth, closely connected to the domestic price level. Inflation

---

[136] Hansson (1995a), pp. 77ff.

is a major cause of uncertainty in an economy because of the way prices are important carriers of information. They give some indication of relative scarcities and as such provide a basis on which economic agents can make decisions about what to do, such as whether or not to make new or more investments, for example. Inflation contains a redistribution effect as well, from holders of liquid assets to those who have placed their savings in real investments, gold for instance, but also away from those who lend money to those who borrow. It has, furthermore, been established that constantly high inflation, while bad, is not as detrimental to economic activity as are completely unpredictable price changes going from high to low and back to high again. An overall increase in the domestic price level is not as detrimental as manipulation of relative prices.

Small scale industries

Defining small scale industries is not an easy task. The criteria have varied with, for instance, time, business sector and writer, regarding capital, number of employees, line of business and mode of production. The situation in Ethiopia is no exception in this regard. Some studies use the employed work force as the sole criterion[137] or fixed asset value.[138] Others rely on a multiple of rather unmeasurable criteria,[139] and yet others focus on a mix of explicit limits and subjective judgements.[140] In this paper the term small scale industry is interpreted according to the HASIDA definition of such economic activity. Unfortunately, due to the relatively limited amount of literature available on the topic in Ethiopian economic life, some of the figures referred to in the text may refer to a slightly different population, if the author quoted has used other criteria. However, since this is to be a qualitative study rather than a quantitative one, discernible trends will have to make up for lack of exact figures.

The role and profile of the SSI sector in the Ethiopian economy

In the years 1960-74 SSIs accounted for 4.48 per cent of Ethiopia's GDP and about 50 per cent of the country's total manufacturing. From the time of the revolution to the late 1980s these proportions had decreased to less than 4 per cent and 37 per cent respectively, while total manufacturing had grown from 8 per cent to 11 per cent of GDP.[141] Beginning in 1990 SSIs again increased their share of the economy with annual growth rates of 3 per cent and almost 10 per cent in the years

---

[137] E.g., Berhanu Abegaz (1994), p 178; and Mulatu Wubneh (1994), p 274.
[138] HASIDA, Proclamation 124/1977, in Teshome Mulat (1994), p. 9.
[139] Roman Habtu (1994), p. 229.
[140] HASIDA Report1984/85, in Teshome Mulat (1994), p. 10.
[141] Teshome Mulat (1994), Table 1, p. 32.

of 1991/92 and 1992/93 respectively, thus accounting for 4.35 per cent of Ethiopian GDP in 1992/93.[142]

When the military came to power in 1974/75 small scale enterprises accounted for 60 per cent of overall manufacturing value added (MVA).[143] After the sweeping nationalisations this share decreased, in favour of large and medium scale firms, to 25 per cent by the mid-1980s, SSIs showing MVA growth rates of about 2 per cent 1980-87 while LMSEs achieved 5 per cent rates.[144] The number of SSIs was then about 7,700, employing nearly 37,000 people,[145] most of whom were working in food processing (grain mills, bakeries, oil pressing etc.), followed in order of importance (in terms of number of units as well as employees) by textiles, woodwork and metal.[146] The then average SSI entity had 23-30 employees, a fixed stock of capital of ETB 100,000,[147] and this segment accounted for 45 per cent of industrial sector employment.[148] 84 per cent of employees had less than 8 years' education and 36 per cent were related to the owner.[149]

In 1985 as well as 1980 LMSE capital-labour ratios exceeded SSI ones, though the latter had caught up (from 50 per cent of that of the LMSEs down to 31 per cent). It was, however, higher in the SSI sector than in private larger firms and higher in metal, chemical and wooden SSIs than in public sector companies. Labour productivity was 40-90 per cent of that in the public sector.[150] Since 1984/85 wages have also been lower in the SSI sector than in the 'large' segment; in surveys carried out later, one in 1990/91 and one in 1992/93, a general trend of increasing capital intensity could be noticed.[151] When asked about their degree of 'motorisation' in 1991/92, 23 per cent of enterprises in a study conducted in Addis Ababa reported no manual operation and the bulk, 71 per cent, answered partly automated/partly manual.[152] While industrial capacity utilisation was 80-100 per cent during the 1980s, falling towards the end, it was 10-35 per cent for HASIDA firms.[153]

While 60 per cent of inputs were obtained from the domestic market, chemicals, textiles and metals were the most import dependent sectors.[154] 6 per cent of SSIs were completely import dependent, which is much less than for large units. In the late 1980s 260 SSIs were legitimate recipients of foreign exchange, in total equiv-

---

[142] Statistical data are, however not consistent on this matter, for instance shares of 4,5 per cent of SSIs to GDP are reported by Berhanu Abegaz (1994), Table 4.3, p. 180, all through the 1980s.
[143] Ibid., p. 179.
[144] UNIDO (1991), p. 22.
[145] The study by HASIDA does leave some questionmarks regarding the population criteria. See Solomon Wole (1992), pp. 172-3.
[146] UNIDO (1991), Table 2.30, p. 52, and Table 2.31, p. 53.
[147] Berhanu Abegaz (1994), p. 178.
[148] UNIDO (1991), p. 11.
[149] Solomon Wole (1992), p. 174.
[150] UNIDO (1991), p. 55, and Table 2.33, p. 56.
[151] Teshome Mulat (1994), Table 3, p. 39, and Table 2, p. 34.
[152] Ibid., p. 33.
[153] UNIDO (1991), p. 37.
[154] Solomon Wole (1992), p. 174.

alent to ETB 14.5 million compared to 29 million in 1987.[155] In the late 1980s only two SSIs were exporting, but they still accounted for 6 per cent of Ethiopia's exports. The SSI sector was able to cover 40 per cent of its annual foreign currency needs.[156]

A study of the Addis Ababa Chamber of Commerce members showed that out of private entrepreneurs more than half were involved in more than one activity, of which trade, especially importing, predominated, and 93 per cent had registered capital of less than ETB 1,000,000. An Investment Office of Ethiopia study showed that of planned investments, of which almost 60 per cent were financed by bank loans, 46 per cent went to industry, and 16 per cent into real estate, in other words a trend away from the service sector to productive manufacturing, but still being imitative rather than innovative.[157] Almost 90 per cent would go to Addis Ababa, where 34 per cent of industrial activities were located in 1984/85.[158]

SSI policies, business environment and transaction costs

Supply constraints, both for domestic and imported inputs, are also beginning to tell. This is particularly true of the small-scale industry sector which, since the Revolution, has suffered from acute shortages of capital and raw materials.

UNIDO[159]

To understand why the small scale sector of the Ethiopian economy is so limited today, one must look at the prevailing SSI environment, but not forget to look at its heritage, its history. Haile Selassie was not interested in realising the potential of small scale industry as an engine of economic growth. His reliance on foreign investors indirectly favoured larger undertakings, since few foreigners aim for small projects, these being more difficult to identify as well as control or at least supervise. And foreign investments were to a large extent run by foreign managers.[160] A survey carried out in 1964 showed that while 74.4 per cent of firms with a registered capital of ETB 20,000 or less were owned by Ethiopians the figure was 43.6 per cent in the range ETB 20,000 to 50,000 and had diminished even further to 32.4 per cent in entities larger than 50,000. Ethiopian participation was lower in manufacturing than in trade and transport related undertakings. Manufacturing was, furthermore, far too capital intensive for a country with its major resource in the form of population.

What attracted investors were high, protective, import barriers, but this was not enough to persuade foreigners to keep their capital in the country. No restrictions were placed on what foreign investors could do with their profits and these disap-

---

[155] UNIDO (1991), p. 53, and p. 116.
[156] Solomon Wole (1992), pp. 174-5.
[157] Solomon Wole (1994), pp. 23ff.
[158] Admit Zerihun (1994), p. 101.
[159] UNIDO (1991), p. 4.
[160] Worku Aberra (1987), pp. 7-8.

peared out of the country in various guises.[161] Between 1961 and 1974 the net inflow of capital has been estimated at no more than ETB 21 million even though FDI came to 311.5 million. Still, there could have been some more opportunities for smaller units. Roman Habtu posits a possibly complementary relationship between smaller units, organised in industrial districts, and larger ones where the former operate on a subcontracting basis, or the latters supply inputs to SSI clusters.[162] Caution is needed though in order for an equal relationship to evolve without demands for rationalisation and improved productivity being forced solely on SSIs. But, the industries to which foreign capital was directed at this point in time had very few linkages with the rest of the Ethiopian economy, a result of the dominate lines of business: food and textiles.[163] These need very limited additional processing prior to consumption and are not much used as inputs for industrial production. Furthermore, in this case agriculture machinery and inputs were imported.

The Emperor was, at least on paper, not unaware of the beauty of smallness. The Second as well as the Third Development Plan mentioned handicrafts, SSIs and policies intended specifically therefore.[164] But of those ETB 1,696 million of public sector allocation of investment in the Second Plan, SSIs and handicrafts received just five million.[165] In addition, foreign incentives were applicable to investments of no less than ETB 200,000 and the degree of protection from foreign competition was dependent upon 'the bargaining persuasiveness of the particular entrepreneur'.[166] As Haile Selassie aged the obstacles facing SSIs grew even more insurmountable as the old Emperor lost some of his influence to governors and administrative personnel. This resulted in a judicial environment quite unfavourable to economic undertakings in general but which hit smaller units hard in particular. 'Judges were accused of widespread corruption', Odesola writes, 'and also delays that worked against the interest of the common man'.[167] In 1969 a report from Ada district (south of Addis Ababa) stated:

> It costs people . . . to get anything done in many of the government offices, because one has to pay almost every official if one is not to be kept waiting for hours or days to see an official. . . . corruption of a serious sort is reported to be rampant among local policemen . . . The characteristic solution to these problems . . . is to avoid . . . these public agencies, especially the court and the police, for they create more problems than they solve.[168]

---

[161] Ibid., p. 11.
[162] Roman Habtu (1994), p. 245.
[163] Worku Aberra (1987), p. 6.
[164] Teshome Mulat (n.d.), p. 11.
[165] ILO (1990), p. 15.
[166] IBRD, Economic Growth and Prospects in Ethiopia, Vol. 2, 1970, Annex, p. i, cited in Worku Aberra (1987), p. 2.
[167] Odesola (1988), p. 11.
[168] Gilkes (1975), p. 47.

During the imperial era the social environment as well discouraged entrepreneurship. The Ethiopian culture was one of feudalism, where the general opinion was that only those who did not figure among the nobility or who did not have access to land were forced into crafts or commerce.[169] This prevalent view had a negative effect on the private sector in general. Becoming a small scale entrepreneur was the last alternative left for those without work or education.[170] Yet people who worked for selfish economic gains were despised by the Orthodox Church too.[171] For all these reasons, numerous potential entrepreneurs were lost to Ethiopia, and with them several years of development of skills and experience that could have formed the basis for a modern SSI sector.

With the military take-over and the initiation of the nationalisation campaign SSIs were affected along with the rest of the economy as established networks were torn apart. Furthermore, it has often been said that the nationalisations as such involved the take-over of medium and large scale firms but this was not the case:

> Successive acts of nationalization since 1975 brought under public ownership not only the major productive establishments of the country, but also such small-scale enterprises as grain mills, woodworks, coffee-cleaning outfits, small hotels, and grocery stores. According to information from all nationalized industrial enterprises, about half of the establishments under its control have an annual gross value of production of less than five million birr. Of these, nearly a third probably fall under the category small-scale industry.[172]

In some respects the situation prevailing initially under the military regime was quite promising for economic activity. A lot of land had been redistributed, providing many people with real estate and raising aggregate demand. The new regime was building up its military strength and thereby providing potential for domestic industries. However, there were also a number of obstacles to growth, for instance, rising fuel prices, wars and costly efforts to transform hitherto foreign managed enterprises, that is Ethiopianising them.[173] These in effect worked as supply constraints, rationing being applied to most inputs with the end result of bias towards large enterprises, employing as many as possible in each unit in order to bring unemployment down and output up. Inevitably, smaller firms were of little interest to the government in such a context, thus ending up far down on the above mentioned list of priorities.

A course of development such as the one described above can be explained quite logically by examining the workings of a socialist economy. As mentioned earlier,

---

[169] Ayalew Zegeye (1995), p. 56.
[170] Taye Berhanu (1995), pp. 236-7.
[171] Ayalew Zegeye (1995), p. 57.
[172] Ministry of Industry, Statistical Bulletin, Addis Ababa 1984, p. 4, quoted from Dessalegn Rahmato (1987), pp. 173-4.
[173] Berhanu Abegaz (1994), pp. 176-7.

linkages between the large firms and the rest of the Ethiopian economy were rather weak, implying two things: smaller units were directly discriminated against in the allocation of resources, and, furthermore, they were even unable to benefit indirectly as subcontractors to larger units since there were no such relations. These phenomena are typical for a socialist economy. Allocation of inputs, capital, labour, foreign currency, technology and so on in such a society is controlled by central government. For this process of distribution to be even minimally feasible, enterprises have to be as big as possible, thus reducing the number of allocative decisions somewhat. That is one side of such a system. The other is that high expectations are placed on economies of scale, hoping to get more than twice the effect out of merging two equally large production units. A third aspect is the prestige involved in being able to present huge factories to the rest of the world, for the state administration as well as the company managers.[174] Coupled with soft budget constraints[175] the end result is a hoarding attitude at all levels, hence little is left over, for example for small scale units, when the list of priorities has been worked through from top to bottom. This hoarding mentality and investment hunger governing larger unit behaviour may also result in widening the business activity from its core of, say, producing machinery, to that of producing steel and in the end perhaps even raising cattle in order to feed the work force.[176] This constant forced diversification robs small scale enterprises of their chances to supply inputs.

In 1977 the PMAC established HASIDA, the Handicraft and Small Scale Industries Development Agency, having been a Department under the Ministry of Commerce and Industry, graduating to a Division in 1975 and, in 1977, becoming a more autonomous body.[177] This authority had as its purpose 'promoting and co-ordinating the development of handicrafts and small scale industries' and consisted of three departments of which the Industrial Promotion and the Project Preparation Department were most relevant to SSIs. SSIs were defined as establishments of at most ETB 200,000, not including buildings and land improvements. Amongst the tasks of this agency were SSI policy formulation and supervision, research, assistance with 'marketing, supply of raw materials and equipment, training, production techniques and management, and obtaining credits from banks'. It was also to 'regulate and issue licences to small scale industries' and prepare 'feasible projects for handicrafts and small scale industries, based on local demand and mainly locally available raw materials'.[178] An overview description of the enterprise had to be handed to HASIDA and a temporary licence was issued while a thorough investigation of the project was undertaken. This then had to be approved by the Ministry of Industry, and thereafter, when the official licence had been granted, the firm had to register with the Ministry of Domestic Trade, negotiate

---

[174] This discussion is based on Kornai (1992), the chapter on investment and growth.
[175] Kornai (1992), pp. 140ff.
[176] This phenomenon is referred to as symptoms of vertical shortages in Kornai (1992), pp. 240ff.
[177] Teshome Mulat (1994), p. 15.
[178] HASIDA (n.d.), pp. 9ff.

with the local administration for land, get an OK from the Ministry of Health and then it could start building.[179] Should credit or connections to infrastructure facilities be required, additional time and effort was needed.[180] The old regulations from 1975 still existed regarding capital investment and there were blank areas regarding what industries the agency covered and a bias at HASIDA in favour of cooperatives. No attempt was made to integrate small units into the Ethiopian economy by tying these to larger enterprises. With HASIDA enforcing the licensing procedures as strictly as it had done since 1975, establishing an SSI was no easier and handicrafts and SSI contributions to Ethiopian GDP actually decreased.[181]

The 1983 Joint Ventures Proclamation, for the reasons mentioned earlier, is not likely to have benefited SSIs to any larger extent. Foreigners remembered the nationalisation lesson from their previous involvement in Ethiopian business, existing SSIs had problems disseminating information about their activities and unrealised ideas for potential businesses were even more difficult for small entrepreneurs to communicate across borders. The mid-1980s were also the sad years in which Ethiopia was on everybody's mind and television screen, due to the drought and starvation. Eshetu Chole writes that '[a]mong the consequences of poor agricultural performance are reduced raw material supplies for industry, reduced foreign exchange and therefore an impaired capacity to finance the purchase of imported inputs, poor prospects for internal resource mobilization and a narrow market'.[182] The tight situation of those small scale units using agricultural products as inputs was reflected by the capacity utilisation of 44 per cent for food processing industries and 11 per cent for textiles.[183] The equivalent figures for LMSEs were 100 per cent and about 75 per cent respectively. The government handled 80 to 100 per cent of the coffee, meat, fruit and vegetables exports.[184] How then could SSIs compete on equal terms despite being one of the few sectors of the economy where private entrepreneurs were actually allowed to work?

Some restrictions were relaxed in 1988. For instance, in January private merchants, licensed ones that is, were allowed to buy grain from regions in surplus and sell to those with shortages.[185] In addition to improving living standards and thus the capacity of the workforce this would also reduce the cost of securing output for further trading, enlarging input as well as output markets for merchants. Furthermore, the limit for SSI private capital investment was raised to one and two million birr for individual entrepreneurs and partnerships respectively.[186] Rather surprisingly, this had proved necessary after that an SSI survey had shown capital accumulation in the sector to be above the old limit. Whether such developments

---

[179] UNIDO (1991), p. 111.
[180] Solomon Wole (1992), pp. 179-80.
[181] ILO (1990), tab 1.3, p. 13.
[182] Eshetu Chole (1994), p. 100.
[183] Berhanu Abegaz (1994), tab 4.9, p. 192.
[184] Mulatu Wubneh (1990), pp. 210-11.
[185] David Rose, Farm Reforms Pay Way for Aid, Manchester Guardian Weekly, January 17, 1988, extracted from Mulatu Wubneh (1990), p. 217.
[186] Teshome Mulat (1994), p. 10.

could be ascribed to beneficial HASIDA effects is questionable, since this agency, ten years after its establishment, had only 290 new SSIs to its name.[187] Obviously the threshold that small entrepreneurs had to overcome to establish their firms was quite high, involving investments in time, money and effort and accumulating considerable sunk costs too, but those managing to pass this initial test seem to have been quite vigorous, if not numerous.

The thirteen resolutions in 1988 to some extent directly mentioned SSIs.[188] The first resolution emphasised the need to strengthen cooperatives in all sectors of society in order to enhance the accumulation process, also in the small scale commodity sphere. The shortage of consumer goods was to be dealt with by allowing SSIs to expand and providing these with industrial zones. Private entrepreneurs were to be allowed to participate, without limits on capital investments, within for instance manufacturing industry, either alone or in cooperation with others, if possessing sufficient capital and managerial skills, and for this a proper legal framework would be created.

Such was the situation that the TGE inherited; a disillusioned and sceptical small scale sector that it would take several years of proper policy management, free of nepotism and corruption, to win the confidence of. This did not tally with the guerrilla background of the EPRDF, former bush-men concentrating on survival rather than economic prosperity who prefer to rely on proven allies rather than neutral techno- or bureaucrats. With such a legacy, the appointment of sympathisers to influential positions would be less surprising.

Entrepreneurs have, for more than 20 years, learnt how to conduct underground economic activities. With economic risks perceived as high, capital investments were kept down, hence trade and services were preferred to immobile manufacturing establishments. Commerce is easier to enter into and leave, and holds the potential for quick profits. And it was the anomalies of the central planning system, the misallocation and hence scarcities that it created, that fed the trade sector. Data from the Addis Ababa Chamber of Commerce show that still in 1993 half its members were traders.[189]

The question is what happens when the policies that give birth to such an environment are removed. As pointed out by Shiferaw Bekele, the previous system favoured those who had contacts and access, the wherewithal for economic success.[190] These formerly successful undertakings will find it hard to survive under market economy conditions. Hence, some go to the wall and their potential replacements are fairly ill-equipped as SSIs.

This last statement deserves some elaboration. It takes time to adapt to life within a capitalistic system if prior experience is lacking, and this goes for all participants, public as well as private. Such is the case in Ethiopia.[191] Entrepreneurs

---

[187] Ibid., p. 16.
[188] Hansson (1995a), pp. 77ff.
[189] Jin-Sang Lee (1995), p. 341.
[190] Shiferaw Bekele (1994), p. 12.
[191] Abdela Jemal (1995), pp. 4-5.

lack knowledge of how to identify new needs and fulfil these. Some SSIs were previously recipients of low-priced commodities supplied by public enterprises under a quota system,[192] requiring no development of competitiveness or even basic search for inputs. This reluctant stance towards free markets was also reflected in a survey undertaken among Addis Ababa's private industrialists. Among perceived policy related problems, low import duties on competing products were mentioned, thus revealing a lingering expectation of special treatment and protection among entrepreneurs.[193]

What then might be the best recipe for creating understanding and lessening the feeling of insecurity among SSIs? Information is one important building block, training and education are others. Information on how to go about starting an enterprise is crucial, including requirements for the establishment of a viable undertaking and the rules and regulations that have to be complied with. Licensing procedures, the first threshold for SSIs to overcome, have been quite cumbersome. Initially, investment licences were only issued centrally by the Office of Investment.[194] This task was later transferred to regional institutions, however, with the establishment of regional investment offices proclaimed at the same time.[195] Requirements for the acquisition of licences seem quite demanding, as does the administrative process itself. The establishment of a system with one stop shops for all licences and registrations, regardless of sector, is underway, but there are reports indicating that SSIs are being excluded.[196] There is also some unclarity about the division of the economy into sectors reserved for private and public actors respectively. The term large scale was, at first, frequently cited as a criteria for exclusive government participation, without really defining the meaning of the concept,[197] but this was later defined properly.[198]

Education and training are other measures for coping with the new business environment. Among Ethiopian entrepreneurs of today, about 68 per cent have completed secondary, or higher, education,[199] the figures including not just small scale establishments where this percentage might be lower. This may explain the relatively high degree of imitative, rather than innovative, SSI investments undertaken, because with training comes innovation and initiative.[200] With cumbersome licensing procedures and low levels of education entrepreneurs choose the easy way out: they observe what others are doing, what undertakings within what sectors seem profitable, and then try to do the same. This is the result of bureaucracy as well as a sheer lack of experience of market economies. The fact that the market for bread, for instance, is not infinite within a given area is not taken into account,

---

[192] Taye Berhanu (1996), pp. 4-5.
[193] Zewdie Shibre and Zekrie Negatu (1995), p. 10.
[194] Negarit Gazeta, Proclamation 15/1992.
[195] Negarit Gazeta, Proclamation 31/1992.
[196] Admit Zerihun and Getachew Belay (1996), p. 172; and Mekdes Aklilu (1995), p. 275.
[197] This was pointed to by Amsale Tshehaye (1996), p. 205.
[198] Negarit Gazeta, Proclamation 37/1996.
[199] Solomon Wole (1996), p. 161.
[200] Esubalew Demissie (1991), p. 47.

hence the current situation of overestablishment and low returns. This imitative behaviour extends to modes of production as well, due to a lack of knowledge about alternative techniques, a problem which is even more severe outside the capital.[201] This might partly explain why the production equipment in SSIs is so old.

That more than half of entrepreneurs are engaged in more than one line of activity is again a sign of risk evasion. With small margins and imperfect information diversification is undertaken, more in order to secure a livelihood than an attempt to make a private fortune. The difficulties in selling an unprofitable undertaking also have to be taken into account. Exit is limited by the scarcity of financial resources and the chances of finding a buyer.[202] The use of family members before taking recourse to external labour is also a common feature. According to one survey 95 per cent of entrepreneurs resort primarily to family and friends.[203] This keeps family unemployment down, but could also reflect how the combined family resources have contributed to the investment. Interesting to note in this respect is then the unwillingness on the part of entrepreneurs to use partnerships as the basis for business undertakings in order to solve problems of investment capital.[204]

The concentration of SSIs in Region 14 (Addis Ababa) is also a reflection of inadequate information. There should obviously be a demand for most products over the whole country, but finding these customers requires investment of time and effort. Addis Ababa has the infrastructure to facilitate business. The city is growing and this is where the largest share of competent manpower can be found.

It might be in order to combine these characteristic observations with a critical view of the obstacles impeding SSI activity and assess how the government is dealing with these situations, if it is in fact providing the transaction cost lowering institutions necessary. The first thing to note then is that no one today knows what an SSI is, since the old HASIDA definition was done away with and was replaced with nothing.[205] HASIDA itself has been dissolved and when the Ministry of Industry was reorganised into three departments during the 1990s, HASIDA was subsumed into the Department for the Private Industry Sector. The Development Agency for Handicrafts and Small Industries, DAHSI, is the replacement today, a reportedly autonomous, but toothless, institution with rather limited means at its disposal. It should be pointed out that the government, as well as the entrepreneurs themselves, would be helped by having a strong DAHSI. It could more efficiently channel directives to the SSI sector, get proper feed-back from its contacts with entrepreneurs and supply statistics on the sector, hence enabling quick indications of where SSIs are heading and why. The assessment made by Solomon Wole, that small investors, the basis for private entrepreneurship development, have been

---

[201] Zewdie Shibre and Zekrie Negatu (1995), p. 15.

[202] Alem Abraha (1996), p. 11.

[203] Mekdes Aklilu (1995), p. 278.

[204] Zewdie Shibre and Zekrie Negatu (1995), p. 16.

[205] Assefa Admassie (1996), pp. 2-3.

completely ignored is perhaps a bit harsh,[206] but it does seem as if SSIs have not received the attention they need and deserve. Some less than encouraging signals were furthermore sent to the small scale sector with the implementation of the 1996 investment incentives regulations.[207] Although introducing income tax and custom duty exemptions these are only applicable where investments exceed ETB 250,000 in the case of domestic investment, and USD 500,000 for foreign undertakings.[208] For joint ventures a USD 300,000 limit is imposed while foreigners reinvesting profits are eligible at USD 100,000 and above. In 1993 no more than 200 of the 32,000 Addis Ababa Chamber of Commerce members had capital assets in excess of ETB 250,000.[209]

Today there are no business or professional associations solely representing SSIs, at least not covering all sectors or having any wider remit. Many of the existing private associations are not very well developed, with an overlap of targeted members and, hence, a very limited number of members.[210] This could be a reflection of previous limits on the rights of Ethiopians to form such associations. Even though this obstacle has been removed the NGOs of today reportedly have difficulties in establishing the channels into government offices that are crucial for the development of communication.[211]

Among SSIs this situation results in a rather vague perception of what the rules of the game actually are. In a 1994 survey 100 per cent of respondents had no idea at all about the Commercial Code of Ethiopia. This has been in place since 1960! The same may well be assumed for more recent laws as well.[212] And what is worse, the lack of communication between entrepreneurs and the government leaves the latter unaware of the formers' unawareness. Perhaps it is not sufficient that Negarit Gazeta, the official bulletin, can be purchased at the government printing works. The bulletin is not accompanied by any index, hence making it necessary for small scale undertakers to go through all proclamations in order to identify those which are relevant to him/her. As legal counsel is beyond the means of most entrepreneurs, interpreting the rather bureaucratic and legalistic language could be another barrier. This has implications not only for the prevailing vague understanding of the rules of the game, but also means that the incentives to private entrepreneurs risk passing unnoticed, not resulting in the push forward of this sector intended to and potential of.

A basic prerequisite for any business establishment is access to investment capital. In a poor country, savings are very limited and as a consequence so too is credit. However, there is more to this issue then meets the eye. According to Assefa Admassie, there are reserves of idle savings, but these do not reach SSIs, a

---

[206] Solomon Wole (1996), p. 166.
[207] Negarit Gazeta, Regulations Nos. 7/1996 and 9/1996.
[208] Special rules regarding customs in Article 11 of Regulation 7/1996.
[209] UNECA (1994), p. 34.
[210] Admit Zerihun and Getachew Belay (1996), p. 176.
[211] Taye Behanu (1996), pp. 10-11.
[212] Ibid., p. 281-2.

problem of channelling rather than supply.[213] The banks are not very interested in serving small firms either, regarding them as risky customers lacking proper organisation and management.[214] Furthermore, the transaction costs incurred by banks for monitoring many small contracts are too high to make it profitable. The Commercial Bank of Ethiopia gives only short term loans, while the Development Bank of Ethiopia (the former AIDB) has a bad reputation among SSIs as directly avoiding the sector through use of rough administrative procedures. This has gone as far as an appeal from private entrepreneurs in 38 African countries, including Ethiopia, to the UN and other international organisations not to use government owned banks, including the DBE, for channelling means intended for SSIs.[215] Funds provided by external sources in the shape of bilateral agreements also have their limitations. Even when meant directly for SSI use, they come with restrictions about from where imports may be bought with such funds.[216]

With high demands for collateral and private contributions to any loans for SSI undertakings, a negative view of banks and financial institutions in general has emerged among SSIs.[217] The opening up of this sector to private investors[218] might not be enough to induce changes. The government is probably the most well-equipped actor to cope with the high transaction costs that loans to numerous small investments imply. Private institutions would set even higher demands for collateral and apply even higher rates of interest, yet the situation as it stands today already causes entrepreneurs to shy away. Allowing machinery to stand as collateral is a step in the right direction, but the effect of allowing the establishment of institutions providing micro-finance[219] risks being limited for the reasons mentioned earlier. Again the result is imitative behaviour on the part of entrepreneurs and duplication of measures undertaken by those who successfully have managed to obtain credits.

One important use of credit is for the acquisition of land for manufacturing SSIs. But land did, with the introduction of auctioning procedures,[220] become extremely expensive. In Addis Ababa, rents ranged from ETB 33.25 to 6,000 per square metre, depending on location,[221] making it very difficult for SSIs to rent premises,[222] and thus rated as one of the most serious policy related obstacles among private entrepreneurs.[223] With limited amounts of land, the result was a 10,000 names long waiting list.[224] The sunk costs incurred by SSIs when going through

[213] Assefa Admassie (1996), p. 4.
[214] Getachew Minas (1995), pp. 160-61.
[215] Mekdes Aklilu (1995), pp. 266, 298 and 301.
[216] Zewdie Shibre and Zekrie Negatu (1995), p. 9.
[217] Mekdes Aklilu (1995), p. 286.
[218] Negarit Gazeta, Proclamation 37/1996.
[219] Negarit Gazeta, Proclamation 40/1996.
[220] Negarit Gazeta, Proclamation 80/1993.
[221] UNECA (1994), p. 43.
[222] Taye Berhanu (1996), p. 5.
[223] Zewdie Shibre and Zekrie Negatu (1995), p. 11.
[224] UNECA (1994), p. 28.

difficult licensing and credit procedures may therefore have been paid in vain since access to suitable land is far from guaranteed. The rocketing of land prices is probably the effect of two factors: the monopolistic structure on the market since the government is the only provider, and a lack of experience on the part of bidders in their assessment of the value of land. Some reports indicate that the stated special attention to investment areas prioritised on part of the government excluded small businesses.[225] The trend seems to be a move away from the system of auctioning,[226] but the amount of Addis Ababa land, where access to most facilities can be secured, is finite.

Lack of confidence in others has already been mentioned in connection with the frequent use of relatives as labour among small firms. This probably has to do with the working experience of employees as well as a lack of formally educated staff. In the former case, many have a background in agriculture where less strict demands on labour prevail regarding work ethic as well as discipline, hence there may be some basis for the distrust that exists. The educational programmes, in the latter case, seem to lack relevance to everyday life and so do not equip new students with appropriate skills.[227]

All these formal obstacles taken together, of course, result in other impediments to SSIs: lack of local inputs, since, for instance, all small entrepreneurs face credit difficulties; lack of spare parts due to imitative, risk averse, investments and insufficient local technical know-how; lack of information for want of channels of communication with government; and hence an inability on the part of officials to provide assistance in spotting new opportunities, perhaps with foreign involvement. However, even more serious are the informal obstacles. Let us look at the Ethiopian customers, entrepreneurs and government in turn. A discouraging picture emerges to SSIs when their market is analysed. The high share of trading SSIs among Addis Ababa Chamber of Commerce members (one study from 1994 reports that 80 per cent were engaged in foreign trade compared to only 9 per cent in manufacturing[228]) reflects even more worrying attitudes than a negative approach to the private sector. While trade, as mentioned previously, offers the chance of quick returns, generally speaking, this is not the case for cross-border trade. High customs duties and tariffs on imported inputs was ranked as the most serious policy related obstacle among Addis Ababa entrepreneurs, and insufficient information on export opportunities were ranked third among market related problems.[229] The truth is that Ethiopian products are regarded as inferior to imported ones, and use of domestic commodities is a sign of low status.[230] This

[225] Admit Zerihun and Getachew Belay (1996), p. 175.
[226] Negarit Gazeta, Proclamation 37/1996.
[227] Zewdie Shibre and Zekrie Negatu (1995), p. 13.
[228] Ayalew Zegeye (1995), tab 4, p. 68.
[229] Zewdie Shibre and Zekrie Negatu (1995), pp. 7ff.
[230] Ayalew Zegeye (1995), p. 69.

seems to be the case irrespective of price or quality,[231] something that makes the problem even more difficult to deal with.

The managers, who are often also the owners, need to change too. Many seem to be content with what they have and view efforts toward improvements as tiresome. Most show reluctance regarding expansion and modernisation. Some look upon the task of management as if it could be done by anyone, and organisational structure, proper accounting and personnel administration are not rated as important.[232]

The government could, for one thing, do more to help SSIs integrate into the rest of the Ethiopian economy. In many other countries small and large scale undertakings complement each other through subcontracting. In Ethiopia, this is not the case. Linkages are weak and the relationship one of competition rather than mutual support.[233] Some reports indicate that foreign suppliers are used instead of small local ones, at times to the point of disregarding higher domestic quality goods, when government officials and public enterprise offices are involved, due to commission. In addition, certain goods labelled as destined for trade fairs or exhibitions are imported tax free and then offered for sale in the same markets where SSIs try to compete.[234]

Access to markets is of course crucial to SSIs, and with it transport, distribution and marketing. But, as in the case of credits, many small contracts are more expensive to set up, monitor and enforce than fewer, but bigger, ones. Consequently, the possibility of discounts on bulk purchases is lost to SSIs when they each negotiate individually. This suggests a need to coordinate the activities of institutions with balanced independent profiles in respect of both foreign and domestic trade. In 1993 243 public undertakings completely dominated activities in for instance wholesale trade, and the current regime has stated that these public companies must remain in order to play a stabilising role.[235] Recently, some giant institutions have emerged and, along with a few merchants operating out of Addis Ababa's huge market, the *Mercato*, completely hoovered up the markets for finished as well as semi-processed goods so crucial to SSIs.[236] Production of these commodities could well be running at maximum capacity, but nothing appears on the markets and prices are rising. While SSIs are forced to shut down, these huge institutions hoard goods until a price level perceived as suitable is reached, and then the goods are disposed of. The background of these firms - Guna, Densho, Ambasel and others - is unknown but indications that point in the direction of linkages with political parties are most worrying.

Some obstacles have formal as well as informal features, for example the decentralisation process. The division of powers between the centre and the regions seems to cause private investors confusion and discourages moves out of

---

[231] Mekdes Aklilu (1995), p. 276.
[232] Abdela Jemal (1995), pp. 5, 8 and 9.
[233] ILO (1990), p. 33.
[234] Mekdes Aklilu (1995), pp. 268 and 276-7.
[235] UNECA (1994), p. 27.
[236] Mekdes Aklilu (1995), pp. 269-70.

the capital.[237] A clear statement of the right for people, irrespective of nationality, capital or goods and services to move or be moved, temporary or permanently, across federal borders is obviously necessary. Private investors are seemingly sceptical to the competence of the authorities in more remote areas as for interpreting and implementing economic policies.[238] There is also a lack of communication, and one survey among private investors indicate that regional policies at times conflict with those of the central government.[239] In some regions a number of check-points have been erected for tax collection.[240] This leaves small entrepreneurs uncertain of what the future might hold,[241] and tends to encourage SSIs to withdraw from planned or potential attempts at wider market identification. And at regional levels there are no DAHSI branches to assist either.

Taxation is another example. The official sales tax rate is 12 per cent in Ethiopia, which is widely regarded as unfair and high among private entrepreneurs. At first, payment of sales tax to the Inland Revenue Administration was set for every three days, an impossible operation. It was, however, later changed to monthly payments.[242] Also, the actual process of taxation obviously contains some elements of arbitrariness. Proper accounting is not undertaken by all businesses, hence the use of arbitrary taxation. But even those who can and do produce financial accounts are treated in the same, arbitrary way.

Are there, then, any incentives to enter the formal SSI sector? What benefits do they get from paying taxes? The legal system and services would, at least theoretically, work just as well (or unsatisfactory) whether acting as a private individual or entrepreneur. Given the difficulties of obtaining credit and land, which requires formal registration, is it worth bothering? SSIs are not eligible recipients of government incentives and typically face competition from duty free imports, smuggling and domestic informal actors paying no tax plus a tax authority, the actions of which are in some respects irresponsible or arbitrary. While the low number of SSI licences in the HASIDA days was a result of a 'lack of supply', that is, unwillingness on the part of the government to issue new ones (this improved somewhat in the late 1980s), today it seems to be lack of demand that is holding back formal business activity.[243] The number of applications for, and the issuing of, temporary licences has outnumbered the permanent ones, the former being somewhat less expensive but also, and more importantly, easier to qualify for. A trend of increasing withdrawals of applications is also noticeable, suggesting that a 'general reluctance to comply with the law . . . has already set in'.[244]

---

[237] Taye Berhanu (1995), pp. 254-5.

[238] UNECA (1994), pp. 44ff.

[239] Zewdie Shibre and Zekrie Negatu (1995), p. 14.

[240] Taye Berhanu (1996), p. 6.

[241] UNECA (1994), p. 29.

[242] Zewdie Shibre and Zekrie Negatu (1995), p. 18.

[243] Teshome Mulat (1994), pp. 35ff.

[244] Ibid., p. 36. These licences make entrepreneurs eligible for, amongst other things, tax relief and land allocations.

Concluding remarks

What we have thus is a society where the population has witnessed a number of regimes, in power for varying lengths of time, but none with any real legitimacy. Throughout history the concept of property rights has suffered serious wear and tear, the rule of law has to a large extent been a subjectively interpreted phenomenon and the country has been divided along class, ethnic and regional lines. Scarce resources have been misallocated to military purposes instead of providing an infrastructural basis on which to build an environment conducive to economic growth. Even today it is still the case that in Ethiopia, land cannot be owned, only leased for longer periods of time.

Corruption was the rule, rather than the exception, under Haile Selassie. Mengistu Haile Mariam brought the situation to a level of uncertainty far exceeding what had previously existed by introducing terror as a means of fostering obedience. Meanwhile, the current regime declared, only months before assuming power, that Albania was the country on which an ideal society should be modelled. Insecurity has, to varying degrees, been prevalent all along, and people have learnt not to place much trust in the regime. It will, henceforth, be even more crucial that the true intentions of the government are known and that the announced reforms are firmly enacted and enforced by law. The government needs to be committed to the liberalisation programme to such an extent that they cannot escape their promises. This is called for in the Ethiopian as well as the international arena.

While SSIs were ignored during the imperial era they were actively discriminated against under Mengistu. The current regime has made some concessions to this sector of the economy, but the indications are that the regime either enjoys insufficient credibility or that their policies are not enough to create a prosperous environment for small entrepreneurs. That SSIs are concentrated to such an extent in Addis Ababa, that so many small entrepreneurs rely on their own funds for investment, that the number of applications for SSI licences is going down, that the number of permanent licence applications is lower than that of temporary ones and, in a more indirect manner, that the capacity utilisation in SSIs is so low, all point to the existence of high transaction costs facing small businesses, but also show the ways in which these entrepreneurs are trying to reduce these costs. Being located in Addis Ababa secures an output market and infrastructure; using their own savings means not having to deal with the difficulties in obtaining loans through banks; and choosing the grey sector of the economy instead of becoming a formally established entity means not having to wait for a licence, thereby escaping taxes as well as other bureaucratic procedures.

If SSIs are to be helped the government must first and foremost identify which these companies are. Secondly, laws and regulations that are consistent, transparent and coordinated are necessary; intentions must be matched by implementation. The private sector, with SSIs explicitly included also in incentives schemes, must be able to act under free competition, supervised and safeguarded

161

by the government and the legal system. Information is furthermore crucial to building confidence in, and an understanding of, the government and its policies, but communication has to go both ways! This is where the role of support associations needs to be emphasised and strengthened. SSI views and observations of failures must be taken seriously and the situation put right. These associations could also serve as sources of statistical data for analysis, and should preferably involve universities and other research institutions in the process.

High transaction costs incurred by many small businesses could be off-set through the establishment of industrial zones, as in Asia. Credits, input purchases, recruitment of staff, training, accounting, distribution, marketing and support services could thus be coordinated at lower costs. Such zones could also help build up linkages and networks. The concentration of undertakings would furthermore allow telecommunications, water, power and other facilities to be provided at more reasonable cost. This could, in sum, make an industrial zone as attractive to investors geographically as Addis Ababa and the problem of expensive land might thus be avoided.

The recent history of violence, fear and uncertainty in combination with poverty, a landscape that is far from accessible, poor planning and strange priorities on the part of previous governments have all helped to create the present situation. It will take a lot of time and effort to regain what has been lost in entrepreneurial spirit but it might take even more to regain the confidence of the people.

7 Tanzania

Pernilla Sjöquist

Introduction

Tanzania has been described as 'one of Africa's economically most distressed, socially most innovative, and politically most controversial countries'.[1] It has been rated one of the poorest countries in the world by the World Bank, and it has attracted international attention for its experiment with African Socialism. Undoubtedly the charismatic leadership of former President Julius Nyerere, and his forefront position in the fight for African liberation, helped to put Tanzania on the global map. In the late 1970s and early 1980s Tanzania experienced, for that country, an unprecedented economic crisis with increasing budget deficits and deteriorating current account positions, all combined with a heavy reliance on foreign aid. Parallel to this, the country endured a rapid growth in its population. Since 1986 Tanzania has in large followed a Structural Adjustment Programme (SAP) under the sponsorship of the International Monetary Fund (IMF) and the World Bank.

Without any doubt, Tanzania can be labelled a transition economy; it is moving away from its attempt at socialism, which led to a high level of bureaucratic co-ordination of resource allocation, towards the implementation of an economic system based on market forces, where market coordination is allowed to play an ever larger role.[2] Although central planning was never adopted, Tanzania developed a socio-economic system where the ruling Party monopolised power and ideology, and where the political system strongly influenced the economy. However, the economic system developed under African Socialism shared many traits with countries adhering to central planning, for instance the high degree of bureaucratic coordination, the presence of soft budget constraints[3] and severe shortages in the

---

[1] Yeager (1989), p. 1.
[2] Kornai (1992), pp. 91-2, describes the characteristics of these two basic coordination mechanisms. Bureaucratic coordination is a vertical relationship between subordinates and superiors in a multi-level hierarchy. These vertical linkages are asymmetrical as the subordinates depend more on the superiors than vice-versa. Thus, the command, i.e. an order which the subordinate has to follow, becomes the typical flow of information. Market coordination, on the other hand, means horizontal linkages between legally equal partners. The motivating factor is financial gains through the price mechanism.
[3] A soft budget constraint is a non-binding budget constraint that does not restrict the behaviour of the firm. This concept was coined by Kornai (e.g., see Kornai 1992), and will be discussed later on.

economy. Not unexpectedly, Tanzania's search for macro-economic stability has been faced with a set of challenges also faced by post-socialist economies. One challenge is the inherited institutional setting which, in all likelihood, is not well-equipped to meet the demands of the new economic order. In particular was the institutional setting of most socialist countries biased against certain types of economic activity, private small scale entrepreneurship being one of them. Such bias may be expected to result in a structure of transaction costs which affects the environment of economic agents and, subsequently, their decisions and behaviour.

This study starts from the basic assumption that sound macro-economic management is closely linked to the structure of transaction costs, and that attempting to specify existing and potential sources of high transaction costs is one of the first steps to move beyond the debate over the advantages and adverse effects of structural adjustment programmes.[4] Thus, its main focus is on the institutional framework of Tanzania, and on possible ways this framework has affected transaction costs facing formal small scale industries. The analysis of the general economic system is made in the light of the situation for small scale industries, and the specific situation of small scale firms is addressed in the latter part of the chapter. As the analysis is based on secondary data and adequate information about Zanzibar proved hard to find, the discussion has been limited to mainland Tanzania.

The remainder of the chapter is organised as follows: the next section briefly discusses the economic history of Tanzania since its independence in 1961. The subsequent section analyses the institutional setting of the country using a transaction cost approach, while the penultimate section extends this analysis to cover the situation for small scale industries in particular. Finally, a concluding section summarises some of the general implications for transaction costs and small scale industry development in Tanzania, as found in this chapter.

Tanzania's economic development since independence

The colonial legacy

Contemporary mainland Tanzania had at the time of independence in December 1961 been under European colonisation since the 1890s, first under German, and from the end of World War I under British rule. Colonialism has put its mark on Tanzanian society and its economy in a number of ways, of which only two will be mentioned here. Firstly, colonialism in Tanzania had created an economy based on plantation agriculture and production of cash crops for export to the European market. Secondly, administrative systems and an economic reward system alien to traditional structures and institutions, as well as a socio-economic structure divided along racial and ethnic lines had been introduced. The Germans had introduced a hierarchical system of government which put Europeans, Arabs and coastal Afri-

---

[4] See Chapter One and Two of this book.

cans in charge of local headmen. The British administration for their part had applied indirect rule under native authority, which in effect meant letting African officials implement colonial directives and customary law. This system led to local chiefs and centrally appointed people holding a higher position in society than the traditional council of elders.[5] Tanzania's colonial legacy has been reflected in the development of the country's political and economical agenda since independence in 1961.

In search of an economic strategy: 1961 to 1967

In 1961, there were a mere 220 industrial establishments, each employing 10 people or more and having fixed assets exceeding TAS[6] 20,000 in Tanzania. The manufacturing sector contributed about 4 per cent to GDP and supported about one per cent of all households in the country.[7] A three year development plan (1961-64) was launched with the prime target of rapid economic growth based on a free-enterprise economy. The new government actively sought to attract investment in industry by designing favourable tariff and tax incentive structures, making existing investment opportunities public, establishing industrial estates and guaranteeing foreign investors against nationalisation.[8]

The First Five Year Plan (FYP), covering the period from 1964 to 1969, continued this strategy and identified market size and availability of capital as the main constraints to industrial development. Changes to the rules of trade and protection of the home market were to address the market constraint, while encouragement of private (including foreign) investment along the lines of import substitution was to lessen the capital constraint.[9] Tanzania experienced rapid growth in industry during this period. In 1965, there were 596 manufacturing establishments, each employing 10 people or more, an increase of almost 160 per cent in four years. The vast majority of investment was channelled into the country's four major urban centres.[10] Available figures on output show considerable increases in most industrial products over the same time period, along with an increase in the share of manufacturing in GDP from 3.6 per cent in 1961 to 8.4 per cent in 1967.[11]

In essence, Tanzania's economy was mainly governed by the same set of principles as had been applied under colonial rule. The end result was an economy heavily dependent on foreign loans and grants, along with an investment and income distribution pattern that continued to favour a small number of farmers, urban wage earners and non-African entrepreneurs. In addition, a number of internal and external disturbances occurred between 1964 and 1967. The violent

---

[5] Yeager (1989), pp. 10-15.
[6] Tanzanian shilling.
[7] Hedlund and Lundahl (1987), p. 15.
[8] Rweyemamum (1979), p. 71.
[9] Skarstein and Wangwe (1986), pp. 4-5.
[10] Rweyemamum (1979), pp. 70-76.
[11] Skarstein and Wangwe (1986), pp. 5, 10.

revolution on Zanzibar in early 1964 and the subsequent formation of the United Republic of Tanzania in April the same year is one example, the loss of support from Tanzania's largest donor countries (UK, USA and West Germany) during the same period another.[12] The latter effectively showed Tanzania's heavy reliance on foreign assistance and its vulnerability to changes on the international arena.

The inward looking phase: 1967 to the late 1970s

The Arusha Declaration of 1967 constitutes a watershed in Tanzania's economic history as it heavily influenced the development of the economy from the later 1960s until the early 1980s. In the 1960s, a political strategy referred to as African Socialism was launched by President Nyerere. Aimed at the creation of a country less dependent on foreign actors in which the state would act as the unifier and provider for the masses, this ideology of socialism and self-reliance was explicit in the Arusha Declaration which provided specific guidelines for a transition to African Socialism and 'one-party democracy' were stated. These guidelines were also incorporated into the Second FYP (1969-74), that strived for Tanzania's self-sufficiency in terms of the basic needs of the people (food, clothing and housing) by formulating an outspoken import substituting agricultural and industrial strategy.[13] *Ujamaa* (familyhood) villages were introduced as the basic economic and social unit in rural areas, the idea being to broaden the tradition of the African extended family to embrace the larger unit of the village. After 1973, a villagisation programme resulted in forced resettlement of scattered populations in rural areas, and legal status was given to the villages.[14]

In accordance with the Arusha Declaration, the public sector was recognised as the official economy, and the commanding heights of the economy (such as banking, major industries and plantations, import and export trade, land and major buildings) were nationalised.[15] In addition to the Third FYP (1976-81), a long term basic industry strategy (BIS), covering 1975-95, was adopted. The BIS focused on the development of industrial activities in the fields of production to meet the basic needs of the people, and on activities which used local resources for production of inputs to domestic agriculture and manufacturing.[16]

This inward looking period was characterised by substantial improvement in some social indicators, for instance increased life expectancy and adult literacy rates, but also with a gradual deterioration economic productivity. Economic indicators for 1967-73 and 1982-84 show a decline of growth in GDP per capita from a positive 2.5 per cent to a negative 2.9 per cent; an increase in inflation from 8.5 per cent p.a. to 30.6 per cent p.a.; and a sharp increase in the debt to exports ratio

[12] Yeager (1989), pp. 65-71.
[13] Hansson et al. (1983), p. 92.
[14] Sarris and van den Brink (1993), p. 11.
[15] Eriksson (1991), p. 6.
[16] Skarstein and Wangwe (1986), p. 7.

from 120.6 to 513.1.[17] Emphasis was put on food production in place of cash crops for exports which, in combination with an overvalued shilling, severely affected the country's ability to earn foreign currency. Restructuring of the industrial sector according to the BIS resulted in increased dependency on imported intermediate and capital goods. The goal of self-reliance in effect transferred resources from agriculture to industry. The role of prices in the allocation of resources was reduced, and price controls were introduced to most sectors of the economy. The villagisation programme and the launching of state run marketing boards and distribution systems failed to increase agricultural productivity. Furthermore, investment in production capacity was not efficiently used and the state sector expanded rapidly.[18]

For a long time, this development was concealed by favourable world market prices for coffee and by a boom in foreign aid. Starting in 1979, however, a series of negative external shocks, for instance, a decline in Tanzania's terms of trade, increasing international interest rates, an expensive war with Uganda and a fall in aid flows, changed the situation. Finally, external pressure in the form of disputes with the IMF and the World Bank about Tanzania's price system and its exchange rate policy, forced the government to adopt economic reforms and SAPs.[19]

Towards a market oriented economic system: the early 1980s and onwards

Although Tanzania's economic crisis in the early 1980s was triggered by external factors, it was nevertheless a logical consequence of the development strategy followed since the adoption of the Arusha Declaration.[20] The first two of a series of economic recovery programmes, the National Economic Survival Plan of 1981 and the SAP implemented in 1983-85, both had limited direct impact on the economy. During 1965-85 official statistics show an average annual decline in real GDP per capita of 0.5 per cent, while household surveys reveal a fall in real income per household of about 50 per cent over the same period.[21] The SAP, however, introduced some elements of systemic reform by initiating trade liberalisation, for instance liberalisation of domestic trade in foodstuffs, the Own Funds Imports scheme and a partial elimination of quantitative controls on imports. Trade liberalisation was generally coupled with relaxation of price controls of the goods in question.

In 1986 the Economic Recovery Programme (ERP) was launched, which proved acceptable to the IMF, and was later incorporated in an agreement between the

---

[17] Hydén and Karlström (1993), p. 1397
[18] Hedlund and Lundahl (1987), pp. 4, 12-16.
[19] Hydén and Karlström (1993), pp. 1396-7
[20] Eriksson and Lundahl (1993), p. 268.
[21] Hydén and Karlström (1993), p. 1399. This has been contested in a survey done by Sarris and van den Brink, who put emphasis on the role of the second economy as an income generator in Tanzania. They conclude that real income did decline somewhat for the urban middle class, but that the earlier reported serious decline during the 1970s and early 1980s should be questioned, especially as far as the rural, but also the urban, poor are concerned (see Sarris and van den Brink 1993, Chapter 6).

Tanzanian Government and the IMF. The focus of the ERP was on short term macro-economic stabilisation and on medium term structural adjustment and economic recovery. It targeted increased agricultural output, higher capacity utilisation within industry, improved physical infrastructure, tight fiscal and monetary policies and a more outward looking trade strategy.[22] It advocated dismantling of the price control system and liberalisation of both internal and external trade. Thus, the ERP signalled a shift in the direction of economic policy of the country and opened the way for a massive inflow of external funds from international donors and the World Bank. The ERP was followed by the Economic and Social Action programme covering 1990-92, which continued along the same lines, but laid particular emphasis on the development of the social sectors of Tanzania, which over the course of time had become neglected.[23]

Annual growth in official GDP ranged from 3.26 per cent to 5.09 per cent between 1986 and 1990.[24] The overvaluation of the Tanzanian shilling was gradually reduced, with the largest devaluations taking place in 1986 and 1987. Not only credits (mostly benefiting the government controlled marketing organisations in the agricultural sector) but also the money supply expanded, keeping inflation high (around 30 per cent in the mid-1980s), making it difficult for real interest rates to become positive. Although foreign currency only in part became subject to free allocation, the foreign trade sector in fact constitutes the key to the entire recovery programme. The own-funded imports scheme and the open general licensing system were two of the driving forces in the recovery process. They made it possible to increase the availability of consumer goods (by some 95 per cent on a national average between 1984 and 1988) and of various inputs in Tanzania's economy. In addition, the scope and the relative size of the private sector increased. Exports of non-traditional commodities, including petroleum products, minerals and manufactures showed the biggest positive change, while the development of traditional agricultural exports, such as coffee and cotton, remained weak. Non-traditional exports made up almost 50 per cent of total official exports in 1990, up from some 32 per cent in 1985. Furthermore, relaxation of price controls continued, the tax and tariff system was revised, an Investment Code (defining areas open to private investment) was introduced, as were new banking laws and bankruptcy legislation.

In essence, the economic programmes in Tanzania have involved both policy changes and reform measures, and a certain degree of change in the economic environment does, in fact, seem to have taken place. African Socialism has been abandoned in favour of a more market oriented development strategy and the role of the private sector has increased. Liberalisation measures have been partial and implemented gradually. In fact, some of them involve official recognition of activities previously banned, resulting in an increase of informal market activities at the expense of parallel and black market activities, thereby reducing the latter's share

---

[22] Eriksson and Lundahl (1993), p. 269.

[23] Eriksson (1991), pp. 9-10.

[24] This paragraph draws on Eriksson (1993a), pp. 13-32.

of Tanzania's economy.[25] It has been argued, however, that, due to the lack of any major reform of the state sector and a certain degree of ambiguity and inconsistency in the liberalisation process, the economic programmes have only partially reformed the economic system and major rigidities still exist.[26]

The institutional setting

Following North's definition of institutions as being formal rules (e.g., statutes) and informal rules (e.g., norms) this section of the case study tries to map the major institutions in Tanzania's economy.[27] Khalil's distinction between institutions as social constraints (such as rules, habits, laws and conventions) and organisations as agents (such as household, firms, and state agencies) is also taken into consideration in the analysis, although in the present chapter the term institution is used to cover both of Khalil's concepts.[28] In other words, institutions refers to both rules, regulations and norms in Tanzania, as well as to the physical organisations which enforce them. In this way a picture of rules and norms operating in Tanzania's economy, and their corresponding organisational form, takes form. The impact of institutions on transactions costs in general in the economy of Tanzania is addressed, but of particular interest to the analysis are those institutions that affect the economic environment of small scale firms.

The role of the Party

When looking at the role of the leading Party in Tanzania, there are three important, and closely interwoven, aspects that have to be considered. First, the Party has been the ultimate shaper of the ideology which has permeated the political and economic life in Tanzania for almost three decades; ideology formed the backbone of also the various institutions that were created. Second, the Party has all along operated as the party supreme in the one party state originally created in the early 1960s, and, thus, as an organisation strongly influenced the structure of the political and economic systems. Third, the effect of the first two aspects on transaction costs, and the subsequent behaviour of firms in Tanzania.

The Party as shaper of ideology At the time of independence, there was already a de facto one party state under the Tanganyika African National Union (TANU) in

---

[25] Bagachwa and Naho (1995), pp. 1393-934. The authors identify the second economy in Tanzania, which constitutes a large part of its economy but which is unrecorded in official statistics, as consisting of the informal sector (unregistered companies involved in legal activities), the parallel market (illegal production and trade of goods that are legal themselves) and the black market (production and trade in illegal and strictly forbidden goods).

[26] E.g., see Eriksson (1991), and (1993a).

[27] North (1990).

[28] Khalil (1995).

place.[29] Formed in 1954, TANU had emerged from the Tanganyika African Association (TAA) and from a number of proto-political interest groups. Opposition to colonialism, combined with British harassment of African interest groups and TAA branches, fuelled the speed with which even remote communities joined TANU in the 1950s. In the national election to the Tanganyika Legislative Office in 1960, TANU won all but one seat.[30] In 1961, TANU represented the unifying force that had succeeded in ending colonialism - and was the only political party of substance in Tanganyika. Thus, 'TANU felt that it had the duty to lead the country as its policies had already won the support of the people'.[31]

In the years following independence, Julius Nyerere, President of Tanzania between 1964 and 1985, started to build an ideological base for TANU, and for Tanzania. It was a socialist approach based on the colonial experience, the practices of pre-colonial African societies, Nyerere's education in Western political philosophy and the then prevailing cold war politics. He concluded that an ideal society was 'based on human equality and a combination of freedom and unity of its members'.[32] At the heart of Nyerere's African Socialism was the creation of the 'new man', an individual who would adhere to the socialist values of hard work and to the moral obligation of contributing for the sake of (the development of) the country.

Ideology as shaper of the political and economic systems Nyerere regarded discussion, equality and freedom to be the essential characteristics of democracy, and he also saw these as being the essential features of a traditional African society. Furthermore, Western-style democracy and multi-party systems were only justifiable in a society divided over fundamental issues. Nyerere did not find this to be the case in Tanzania, which had been unified in its fight for independence and which, according to him, needed to remain united in order to improve the situation of its people. Subsequently, he did not see any incongruity in speaking for equality and democracy, and at the same time arguing for a political system based on one single party. The role of this party was to be a two-way channel for ideas between the people and the Government; securing grassroots' participation and popular election of political candidates, while at the same time reducing bureaucracy and increasing control of the Government.[33] In fact, voluntary participation and mass support can be regarded as the two legs of Nyerere's socialism.[34]

The formal introduction of 'one-party democracy' in 1965,[35] was triggered by the revolution on Zanzibar and the subsequent creation of the United Republic of

---

[29] Kweka (1995), p. 65.
[30] Yeager (1989), pp. 21-5.
[31] Kweka (1995), p. 65.
[32] Nyerere as quoted in Kweka (1995), p. 63.
[33] Kweka (1995), pp. 60-67.
[34] Hedlund and Lundahl (1989), p. 19.
[35] Nyirabu (1994), p. 2. One party democracy was incorporated in an interim constitution which actually allowed for two parties to be present in Tanzania: the Afro-Shiraz Party (ASP) on Zanzibar

170

Tanzania in 1964. It legalised a political structure which had already been taking form, in which TANU held political supremacy. In 1963, the colonial native authorities were replaced by district councils, to which district TANU organisations were empowered to approve all candidates. Private trade unions and cooperative societies were reorganised and became official affiliations of TANU. After 1965, policy decisions were made by the Party and merely ratified by the National Assembly. The National Executive Committee of TANU was given the parliamentary right to summon witnesses and subpoena evidence from both Party and Government leaders. In addition, the Preventive Detention Act of 1962 and subsequent legislation allowed for the arrest of TANU critics within the trade unions, as well as local inhabitants considered by the regional and area commissioners to be endangering peace and good order.[36]

Ideology in socialist Tanzania produced a set of objectives centred around economic development, putting emphasis on distribution and economic equality, rather than on economic growth. The resulting incentive scheme was complicated, mixing elements of central control with decentralised decision making within the framework of Governmental guidance, voluntary participation and moral exhortation. To help create the new man, a set of non-material incentives based on the African tradition of the extended family was advocated: 'the *carrot* of moral rewards for providing for your nearest relatives, and the *stick* of social disgrace for those who do not pull their weight'.[37] These ideas all came together in the Arusha Declaration of 1967, which incorporated a new economic system for the new state and the new ideology. In the Declaration, capitalism was declared the main enemy; foreign interests and the commanding heights of the economy were nationalised; moral exhortation was to replace material incentives; the Leadership Code preventing TANU and Government leaders from engaging in economic activities outside the political system was introduced; and an explicit focus on agricultural development as the means to achieve self-reliance was formed. A second ideological milestone came in 1971 when the Party Guidelines were issued. This document aimed at revitalising the Party and its socialist values and attitudes towards domestic capitalist stiffened. One result was the loss of one-fifth of the country's Asian population in 1971 alone, following expropriation of their private houses.

In general, the role of the governing Party in Tanzania under African Socialism was significant. In implementing its ideology (which was not always done successfully) it shaped a highly integrated political and economic system through which the rules of the game could be set. At present, this aspect of the Tanzanian socialist system finds itself in transition, a development that started with the 1991 Zanzibar Resolution. Here, the national committee of the Chama Cha Mapinduzi (CCM), in order to keep up with changing times, reinterpreted the Leadership Code to allow

---

and TANU in Mainland Tanzania. In 1977, the two parties were merged to form the Chama Cha Mapinduzi (CCM).

[36] Yeager (1989), pp. 66-9.

[37] Hedlund and Lundahl (1989), p. 22; emphasis in the original. This and the following paragraphs draw heavily on Hedlund and Lundahl (1989).

for party members to own shares in private businesses, and legitimised some economic activities previously labelled as capitalist activities.[38] Finally, the introduction of the multi-party system in 1992 and the elections held in 1995 reflect the reshaping of the ideological environment in Tanzania.

Party, ideology and transaction costs

The attitude towards capitalism and private enterprise under African Socialism has not been conducive to private entrepreneurship in Tanzania. In fact, a sharp anti-market philosophy prevailed, which, for instance, could be seen in daily news commentaries which strongly discredited anything capitalist in the country.[39] The role of the private sector within the socialist framework in general has been ambiguous. Apart from the declaration of the public sector as the official economy, a number of Government Acts and Directives have directly and indirectly discouraged private entrepreneurship.[40] As late as the 1987-2000 Party programme, the private sector was only seen as temporarily serving a purpose in the transition period from capitalism to socialism, after which it was to be abolished.[41]

The distrust of private entrepreneurs, and the fear of an emerging economic and political elite, were manifested in the 1983 crackdown on 'economic saboteurs and racketeers'. This event was triggered by the belief that the shortage of goods in the formal sector and the rapid expansion of the second economy was due to deliberate hoarding with the aim of overthrowing the Government.[42] After the introduction of the reform programmes in 1984, the situation for the private sector has changed somewhat. The most significant recognition of change, at least in symbolic terms, was the adoption of the Investment Code in 1990 (defining areas open for private, including foreign, investment).[43] However, the very need to define areas open for private investment underlines the ambiguous position this sector has had on Tanzania's ideological setting.

In essence, both the institutional aspect and the organisational aspect of the Party, that is the ideology and the political system, have created a high degree of uncertainty among private economic agents. The official ideology has been alien to private entrepreneurship, and developments up until 1984 indicated increasingly hard restrictions under which these enterprises could operate. The combination of the 1983 crackdown and the introduction of economic liberalisation measures the following year, implied extremely fast changes in the policy framework of the country. In addition, the step-by-step approach of the reform process in general, the lack of an explicit commitment to transform the economic system and the

---

[38] Nyirabu (1994), p. 11.

[39] Hydén and Karlström (1993), p. 1396.

[40] Bagachwa (1996), p. 24 Apart from the previous mentioned Nationalisation Acts and the Leadership Code, which effectively excluded capitalists from engaging in politics, the 1974 Ujamaa Village Act excluded individuals from owning small industrial enterprises in villages.

[41] Eriksson (1991), p. 38.

[42] For an extensive account of the crackdown, see Bagachwa and Maliyamkono (1990), pp. ix-xix.

[43] Eriksson (1991), pp. 36-7.

occasional discrepancy between directives and their implementation, have resulted in uncertainty regarding in what direction the country is going.

Thus, first and foremost, the role of the Party has tended to increase overall transaction costs, by creating and maintaining uncertainty about the rules of the game in Tanzania.[44] Lack of trust in the intentions of the political leadership means that business commitments and investment decisions are short term in nature and limited in size. Search costs may increase because information about the behaviour of the potential partner, as well as the price and quality of the product, have to be investigated and reinvestigated thoroughly by own means before any decision to enter a contract can be made. Furthermore, contracting costs rise as the contract, or the agreement between two parties in a business deal, has to cover a number of possible scenarios. So too do costs of third party protection, because the contract has to take into account possible encroachment by a third party. This could be the government in the case of nationalisation, or restrictions allowing state enterprises only in economic activities where the government can be anticipated to show particular interest.[45]

Furthermore, following a redistribution oriented, as opposed to growth oriented, ideology, a number of regulations that affected transaction costs in Tanzania were introduced. Restrictions on certain commodities and credit arrangements favouring the state sector - the official economy - are likely to have raised transaction costs for those operating outside of it. The implication is that search costs and third party protection costs, to mention but a few, have increased due to the ideology of the ruling party in Tanzania. Some of these transaction costs may have decreased when liberalisation measures were introduced (e.g., liberalisation of domestic and external trade permitted economic activities that were previously regarded as capitalist but that were carried out anyway), although under a great deal of uncertainty and risk.

It is worth pointing out, however, that as long as there is no explicit commitment to transformation of the economic system and the official ideology remains ambiguous in its relation to private economic activity, the threat of reversal of reform measures and a reintroduction of restrictions on private economic activity is always present. Recent changes in the political system, that is, the introduction of a multi-party system, may have reduced this source of uncertainty, while at the same time increasing short term uncertainty about the political environment and the ideological base of Tanzania. Thus, because of the current transformation process, extra transaction costs, due to lack of trust in the system, can be expected to play an important role in the decision making process of firms in Tanzania.

---

[44] Ibid., pp. 37-9.
[45] See Chapter Three of the present volume for a description of the different transaction costs mentioned.

Government organisation   Mukandala argues that under African Socialism, the ruling party had overall control of the state in Tanzania. The Government was either part of, or answerable to, the Party, and government and party functionaries overlapped to a high degree. Formulation of political policy was dominated by the Party, particularly by its National Executive Committee and its Central Committee; and the role of Government was mainly to implement these policies under supervision of the Parliament. In addition, the Parliament constituted a committee of the National Congress of the Party. Distinguishing between the roles of party and government was in most cases troublesome.

Administration became the fastest growing sector of the economy in the 1970s, and by the mid-1980s it made up just short of 30 per cent of government spending.[46] In 1988, the public sector comprised 303,000 workers of which 142,166, or some 47 per cent, were to be found in central government and the rest in local government or in other services.[47] In general, bureaucrats played a secondary role to politicians, something which was abundantly clear in terms of policy making. However, this was often compensated for by a tendency among bureaucrats to 'leave policies that they did not like to die a natural death'.[48] The situation changed somewhat in the 1980s, as policy decisions, due to internal pressure as well as to the involvement of international agencies such as the World Bank and the IMF, started to rely more on technocratic, as opposed to ideological, expertise. The economic crisis in the early 1980s, and the decline in governmental resources, led to the bureaucracy having increasing difficulties in transferring information to its different branches. As a consequence, some measures to decentralise were taken, such as the introduction of popularly elected Executive Officer at the district level.

Fiscal policy and taxation   In the years following independence, fiscal policy basically followed the policy adopted by the colonial administration, and was generally of a conservative nature. As the ideology of African Socialism took form in the 1960s, government budget deficits came to be seen as an instrument of development policy.[49]

There seems to be a general consensus that the rapid expansion of the public sector of the 1970s, together with a lack of appropriate policy responses to external shocks, were the main factors behind the economic crisis in Tanzania.[50] The Government's aim was to manage economic difficulties by instituting tight controls, and it used the budget as its principal policy instrument.[51] Between 1976 and

---

[46] Sarris and van den Brink (1993), p. 25.
[47] Mukandala (1995), p. 66.
[48] Ibid., p. 67.
[49] Bukuku (1992), p. 3.
[50] E.g., see Ndulu (1988); Bagachwa and Maliyamkono (1990); Sarris and van den Brink (1993); Eriksson (1993a); and Hydén and Karlström (1995).
[51] Wagao (1992), p. 5.

1987, the public sector deficit ranged from 7.5 to 14.5 per cent of GDP at market prices. Moreover, in the 1980s there was a sharp increase in the proportion spent on administration and servicing the public debt at the expense of education, health and economic services.[52] This marked a considerable divergence from the basic needs approach to which the Government committed itself when adopting the Arusha Declaration.

Taxation was introduced in 1897 by the Germans as a mean to incorporate indigenous agricultural producers into the money economy. Today, consumption and excise duties alongside income and personal taxes constitute the bulk of Government revenue which between 1967 and 1986 made up 70 to 80 per cent of total revenue.[53] Osoro argues that tax reforms since the end of the 1960s were in general aimed at raising revenue to match the rapidly growing fiscal spending in the country. The whole focus has been on base broadening and rate increasing measures which in the process, however, this has created a highly complex tax system which lacks in administration and enforcement.[54] Apart from administration, the granting of generous tax exemptions has further reduced revenue productivity. There are a number of possible exemptions from sales tax (e.g., on industrial inputs and machinery) as well as from customs where 'the Minister of Finance has discretionary powers to exempt goods and individuals from full or partial payment of duty'.[55] Furthermore, the tax structure could be accused of discriminating against production in favour of imports and of having become a part of the soft budget constraints facing the parastatal sector in Tanzania.[56]

Strömberg has investigated the tax structure and collection procedure encountering small scale industries in Tanzania. Company profits tax (50 per cent for resident private and public companies), tax on employees' wages, withholding tax, wealth tax, and estate duty all have to be paid once a year to the Income Tax Authority. Sales taxes are levied on locally manufactured goods, on imports and on a few services and are payable on a monthly basis to the Customs and Sales Tax Department. Import duty is paid at the port, and is usually administered by the importer's agent. Finally, stamp and excise duties, along with various registration and licensing fees, have to be paid to the Internal Revenue Department. These departments are all accountable to the Ministry of Finance and each has its own office in every region of Tanzania. In most cases, a small scale company has to send a representative to visit the different tax departments in person and pay the tax in cash.[57]

Monetary policy Under African Socialism prices were regarded to have little or no role to play in the allocation of economic resources, and fixed nominal prices were

---

[52] Sarris and van den Brink (1993), p. 23.
[53] Ibid., p. 25.
[54] Osoro (1993), pp. 1-10.
[55] Ibid., p. 23.
[56] Eriksson (1991), pp. 27, 41.
[57] Strömberg (1995), p. 64.

seen as being important in their own right. This included unchangeable nominal exchange as well as interest rates. 'Changes in nominal prices were seen as a symptom of profit making and thus of a capitalist mentality'.[58] This ideological standpoint shaped the pricing system with its emphasis on administrative price controls, as well as influenced both interest rate and exchange rate policy.

As pointed out by Caselli, the development of a well functioning money and stock market was not in line with the official ideology. Instead mobilisation and allocation of financial resources were to take place through an appropriate organisational structure and, starting in the early 1970s, through financial and credit planning. The key monetary policy instrument has been control of credit. The powers of the Bank of Tanzania (BoT) were extended far beyond that of a traditional central bank on matters of credit control, and selective control of credits extended by commercial banks and other financial institutions was made possible for the BoT.[59]

Ndulu points to 'the close relationship between the fiscal deficit, balance of payments and money supply process' in Tanzania.[60] Mainly because of underdeveloped financial and capital markets, financing of government deficits was restricted to monetary expansion. As a result, Ndulu was able to find close to a one-to-one correspondence between growth in fiscal deficit and expansion of the money supply in Tanzania. Between 1978 and 1981 net claims on the government contributed to 90 per cent of monetary base expansion.[61] Net claims on the government by the banking system increased by almost 20 per cent annually in the late 1970s, and close to 30 per cent annually for the first three years in the 1980s. At the height of the economic crisis, from 24 per cent up to as much as almost 72 per cent of the financing of the public deficit was in the form of bank borrowing. Since 1986 the proportion has been reduced quite considerably, although loans to loss making parastatals through the banking system have continued, which in effect constitutes money creation.[62]

Inflation in Tanzania, after having fluctuated around 12 per cent in the 1970s, jumped to 36 per cent in 1980 and reached a peak of 43 per cent in 1984. Between 1985 and 1989, inflation stayed close to 30 per cent, after which it finally came down to 19 per cent in 1990.[63] According to Ndulu, the inflationary process in Tanzania was fundamentally structural in that it was determined by supply side constraints and channelled through increasing costs. The government exercised monetary accommodation of these pressures in the form of food subsidies (until 1984) and, despite declining savings rates and lower investment productivity, maintained high investment rates in industry. Between 1966 and 1981, savings varied from 8 to 10 per cent of GDP, while net investment for the same period rose

[58] Hydén and Karlström (1993), p. 1396.
[59] Caselli (1976).
[60] Ndulu (1988), p. 3.
[61] Ibid., p. 4.
[62] Sarris and van den Brink (1993), p. 31, 44-6.
[63] Eriksson (1993a), pp. 8, 31.

from 7 to 27.5 per cent of GDP.[64] The BoT reports some increase in deposits since the start of the reform process, as nominal interest rates have been raised to match inflation and taxes on savings have been reduced.[65]

After the introduction of the Tanzanian shilling in 1966, the exchange rate remained unchanged at TAS 7.143 per USD for fifteen years. By 1980, the TAS had depreciated by some 14.5 per cent, and in the early 1980s it was brought down somewhat more. This was counterbalanced by the high domestic inflation rate, however, and in effect the TAS appreciated in real terms. Thus, the foreign exchange situation in Tanzania since the 1970s may be characterised as an accelerating overvaluation of the TAS.[66] Currency devaluation as a tool for the adjustment of the balance of payment was highly debated with the IMF in the early 1980s. One of the main concerns from the Tanzanian side was the threat of an inflationary spiral due to changes in the real exchange rate between tradeable and non-tradeable goods and expected slow response in production of export crops. Another concern was the expected income distribution effects of the extensive and rapid devaluation scheme suggested by the IMF. However, as Tanzania was finalising the ERP agreement with the IMF in 1986 the attitude changed and the Government agreed to letting the exchange rate be adjusted on a monthly basis. By December 1990, it had reached TAS 195 per USD.[67]

Industry policy As stated before, early industry policy was generally open to free enterprise, but considerable changes took place following the adoption of the Arusha Declaration. The Second FYP reflected the ideology of socialism and self-reliance and argued for increased production of domestic consumer goods, along with intermediate and capital goods. The long term BIS, adopted in 1974, has had a real effect on the industrial development in the country. Although agricultural development was the major focal point of the Arusha Declaration, and thus at the political centre, the BIS helped to push agriculture to the economic periphery at the expense of larger scale and capital intensive industrialisation.[68] Skarstein and Wangwe clarify that under the BIS

> exports of manufactured goods would be seen as an extension of the home market, i.e. the export market would develop after the home market had been fully developed and catered for. [The strategy of BIS] represented a significant shift towards the development of domestic resources to meet domestic needs whereby most of the materials required for industrial development would be produced in the country.[69]

---

[64] Ndulu (1988), pp. 4-9, 46.
[65] Eriksson (1993a), p. 28.
[66] Berglöf (1990), pp. 22-3.
[67] Bagachwa (1993), p. 94.
[68] Hedlund and Lundahl (1987), p. 11.
[69] Skarstein and Wangwe (1986), p. 35.

The authors point out that the choice of technology was restricted by, for example, the source of external finance and available technical managerial skills, and that as an effect industrialisation in Tanzania under the BIS was marked by heavy dependence on imported inputs, machinery and know-how. In most cases the employment effect of the industrialisation effort was rather limited, particularly in the rural areas. Thus, in most cases the implementation of the BIS worked against the development goals outlined the very same document, and against the objectives of socialism and self-reliance.

Linkages played a pronounced role in the BIS as a means to achieve structural change, although the emphasis was more put on inter-sectoral linkages (e.g. between industry and agriculture) than intra-industrial linkages (e.g., linkages within the manufacturing sector). The BIS identified a list of core industries which were to constitute the base of industrial production in Tanzania: the iron and steel industries; metal working and engineering; industrial chemicals; paper; textiles; leather; construction materials; and electricity. Studies have shown that, typically, these basic industries did show stronger than average backward linkages, but that this was not the case for forward linkages. Moreover, the basic industries proved to be highly import intensive, displaying low income effects. The linkages between, and the precise role of, small and large industries were vague and unclear in the BIS. In general, the planners seemed to have regarded small scale industries as connected with a number of sacrifices in terms of cost, quality, consumer choice, speed and efficiency. In conclusion, the planners sent 'a message of bias against the small-scale of industries'.[70]

Rules about registration and licensing constitute a part of the industry policy that directly affects firms in any economy. In Tanzania, enterprises are required to be registered (for small scale units) and sometimes licensed (for units with investments in buildings and machinery of above TAS 5 million). Failure to comply with these requirements constitutes illegality. Bagachwa describes the registration process as starting with the company name having to be accepted by the Company Registration Office. Second, the articles of association have to be presented to the Company Registrar were registration is received for a fee. Third, if the company is to be licensed, it has to apply to the relevant municipal authority, such as the City Council, where the application has to be approved by as many as six different authorities, ranging from the Health Officer to the Principal Assessor, for a fee. Fourth, the licence has to be taken to the Trade Officer where it is lodged and the appropriate ward number according to location is allocated. This fourth step can take up to three months. Finally, the enterprise has to be registered by the National Provident Office for employer insurance purposes.[71] The licence has to be renewed each year for a fee, which hinges upon the company first having received a number of clearances from various authorities.[72] In short, licensing and registration procedures are rather long drawn out and costly affairs.

---

[70] Ibid., pp. 52, 169-90.
[71] Bagachwa (1993), p. 108.
[72] Levy (1993), p. 76.

Internal and external trade policy The external position of Tanzania has been a major source of concern since the late 1970s. In 1976 the trade deficit amounted to some 2 per cent of GNP. In 1978 it had jumped to about 15 per cent, while in 1988 it had surged to 26 per cent of GNP. Agricultural primary products, that is coffee, cotton, sisal, tea, tobacco and cashew nuts, are Tanzania's six top foreign exchange earners. Together they account for about 60 per cent of total export earnings, although the volume of all six has declined significantly since the mid-1960s. Capital and intermediate goods make up the bulk of imports, while food imports account for 40-60 per cent of consumer imports. Before 1985, most of the current account deficit was financed through capital transfers. After 1985, an increasing share has been financed by net external borrowing.[73] It is within the areas of trade policy and price deregulations, that the most comprehensive reform measures of the 1980s are to be found.

Under African Socialism, the pricing system, which stipulated administratively set prices for a number of goods and services, was an integral part of the internal trade policy. Early on the pricing of foodstuffs (which was made more flexible in the mid-1970s in order to increase production of food) and non-food items (including crops produced for of export) were subject to a high degree of administrative intervention. In addition, a pan-territorial pricing system was used with the purpose of equalising producer and consumer prices in all regions.[74] In the early 1980s, more than 400 categories of goods were subject to price control, a number that had been reduced to just three by 1991. Prices for manufactured imports were fully deregulated by then. Up until 1984, all domestic wholesale trade was confined to state agencies, which often exercised monopolistic powers. More than 50 categories of goods, including consumer goods, were subject to such restrictions. By 1991, just three categories were still controlled.[75]

Most imports and exports were originally confined to state agencies. Despite the subsequent lifting of restrictions there is still a strong monopoly with respect to the major export crops. Foreign currency for trade purposes used to be allocated administratively, but since the mid-1980s this has also been subject to significant change. The introduction of various export retention schemes since 1982, the Own Funds Import Scheme in 1985, the Open General Licence Facility in 1988 and the introduction of free foreign exchange auctioning in 1993[76] have all relaxed the constraint on procurement of foreign currency by legal means. In 1988 the complex tariff structure was simplified when some specific duties were abolished and by 1990 tariff rates had been reduced to four *ad valorem* rates. Export taxes are almost non-existent in Tanzania today.[77]

---

[73] Sarris and van den Brink (1993), pp. 19-20.
[74] Hansson et al. (1983), p. 98.
[75] Bagachwa (1993), p. 96.
[76] Eriksson (1995), p. 18.
[77] Bagachwa (1993), p. 96.

Above, policies have been identified as institutions which affect the behaviour and decisions of economic agents operating in Tanzania. The picture that emerges indicates that the Government did not consider the lowering of overall transaction costs of the economy to be its major concern. Rather, policies and regulations were focused on redistribution, and development was to be achieved through a system of tight controls and an active steering of the economy in a predetermined direction based on socialism and self-reliance.

As to the organisation of government and of the political system in Tanzania, two interesting aspects emerge. The sheer size and scope of the political system which infiltrated most levels of society and the high degree of interaction and interdependence that existed between the Party, the Government and the public sector. Given the integration of powers between the legislature (in effect the Party), the executive (in effect the Government and various parastatals) and the judiciary that prevailed in Tanzania, the political system to a large extent had to rely on self-enforcement of contracts. In fact, for most contracts within the system, such as policy decrees, the system itself had to be self-monitoring and self-regulating. Consequently, there were neither checks nor balances, nor was there any powerful third party that could enforce contracts drawn up within the political system. In effect, the political system in Tanzania with its vast size and range must have contributed considerably to the creation of high overall transaction costs. This particular situation, however, is bound to change as a new political order under a multi-party system emerges.

As to rules and regulations, and the subsequent behaviour of firms, there are many mechanisms that can influence transaction costs. Constantly present throughout, though, is the importance of ex ante transaction costs, mainly in the form of costs for search of information about restrictions, as well as exemptions from restrictions. The time factor seems to be another major source of transaction cost. The examples of obligatory procedures in the case of registration and remittance of taxes both indicate that potential entrepreneurs need to be well-informed about a number of requirements and procedures. In addition, they have to possess a great deal of patience, and should probably secure an alternative source of income while their application is being processed by various authorities.

In short, the non-transparent nature of government policy, as well as the organisational structure supporting these policies, seem to impose significant transaction costs on registered and tax paying (i.e. formal) enterprises in Tanzania. This points to a number of small scale entrepreneurs in effect being pushed into operating in the informal economy, regardless of whether they actually intended to or not. On the question of taxation there is another side to the coin, namely tax evasion. Administrative demands for taxation are a source of high transaction costs to a company only as long as taxes are paid. Tax evasion is an effective mitigating strategy when tax enforcement is poor. As a consequence, the defective taxation system in Tanzania may work as a disincentive for small scale enterprises to register, and for investments to grow sufficiently in size. Instead it may encourage the expansion of operations by means of adding new, equally small and non-registered enterprises to existing ones.

The state sector

The state sector comprises majority owned state enterprises and institutions, which in Tanzania are referred to as parastatals. Official financial institutions, which for the most part are fully state owned, have here been separated from other parastatals in order to highlight their particular role in the economy. In accordance with the official ideology adopted after 1967, the state sector has played a significant part in Tanzania's economic development. By its sheer size in some industries, and by its key position in others, the state sector must be regarded as one of the most important institutions affecting the economic environment in the country.

Parastatals: size and scope of the sector[78] According to Eriksson, there were about 400 parastatals in Tanzania in the late 1980s, of which more than 75 per cent were commercial.[79] They were found in all sectors of the economy. There were agricultural parastatals, for instance state farms and marketing boards, such as the National Milling Corporation (NMC), responsible for the marketing of agricultural inputs and outputs as well as the processing of certain farm produce. Parastatals were engaged in industry and manufacturing, domestic wholesale and retail trade, and exports and imports. Mostly due to uncertainty about the reliability of official figures, the share of the state sector in the economy of Tanzania is difficult to gauge. Estimates show that parastatals have been more heavily represented in certain economic sectors than in others, manufacturing being one such sector (contribution from parastatals to industry value added is almost 50 per cent). In some industries, parastatals have held an almost monopolistic position (e.g., steel and basic metal production, fertilisers, pharmaceuticals, tyres and tubes, textiles, leather goods, shoes and paper products), this being the case also in some parts of agriculture (e.g., wheat, rice, sugar and sisal production, marketing of cash crops). In addition, agricultural cooperatives (reintroduction in 1984) bore a strong resemblance to state organisations, and were officially subordinated to the Party.

It ought to be pointed out, though, that despite the ambiguous role of private ownership and the general emphasis put on the state sector, the Tanzanian economy nonetheless remained mixed. The private and the state sector operated side by side, although private activities were suppressed and barely acknowledged. Private economic activities remained important mainly in agriculture, but also in the manufacturing of household metal products, electrical equipment, soap, paints,

---

[78] Unless otherwise stated, the sections on parastatals draw on Eriksson (1991).

[79] Commercial parastatals, or parastatal enterprises, are parastatals supposed to generate revenue for the central government from dividends on profits. Non-commercial parastatals, or parastatal organisations, do not operate on such commercial lines and include e.g., government run research institutes (see Bukuku 1992, p. 9).

and plastics.[80] Retail trade and construction are other areas where the private sector has been important.[81] Nevertheless, in industries where private interests were permitted, parastatals took priority over private enterprises in the eyes of the Party and of the Government. They received preferential treatment in various ways, for example in allocation of inputs, licences, credits and foreign currency. International donor organisations have also shown a tendency to channel aid through the official, parastatal structure.

Eriksson argues that the reform process in Tanzania has not so far resulted in privatisation of state enterprises to any noticeable extent. A limited number of joint ventures have been established with existing parastatals, and some parastatals have been dismantled. Concerns have been raised about the proper size of the public sector, the magnitude of a privatisation scheme for state enterprises, the timing of any such privatisation and, finally, to whom the chance of investment under a privatisation scheme should be offered.[82] There are signs of changes within agricultural marketing, with the NMC having closed branches and retail shops as well as having laid off 300 workers. The overall staffing level within the state sector has been frozen.[83]

Parastatals: the decision making process The decision making process for parastatals in Tanzania involved a number of levels and institutional bodies. Major decisions could be categorised as follows: (1) *Policy*: decisions about the purpose and the nature of business of the parastatal were taken high up in the central hierarchy, that is, by the National Assembly, the CCM and the Office of the President. (2) *Establishment and Investment*: decisions on entry and exit, approval of corporate plans and of investment plans were centralised, involving four to six institutions in each case, ranging from the Worker's Council to the Ministry of Finance and Planning. Major decisions on the location and size of a unit were initiated by the Central Committee or the National Executive Committee of the CCM. (3) *Appointment Decisions*: appointment of general manager and of the board of directors was done by the parent Ministry of the respective parastatal in agreement with the President. In general, no leading position within parastatals or cooperatives was ever filled unless the person had first been approved by the Party. In short, a *nomenklatura* like system was at work in Tanzania.[84] (4) *Operations*: physical planning of the production of parastatals was never adopted, instead command and pressure from the Party and the Government influenced operational decisions. Decisions on day-to-day issues were supposed to be delegated to managers at the enterprise level, but in reality not even such decisions

---

[80] Skarstein and Wangwe (1986), pp. 19-20.

[81] Eriksson (1991), p. 7.

[82] See for example Bukuku (1992); and Msambichaka (1992).

[83] Eriksson (1993a), pp. 13-17.

[84] *Nomenklatura* refer to the 'right of all levels of the Communist Party apparatus - from the central party committee down to the enterprise committee - to "recommend" and "approve" appointments for all managerial positions in the economic (and public) administration hierarchy, and managerial positions in enterprises' (Winiecki 1991, p. 4).

were taken without prior approval from different supervisory bodies. This included decisions on employment levels and wages, as well as output prices. In addition, since trade in most inputs and outputs was confined to state agencies, parastatals were not free to choose their suppliers and customers.

Recently, there are signs of the appointment process having become more meritocratic as formal procedures have been introduced, and as the boards of directors seem to take a more active part in the appointment process. Changes have been very slow in materialising though. Nevertheless, liberalisation of domestic trade and of prices has increased the possibility for parastatal managers to make independent operational decisions.

Parastatals: incentives and soft budget constraints Despite the fact that the bulk of parastatals in Tanzania are commercial, many of them are chronic loss makers.[85] The goal of profit making was in many instances confused with other objectives, and parastatals were 'seen as objectives rather than means'[86] to achieve certain goals. In addition, other success criteria than just profits were applied to commercial parastatals, loyalty probably being the most important of them. In particular, there was no system of rewards and punishments based on performance in state enterprises. Furthermore, given the low compensation levels in the public sector, employees have been forced to divert time and effort to other income generating activities, and there are numerous reports on abuse or theft of public property, as well as fraud and corruption.

All of this was made possible or has been facilitated by the presence of soft budget constraints, which implies that firms do not operate under strict financial restrictions. Eriksson, who has investigated this phenomena in Tanzania's economy, contends that the budget constraint is not binding and 'cost over-runs are covered by some other organisation, typically the state'.[87] The budget constraint of parastatals in Tanzania has been softened by a number of mechanisms, including direct subsidies via the government budget, soft credits from the banking system, non-uniform and negotiable taxes, administrative prices set on a cost-plus basis, guarantees issued by the Government, and privileged or free access to import support from donor agencies. The mechanisms used varied between different sectors, as did probably the degree of softness.

One important aspect of soft budget constraints is that they influences the ex ante behaviour of the firm since no particular attention has to be paid to cost or price awareness, particularly on the input side. Certain trends toward a hardening of soft budget constraints can be discerned since the reform process started. This is particularly noticeable within industry and commerce where parastatals are facing greater competition due to liberalisation measures, and consequently the government seems to have become less inclined to bail out loss making parastatals.[88]

---

[85] Eriksson (1993b), pp. 16-18.
[86] Moshi (1990), as quoted in Eriksson (1991), p. 25.
[87] Eriksson (1993b), p. 1
[88] World Bank (1988), p. 23

The financial system In the inland areas of contemporary mainland Tanzania, which have been home to agricultural-kinship societies since the dawn of mankind, money did not come in to use as a means of exchange until the 19th century. The coastal areas on the other hand (and also Zanzibar) have a rather different history based on trade, and numerous archaeological findings of Roman, Arab, Persian and Chinese coins uncover a long tradition of the use of money. When the Germans arrived in the 1880s, the Indian rupee was the prevailing currency due to commercial connections with India and Indian immigration. Tanzania's first commercial bank opened in 1905, and the country was a member of the East African Currency Board under British colonisation. Ever since the BoT was formed in 1966, Tanzania has had an independent financial system.[89]

The banking sector was one of the industries which was nationalised in 1967. As previously mentioned, the financial system was highly inter-linked with the government sector and it played a major role in the economic development of Tanzania by being a tool for implementing monetary policy. It was also an operating device for the softening of the budget constraint facing parastatals; the 'banks have mainly fulfilled the task of accommodating the financial needs of the state sector'.[90]

The financial system in Tanzania consisted of a dozen different financial organisations, each in practice enjoying monopoly power within their respective areas of operation. New banking legislation allowing for the establishment of private and foreign banks was adopted in 1991, and by February 1993 at least two foreign banks had secured operating licences.[91] The BoT is directly subordinate to the Ministry of Finance, while the commercial banks are directly subordinate to the BoT. Eriksson argues that the financial system in Tanzania has over time developed to resemble, in some aspects, the monobank system of the former socialist economies in Eastern Europe. She bases this argument on the frequent political interventions in decisions on credit allocation, together with other operational decisions, as well as the prevailing tendency of lending being 'determined by government priorities rather than market criteria'.[92]

The National Bank of Commerce (NBC) is the major commercial bank in Tanzania, and it has been a major tool by which credit has been extended to the state sector. Formal lending criteria, such as credit worthiness and collateral, were established for both the public and the private sector, although these were infringed upon by other decision giving priority to the state sector. In addition, interest rates were generally lower for state enterprises than for private. Recorded NBC lending since 1984 shows a bias towards the parastatal sector at the expense of the private, and towards agriculture at the expense of industry. The overall share of the private sector in NBC lending has increased steadily, however, and by 1992

---

[89] Caselli (1975), pp. 21-5, 111 ff.
[90] Eriksson (1991), p. 28.
[91] Eriksson (1993b), p. 41.
[92] E.g., see Eriksson (1991), p. 15, and (1993a) p. 41.

private sector recipients were predominant in commerce and industry lending.[93] The NBC has been accused of poor service, complex and time consuming loan procedures as well as having a poor communications record.[94] For example, to open a savings account the NBC required references and permitted only a limited number of withdrawals per week. High nominal interest rates (still resulting in negative real interest rates) were offered on savings accounts up to a certain amount, after which capital had to be invested in short term certificates or in fixed term deposits with lower interest rates. On top of this, no interest at all was paid on current accounts, although parastatals were obliged to maintain their current accounts with the NBC.[95] Studies indicate a high degree of disorganisation within the NBC as consolidation of branch data at the head office was non-existent until the bank was computerised in 1991, and as there were signs of internal policies being 'neither understood nor followed in most of the branches'.[96]

Parastatals, banks and transaction costs

First and foremost, the above points to how parastatals, apart from having been a major obstacle to achieving allocative efficiency, have served to raise transaction costs in Tanzania. By being the high priority sector, backed up by an extensive regulatory framework, parastatals have in many cases excluded other economic agents from easy access to resources, credits, foreign currency, distribution networks and markets. Mitigating strategies of non-parastatals involve activities and organisational structures that, although being probably the most efficient given the circumstances, could become even more efficient had not rules and regulations that constantly favoured parastatals been in place.

Furthermore, the structure and the operations of the parastatals, in combination with the negative official attitude towards private ownership, are bound to create difficulties for an outside private firm to become a supplier or a subcontractor to a parastatal. The outlined decision making process implies a high degree of integration within the parastatal sector and little power for local management to act independently. The structure of incentives and the soft budget constraints suggest a low level of accountability and low cost awareness on the part of management. Thus, even if alternative competitive suppliers or subcontractors were available, parastatal managers would probably show little interest in them. First, there was no need to identify cost reducing activities for the parastatal manager since cost was not a constraining factor. Second, pushing for new arrangements was not considered necessary as managers were not held accountable for the financial outcome of the parastatal. Third, even if these first two actions were taken, the parastatal manager was in the end limited by, and subject to, the comprehensive decision making process of the parastatal corporation. Feasible mitigating strategies on

---

[93] Eriksson (1993b), pp. 43-4, 85.
[94] E.g., see World Bank (1988), p. 24; Hyuha et al. (1993), p. 25; and Strömberg (1995), pp. 65-7.
[95] World Bank (1988), p. 24, footnote 22.
[96] Eriksson (1993b), pp. 42, 45.

behalf of any agent in dealing with parastatals include networking and lobbying, but bribery and corruption. All of these activities raise transaction costs in the economy, particularly ex ante costs such as search and bargaining costs.

The parastatal sector and the financial system stand out as two highly inter-linked institutions; financial institutions have allocated credits and foreign currency to parastatals, accumulated overdue parastatal commitments and differentiated between private sector and state sector interest rates. Thus, the financial system has, first, affected transaction costs by implementing policies that themselves were transaction cost generating. Second, the lack of credit in the private sector, due to the preferential treatment of parastatals by the financial system, has tended to strain private enterprises' ability to invest in their own operations. Their only solution may be to turn to the informal sector for funding. Informal financing as a mitigating strategy may involve high interest rates in some instances, but low or non-existent interest rates in others. Nevertheless, informal funding is based on personal trust, and on considerable, often time consuming, investments in activities such as networking and reputation building. Furthermore, there is a size limit to informal credit operations because monitoring costs tend to increase rapidly with the number of entrants and with distance. In short, there is scope for a reduction of transaction costs in the economy as a whole if trust is of a general nature, that is if economic agents can put their trust in a well-functioning financial system and its operational procedures, as opposed to of a particular nature, that is when economic agents can only trust one particular person or a limited group of people.[97]

This leads to the third and final point about transaction costs and the financial system in Tanzania, which is the low level of financial integration. The description of the financial system implies potential investment resources not being channelled properly into profitable investments. Monetary policy has in general not been conducive to savings within the official financial system as real interest rates were often low or negative. The banking system itself has not been a good promoter of savings, as such activities were coupled with discouraging administrative requirements. Other financial intermediaries, such as a functioning capital market, have, so far, been lacking or of moderate importance.

An example of both point number two and three above, is the separation of the Asian business community, which constitutes a substantial part of the private sector in economic terms, from the rest of the economy. The Asian business community has in effect developed its own financial institutions. The underlying reason seems to be a lack of trust in governmental policy regarding private ownership, which has spilled over into a lack of trust in the financial system.[98] Although this arrangement may reduce transaction costs for the participants in the system, when compared to having to invest in complicated and time consuming application and feedback procedures, it is also the outcome of high transaction costs in

---

[97] See Platteau (1994b) for a discussion on generalised trust and morality, as well as distrust and limited morality.
[98] Eriksson (1991), p. 41.

the economy, and in fact constitutes a suboptimal solution for the economy as a whole.

Property rights

Private property rights The Arusha Declaration stated that 'major means of production should be owned by the state on behalf of peasants and workers',[99] which was manifested in the subsequent nationalisation of the commanding heights of the economy. However, nationalisation extended beyond the core industries and came to include private rented buildings and farm estates, as well as retail trade activities such as small butcheries and bakeries under private ownership.[100] The Government has tried to play down the threat of nationalisation by the introduction of the Investment Code in 1990, which acknowledges the existence and importance of the private sector and identifies areas open for private investments. In addition, the President has declared that the word nationalisation should be erased from the political vocabulary in Tanzania.[101] Still, the wording of the code implies that private property might still be nationalised in 'due process of law providing for payment of full and fair compensation'.[102] How any such compensation would be calculated is not stated. Again, it is worth mentioning that, in general, the economy of Tanzania remained mixed, even after nationalisation.

Eriksson also points to the lack of legislation providing for bankruptcy and the unclear role of patent legislation in Tanzania. Historically, informal rules were in general given a higher status that formal legal rights. Policies were backed by Government decree and not by formal legislation. The increased scope of private enterprise following the trade liberalisation measures in the 1980s, was not given a legal framework until the Investment Code of 1990. Also, the old legislation regarding confinement of goods to the state sector was still in force as late as 1991, although in real life a lot of deregulation had already taken place.[103]

Land property rights Coldham explains that in 1961 virtually all land was held according to right of occupancy, a system dating back to the period of British administration when all land was public land vested in the Governor who had the authority to grant rights of occupancy. Customary rights were incorporated into occupancy rights. After nationalisation, land was officially owned by the state, but the villages had the right to cultivate it. Coldham holds that the compulsory villagisation programme in the mid-1970s was basically a policy without any legal framework to define land rights of both villages and villagers; it was based on the assumption that land tenure could, and should, be handled by administrative means. As a result, a number of disputes over land and land compensation have

---

[99] Skarstein and Wangwe (1986), p. 17.
[100] Bagachwa (1993), p. 105.
[101] Mukandala (1995), p. 63.
[102] Eriksson (1991), p. 36.
[103] Ibid., pp. 35-6.

been filed 'in the more relaxed climate of the 1980s'.[104] However, in accordance with the 1991 Commission of Inquiry into Land Matters, land has been proclaimed valuable, and the development of private land ownership has been accepted. However, no enthusiasm to introduce a comprehensive programme of registration of individual land titles has been shown. Eriksson states that customary law and the right to inherit land were basically not infringed upon in areas where cash crops were intensively grown. Finally, long term leasing of land, or rather of what is built on it, was introduced in the 1983.[105]

Property rights and transaction costs

In line with the negative attitude towards private ownership that prevailed under African Socialism, private property rights were poorly defined, or undefined. The ideology regarded state ownership, and sometimes communal ownership, as the means to achieve the goals of socialism and self-reliance. Over time though, there seems to have been a certain mix-up between these goals and means in terms of state ownership and parastatal expansion. In addition, informal rules have often been more important than formal rules in the historical context of Tanzania, something which continued to be the case in certain areas of its economy. In sum, the private sector was operating under a dual legal system in Tanzania; the official system with its weak definition of property rights, and the traditional based on a set of normative rules. The enforcement of property rights has in effect inter-linked the two systems to a certain degree. Poor enforcement of property rights under the official system has lead to corruption and bribery being accepted as an informal rule.[106]

According to Eggertsson, property rights are seen as fundamental to the issue of transaction costs since 'transaction costs are the costs that arise when individuals exchange ownership rights to economic assets and enforce their exclusive rights'.[107] Badly defined and poorly enforced property rights ought to have increased overall transaction costs in Tanzania's economy by increasing risk and uncertainty. Potential illegality of a contract has to be included in the negotiations about its terms, and monitoring and enforcement of contracts have to be done by the respective contracting partners since there is no adequate legal framework to rely upon. Also, a perceived threat of nationalisation implies high costs for protection of third parties. Poorly defined, protected and enforced property rights are likely to result in private entrepreneurs being reluctant to engage in long term and high cost investments. Land, apart from being essential for agricultural production, is also important as collateral for credits. Uncertainty about property rights to land ought to have had an effect on the possibility for private entrepreneurs to receive formal credit, and thus, on transaction costs in the financial market.

---

[104] Coldham (1995), p. 231.
[105] Eriksson (1991), p. 17.
[106] This has been pointed out by Eriksson (1991), p. 36.
[107] Eggertsson (1990), p. 14.

Small scale industries in Tanzania

Definitions

Small scale[108] No coherent definition of small scale industries exists in Tanzania. Instead different public agencies and organisations use their own classification as to what a small scale enterprise constitutes. TANU's definition in its Party Directive of 1973 was:

> Any unit whose control is within the capability of the people whether individually or collectively in terms of capital required or know how; it includes handicrafts or any organized activity based on the division of labour.

According to Bagachwa, the Small Industry Development Organisation (SIDO) in principle embraces this highly flexible definition. However, in order to conduct surveys and statistical reports it has been forced to add its own categorisation. Since 1994, SIDO has defined small scale enterprises as 'privately owned economic units with less than 50 permanent employees which have a minimum turnover of USD 6.000 a year and a minimum investment of USD 400'.[109] As to official figures, the National Accounts of Tanzania give an estimate of small scale manufacturing units based on firms with five to ten employees, along with an estimate of handicrafts based on manufacturing firms engaging fewer than five people. The Bureau of Statistics annually conducts a Survey of Industrial Production which defines small scale industries as establishments with less than 10 workers. Finally, the NBC distinguishes between Small Scale Industries (SSIs) and Small Scale Enterprises (SSEs) based on its credit thresholds. In 1990 SSIs covered firms within a threshold level of TAS 20 million, while firms that were over this limit but below TAS 50 million were classified as SSEs.[110] The NBC also requires any small scale business to be: (i) labour intensive; (ii) export oriented; (iii) import substituting; (iv) predominantly based on local materials; and (v) to demonstrate good potential to generate inputs into other industries, that is to comply to the general guidelines under BIS.

Informal vs. formal There is a continuing discussion among practitioners and academia about the definition of informal and formal sectors in an economy. Some make a distinction between wage earning and self-employment, and thus regard the informal sector as consisting of all income opportunities outside formal employment including both legitimate (e.g., activities such as self-employed artisans and

---

[108] Unless otherwise stated this section draws on Bagachwa (1996), pp. 9-10.
[109] SIDO [(1984?)].
[110] Note that this definition does not follow the commonly held definition of SSIs as small firms engaged in industrial activities (e.g., manufacturing) and SSEs covering small scale firms engaged in other activities (e.g., service activities).

shoemakers) and illegitimate (e.g., pushing drugs and petty theft) activities.[111] In the case of Tanzania, definitions of the informal sector range from being based primarily on size (equalising the informal sector with micro enterprises employing less than ten workers), or function (traditional crafts constituting the informal sector while modern small scale factories constitute the formal), - or a combination of the two - to include access to organised markets, to credit institutions, the degree of regulation and competitiveness of the market, family or non-family ownership, and access to formal schooling and training.[112] Whichever definition is used, the category labelled the informal sector usually tries to capture activities that are unrecorded in official statistics.

For the purpose of this study, a strict application of the judicial sense of the term formal has been used, that is the main focus is on small scale enterprises that are registered and/or licensed, and that exercise legitimate economic activities. This includes private sector employment as well as primary and secondary self-employment activities, as long as they are registered. This distinction along legal lines is found to be essential in the analysis of how institutions and transaction costs affect SSIs in Tanzania, as formal SSIs operate within the structure of transaction costs set by the economic system itself. However, it also implies that previous empirical work done on SSIs in the country, formal or informal, has to be carefully interpreted.

The role of small scale industries

Principally, the ideology of African Socialism was not negative to small scale economic units. On the contrary, small scale production was seen as an important mechanism by which self-reliance within rural areas, and equality between urban and rural areas, could be attained. Based on their low need of sophisticated know-how and capital, their potential as employment creators in rural areas, and their possible role as carriers of technological change in rural areas, the 1973 Party Directive regarded 'Small Scale Industries as necessary for our country's development'.[113] Even though there seemed to be a general agreement about the importance of small scale enterprises at the time, the role of these enterprises in terms of industrial development was not explicit.

The BIS regarded local small scale businesses as an important means of spreading economic activity and thus increasing rural development and reducing transportation bottlenecks.[114] As pointed out earlier, the BIS, although accepting the need for both large scale and small scale industries, was vague about the roles of the two, and was biased against small scale operations in its policy recommendations. Furthermore, as pointed out by Bagachwa, in theory the industrial

---

[111] See e.g., Hart (1973), p. 68.

[112] See e.g., Bagachwa (1993), p.107, and (1996), p. 10; Bagachwa and Naho (1995), p. 1388; and Strömberg (1995), p. 4.

[113] SIDO [(1984?)], p. 2.

[114] Havnevik et al. (1995), p. 62.

structure was supposed to combine small and large as well as centralised and decentralised enterprises. Large scale centralised industries were supposed to predominate at the national level while development authorities were supposed to organise and assist medium and small scale activities at regional and district level. Finally, village committees were supposed to organise and supervise rural industrial activities at village level. In practice, however, large scale centralised enterprises came to dominate the national as well as the regional and district levels, and the development of village based SSIs was almost totally neglected.[115]

It is worth noting that 'small' did not usually imply 'private' under these circumstances. The 1973 Party Directive 'required the Party, Government, Cooperatives, and Parastatals to be responsible for persuading, encouraging and supervising the establishment and running of small industries on socialist principles in villages and towns'.[116] This was interpreted to mean that there should be no room for individually owned small industries in Ujamaa villages, a policy later legally formalised into the 1975 Villages and Ujamaa Villages Act. Moreover, when selecting candidates for its projects, SIDO paid particular attention to ownership criteria and the applicant's organisational structure. 'Preference is given to sound industrial co-operatives, and small public organizations over partnerships and limited liability companies'.[117] In sum, small scale production was recognised early on as being important for Tanzania, given the underlying assumption that small enterprises were means to achieve the goals of socialism and self-reliance. Therefore they should not be in private hands.

In practise, small scale industries typically remained under private ownership. However, these small firms are for the most part to be found in the informal sector. It is indicative that most empirical studies focus on the second economy[118] in one way or another, and the important role it plays in the country's economy. Bagachwa and Naho estimate the second economy in Tanzania to have made up some 15 per cent of total (official plus second economy) real GDP in the 1970s and more than 20 per cent for most of the 1980s. The share of the second economy of official real GDP for the same time periods was estimated at some 15 to 20 per cent and 25 to 30 per cent respectively.[119] Tripp has calculated that a minimum of 80 per cent of urban household income come from activities in the informal sector.[120] Finally, Bagachwa shows that small scale industries are less capital intensive than parastatals, and that average labour productivity within the informal sector is higher than for parastatals in both rural and urban areas.[121]

As most studies conducted in order to estimate the role of the small scale sector in Tanzania have focused primarily on the informal sector, the exact role of the

[115] Bagachwa (1993), p. 101.
[116] Havnevik et al. (1995), p. 259.
[117] SIDO [(1984?)], p. 14.
[118] See the definition of the second economy given in footnote 25.
[119] Bagachwa and Naho (1995), pp. 1393-5.
[120] Tripp (1989), p. 9.
[121] Bagachwa (1996), pp. 20-22.

formal small scale sector has been rather difficult to survey. Nevertheless, the picture that emerges indicates that small scale businesses in general, regardless of form, are, and have been, important factors in the Tanzanian economy. They generate income and employment opportunities along with much needed inputs and consumer products. In particular, most sources on Tanzania indicate small businesses becoming increasingly important in practical terms during the economic crisis in the early 1980s. Equally important, however, is the observation that formal sector activities are by and large shunned by entrepreneurs.

Supporting institutions for small scale industries

This section looks at two support organisations for small scale industries in Tanzania which both are integral parts of the institutional framework outlined so far, namely SIDO and NBC. Aside from these, there are a number of domestic and international NGOs that operate in support of SSIs in the country. However, due to insufficient information, these organisations will not discussed here,.

The Small Industries Development Organisation[122]   In 1966 the National Small Industries Corporation (NSIC) was established to promote development of small scale industries in Tanzania. Following the 1973 Party Directives SIDO, a parastatal under the Ministry of Industry, replaced the rather malfunctioning NSIC.[123] The principal task of SIDO was to promote SSIs and to coordinate all policies and programmes towards SSIs in the country. It is interesting to note, though, that SIDO's small industry development plans have not been incorporated into the national development plans, and that the Small-scale Development Plans have tended to lag behind the national plans. From the Government SIDO receives limited financial support, which has declined since the early 1980s both in absolute numbers and as share of SIDO's total development budget. Between 1974 and 1984, 56 per cent of SIDO's total development budget was covered by domestic resources, the rest came from foreign sources.[124] Eriksson has calculated that for each year between 1981 and 1992 SIDO reported losses exceeding TAS 5 million. In fact, SIDO belonged to the top ten loss making parastatals in Tanzania not less than five times during this period it.[125]

The primary function of SIDO's industrial extension service is to provide small entrepreneurs with information about industries suitable for immediate establishment as well as production techniques required in these industries. To this end, SIDO has a network of Regional Extension Offices which are supposed to conduct economic surveys, prepare techno-economic profiles and feasibility studies, and assist small enterprises in procurement of raw materials and marketing. Selection of the industries that are to be promoted is done according to the priorities set by

---

[122] Unless otherwise stated, this section draws on SIDO [(1984?)].
[123] Havnevik et al. (1985), pp. 64-5.
[124] Ibid., pp. 125, 267-70.
[125] Eriksson (1993b), p. 68.

the BIS and the Government, and there is a possibility to mix projects proposed by entrepreneurs (tailor made projects) and projects initiated by SIDO (open projects). Between 1976 and 1983, SIDO conducted 60 industry prospect studies, 819 feasibility studies, 698 technical profiles and it held 141 technical seminars. Bagachwa reports that SIDO prepared 609 feasibility studies, 565 technical profiles and 82 market surveys between 1985 and 1989. Most of these industry extension services were carried out in urban areas.[126]

Under the 'hire purchase scheme', SIDO is responsible for procuring machinery, equipment and tools and renting them to SSIs on a hire purchase basis at interests rates below the commercial. After the last instalment has been paid, ownership of the property is transferred to the SSI. Between 1974 and 1984, TAS 53.3 million were authorised in hire purchase loans for the use in rural areas while TAS 256.5 million, or some 83 per cent of the total funds for the period, were approved for urban areas. Between 1985 and 1989 a total of 203 projects amounting to TAS 287 million were financed under the hire purchase scheme.[127] Investigations show extreme delays or non-delivery of machinery in some cases, while on the other hand there are instances of machinery being delivered without SIDO first having received the required down payment from the entrepreneur, as well as SIDO disbursing loans exceeding the amounts authorised.[128]

Through the industrial estate programme SIDO provides basic infrastructure, that is roads, water, sewage, power and telecommunication for factories inside its industrial estates. In 1985 a total of 154 sheds were in operation in 16 estates. SIDO is the owner of all sheds in an industrial estate, while the entrepreneurs pay rent for using them.[129] Bagachwa identifies a number of problems encountered by the programme, such as 'intermittent supply of water, power interruptions, lack of raw materials, scarcity of experienced entrepreneurs and low recovery of rental incomes (estimated to be 10 per cent)'.[130] Reviews have shown that projects inside the industrial estates exhibit higher unit costs, lower levels of capacity utilisation and higher machine intensity than industries outside.

Finally, to provide proven technology and to minimise 'entrepreneur's expenses on research and product development',[131] SIDO runs transfer of technology programmes. One of its major programmes has been the Sister Industry Programme (SIP). Under the SIP, Swedish small scale enterprises (senior sisters) provided Tanzanian SSIs (junior sisters) with know-how, supply of machinery, start-up raw materials and initial training for entrepreneurs, managers and workers. The senior sisters also assisted in plant installation. This programme started in 1976 and was funded by the Swedish International Development Cooperation Agency. By 1990, 34 ventures employing some 1,400 people had been established under SIP at a cost

---

[126] Bagachwa (1993), p. 103.
[127] Ibid., p. 102.
[128] Havnevik et al., pp. 210-13.
[129] Ibid., pp. 164-75.
[130] Bagachwa (1993), p. 101.
[131] SIDO [(1984?)], p. 35.

of USD 75 million (constant 1990 prices).[132] SIP projects have been found to be relatively capital intensive and highly import dependent, and to have had rather limited employment generating effects. As a result of the foreign exchange shortage many SIP industries operated below capacity level, although, in some cases, this constraint resulted in backward linkages because the SIP enterprise was forced to find local suppliers. Managerial constraints have been identified as the major challenge for the survival and development of SIP industries.[133]

SIDO has various other programmes for entrepreneurial development which cover both basic skill development and upgrading of skills by entrepreneurs, managers and workers. Finally, SIDO also targets the handicraft sector with technical and financial services as well as help with training and marketing.

The National Bank of Commerce In 1981, the NBC established the NBC Term Finance Unit to deal with SSI and SSE[134] financing, through which it provides medium and long term loans along with consultation services and seminars to the sector. A maximum of 80 per cent of an investment could be borrowed for up to ten years at commercial interest rates. According to Bagachwa, 116 SSE projects had received loans worth TAS 508 million as of June 1990. However, as pointed out by the author, funding of small scale operations by the NBC has suffered from substantial delays; on average some 79 weeks may elapse between the submission of the loan application and the disbursement of the loan itself, but cases of delays of up to three years have been reported. Procurement of equipment and tools by the NBC in Dar es Salaam, and the subsequent distribution of these, has been an additional source of delay for small scale clients.[135]

Strömberg has investigated the loan procedure adopted by the NBC. In order to be granted a loan from the NBC, a small scale industry entrepreneur has to provide two references and deposit TAS 100,000 in a savings account with the bank. In addition to this, a feasibility study, the memorandum of association, the corporation certificate and a letter of intent to borrow have to be presented, along with financial statements covering the last five years of operation, which should have been audited at least once during this period. The NBC also requires real property or fixed assets as collateral for the loan, which has to be fully secured. Since 1991, the situation for micro enterprises[136] has been somewhat different as lending with-

---

[132] Bagachwa (1993), p. 112.

[133] Carlsson et al. (1988), pp. 71-7.

[134] See page 189 for NBC's distinction between SSIs and SSEs.

[135] Bagachwa (1993), p. 103, and (1995), p. 35.

[136] Strömberg actually refers to these enterprises as informal enterprises, but since she does not follow the same legal distinction of informal and formal as done in this chapter, the usage of this particular term was found inappropriate. All other evidence in Strömberg's paper indicates that the term micro enterprises, regardless of legal form, is a more accurate description of the circumstances referred to in the passage. However, it is not clear if Strömberg is also referring to the distinctions between SSIs and SSEs made by NBC, i.e. if micro enterprises (or the informal sector) imply SSIs as defined by NBC's threshold level, and if the term small scale industries also is applicable to SSEs as defined by the lending threshold of the NBC.

out collateral was introduced for this group;[137] small scale units in this category need only to deposit TAS 30,000 in a holding account and present a project profile (for which help is offered by the Community Development Officers) to be entitled to a loan from the NBC. The NBC treats the holding account as security, and has the right to auction off the project machinery if the loan is not repaid in due time.

In 1995 the NBC reported less than a 50 per cent recovery rate on its loans to small scale units, and to have frozen all lending facilities to this sector. The freeze did not apply to micro enterprises, however, as these loans were backed up by foreign currency funds provided by international aid organisations.[138]

Small scale supporting institutions and transaction costs

As a supporting institution SIDO deserves special attention; it is the implementing as well as coordinating body for policies targeting small scale industry development in Tanzania. It is in this light that the separation of SIDO's Small-scale Industrial Development Plans from the National Development Plans (and the low levels of financial resources provided by the Government) should be seen. Apart from being an outcome of the hardening economic situation facing Tanzania in the early 1980s, this may be a further manifestation of the vaguely defined role of small scale industries as outlined so far. To explore fully how, and to what extent, SIDO's undertakings generate or reduce transaction costs, a full evaluation of its operations is needed, which is beyond the scope of this chapter. However, some general implications may be presented here.

In theory, many of SIDO's support programmes would result in reduced transaction costs for small scale industries - if implemented properly. For instance, the industry extension service could reduce information asymmetries and high search costs facing small scale industries in the economy of Tanzania. Easy access to information about foreign and domestic market demand, new technologies, potential suppliers and emerging subcontracting opportunities would significantly lower ex ante transaction costs for many SSIs. Furthermore, improved access to tools, machinery and equipment at a reasonable cost under a hire purchase scheme, as well as access to physical infrastructure in an industrial estate, would reduce costs in terms of time and money spent in trying to operate in an economy marked by shortages, as in the case of Tanzania.

Unfortunately, SIDO seems to have experienced operational problems due to lack of a clearly defined set of priorities, poor communication between the headquarters in Dar es Salaam and the regional offices (as well as between the industrial estates and the regional offices), and a shortage of staff with the required high level of technical and economical competence. As a result, feasibility studies have often been weak and projects have suffered from badly specified technical requirements. Numerous sources of delays within the SIDO framework seem to

---

[137] Bagachwa (1996), p. 35.
[138] Strömberg (1995), pp. 65-7.

have emerged mainly due to organisational problems.[139] Thus, SIDO may work as an example of the distinction made by Khalil between institutions and organisations; the weak support provided by SIDO seems to stem mainly from its organisational problems (the organisation as an agent), and not from its underlying set of norms, rules and regulations (the institution as social constraints).[140]

For the individual SSI, this implies that much of the transaction cost reducing effects of a SIDO programme have been lost, since the SSI may not be able to by-pass information and distribution bottlenecks by participating in the programme. When entering a SIDO programme, the SSI might have expected to avoid transaction cost increasing activities such as searching for adequate information about markets and suppliers, and to reduce insecurity and high monitoring and enforcement costs. However, the SSI has entered into a contract with SIDO which has to be monitored and enforced, a situation that does not necessarily mean that its position is stronger *vis-à-vis* SIDO that it would be *vis-à-vis* any other contractual partner. As a result of problems experienced when dealing with SIDO, such as long delays and poor quality of implemented infrastructure, entrepreneurs in Tanzania may have lost trust in SIDO's ability to promote their activities. It is also worth noting that a major share of SIDO's development budget has been channelled into supporting manufacturing units in industrial estates, which implies that a substantial part of SIDO resources has reduced transaction costs (in the best of cases) for only a rather limited number of SSIs operating inside its estates.

Lack of access to credit is often identified by the SSIs themselves as one of the most binding constraints, particularly when undertaking new business investments,[141] leaving a valuable transaction cost reducing role to the NBC. In particular ex ante transaction costs could be reduced if the NBC was able to provide SSIs with easily accessed information about availability and cost of credits, and if it had simple and fast application procedures. The time factor seems to constitute a major source of transaction costs for SSIs when dealing with the NBC, just as with registration and licensing. An average time lag of 79 weeks - or some one and a half years - between application for and disbursement of a loan implies SSIs having to find alternative sources of funding. This can be done by turning to the informal financial sector, or by securing funds by allowing partners into the business. Both strategies could be expected to result in only rather moderate amounts being borrowed, and, most possible, on a short time basis.

When it comes to simple application procedures it should not be forgotten that, in accordance with good banking practice, the NBC has to adopt a certain degree

---

[139] Havnevik et al. (1985), Chapter 5.

[140] See the section on the institutional setting, page 169, for a brief description, or Khalil (1995) for a more thorough investigation.

[141] E.g., see Levy (1993); and Parker et al. (1995). In Levy's study, lack of access to finance was identified as the principal constraint by all the surveyed small scale industries within the furniture sector in Tanzania. In the study made by Parker et al., access to finance was not regarded as a primary constraint on current operations as 37 per cent of the sampled enterprises had just received a loan, while 90 per cent of the firms cited cost of credit and 50 per cent cited access to credit as major constraints for undertaking new investments.

of formality when dealing with loan applications from businesses of any size. However, these requirements tend to mean higher transaction costs for small scale units than for large scale. Apart from the likelihood of various charges taking a larger share of the total budget of an SSI than of a large company, most SSIs have only limited ability to internalise administrative functions and employ financial managers with the skills and time to deal with financial institutions. Instead, SSIs have to rely on external services for tasks such as accounting and auditing, which, generally speaking, will impose search, bargaining and monitoring costs on the SSI, assuming that the market for such producer services is not fully efficient. Added to which, it may be noted, the time spent dealing with the NBC reduces the time that can be spent on other, profit generating activities.

Finally, it is interesting to note that when dealing with the NBC, and maybe also with SIDO, there is an advantage in being *very* small, as opposed to just small. As long as a company belongs to the category of micro enterprises many of the transaction cost generating rules and requirements can be avoided, and access to credit may actually be made easier. A micro enterprise which grows, and graduates, so to speak, into an SSI, faces stiffening requirements; collateral requirements being but one example. Although this can in part be explained by the financial needs growing with the company, it indicates a situation in which there are few financial incentives for small scale industries to develop and grow. Thus, in Tanzania, large scale and long term SSI investment may be hampered by both lack of timing and access to formal credits, as well as by a financial institutional setting which adversely affects the growth of small scale enterprises over a certain threshold level.

Concluding remarks

Most of the outlined sources of transaction costs apply equally well to both small and large scale industries operating in Tanzania. However, the analysis thus far has carried certain implications for formal small scale industries. First and foremost, formal small scale industries and traditional cooperatives in effect happened to symbolise two aspects alien to the ideology and the policy framework that prevailed in Tanzania for almost 20 years, namely private ownership and small scale. In other words, formal small scale industries can be expected to have suffered from the combination of a generally hostile attitude towards private business, and from an unclear role of small scale industries within the industrial policy framework. Apart from the general insecurity about private property rights and its expected adverse effect on the expansion of private - including small scale - businesses in Tanzania, property rights have also tended to restrict SSIs in their dealings with the financial sector. For instance, since land is formally owned by the state and banks generally do not accept leasehold land titles as collateral, SSIs are usually limited in their borrowing to the value of the physical construction on the land itself. Furthermore, in the industrial estates run by SIDO, that agency is the owner of the buildings in which SSIs operate. This leads either to SSIs being restricted to SIDO programmes in order to obtain credits, or that an agreement has to be worked out between SIDO and a bank, most probably the NBC.

Second, formal rules and regulations as formulated by Party and Government, may have had sever transaction cost effects on small scale industries. The examples given of licensing requirements, of taxation procedures and of access to credits, all indicate high transaction costs for SSIs. These activities involve substantial information gathering about the correct procedures to follow as well as any possible exemptions from regulations, all of which are extremely time consuming and often costly. On the whole, legislation and regulatory practices in Tanzania do not seem to have identified the particular needs of SSIs as compared to large scale enterprises, which in any case have more resources to work through the necessary processes and paperwork.[142] In addition, transaction costs of this sort may be increased by the prevalence of corruption in the public sector. For example, Tripp found that in order to work through all the bureaucracy to obtain a business licence, an entrepreneur may have to give bribes amounting to three or four times the cost of the actual licence.[143] Moreover, licences must be renewed annually and this requires clearance from a number of public authorities, which, according to Levy, often requires side payments or kickbacks. Levy found 'lubrication' to be a pervasive feature of the tax collection system too, with tax officials sometimes visiting firms to 'negotiate' their tax burden as often as five times a year (on average) for sales taxes, and two times a year for income tax.[144]

Third, small scale industries in general can be expected to have been excluded from one of the greater market opportunities in Tanzania: the parastatals and the public sector. Given the incentive structure and the decision making process, as outlined, parastatals have had little incentive to turn to SSIs for purchase or outsourcing. This particular situation may be changing though, as the economic reform measures finally reach the parastatal sector.[145] Preferential treatment of parastatals, regulations on resource allocation (including allocation of foreign currency) and on distribution often excluded formal SSIs from having easy access to inputs, foreign currency and imports. However, this is the field in which economic reforms have been most extensive, and transaction costs in this areas may be decreasing in Tanzania. The economic reforms have also led to intensified competition in some sectors, which may reduce the risk of opportunism and failed contracts and, thus, lead to reduced transaction costs as the risk of information asymmetries declines. In the process there are both winners and losers among the SSIs.[146]

---

[142] Bagachwa (1996), p. 28.

[143] Tripp (1989), p. 31.

[144] Levy (1993), p. 76.

[145] Levy reports that seven of his sampled 20 SSIs in the furniture sector had won their first tenders to supply government agencies in the 1980s. Six out of the seven had done this after 1987 (see Levy 1993, p. 68).

[146] Bagachwa (1996), pp. 28-31.

198

Moving on to more general findings, the thinking behind the economic system established after the adoption of the Arusha Declaration in 1967, does not appear to have concerned itself much with lowering overall transaction costs in the markets of Tanzania. On the contrary, the economic system can be accused of having increased transaction costs by creating information asymmetries, distribution bottlenecks and severe shortages. There are reasons to believe that formal small scale industries have been more adversely affected by these transaction costs than large scale industries, and that such transaction costs may be one reason behind the growth of the second economy in Tanzania during the late 1970s and early 1980s. Moreover, transaction costs can be expected to remain high - maybe even increase in some areas - during the transitional period, as uncertainty among economic agents is high and as many of the main features of the old system still remain in place despite the reforms.

A number of empirical studies have shown that there are active and innovative entrepreneurs in Tanzania, not least within the informal sector, and the question now is how to incorporate these into the formal economy. This chapter has pointed out that certain obstacles preventing this from happening are a built in feature of the institutional framework. The obstacles referred to here are: the licensing and registration procedures, and the requirement of yearly renewals; the system of taxation collection; issues regarding property rights and collateral; complex and time consuming credit procedures; and the still uncertain position of private businesses and the threat of nationalisation.

A firm may successfully avoid transaction costs connected with these obstacles by staying out of the formal sector. One way of doing this is to remain very small in size and expand operations by adding new, equally small business to the existing ones. Thus, some aspects of the institutional setting may work both as a disincentive to enterprises currently outside the formal sector to enter it, and as an obstacle to dynamic growth of small scale enterprises in Tanzania.

199

8 Institutions and SSIs: some lessons from diverse experiences

Örjan Sjöberg

'Why', Alice Amsden recently asked, 'isn't the whole world experimenting with the East Asian model to develop?'[1] It is true, after all, that although it did take quite some time before the world noticed what was afoot in East Asia, the miracle is now recognised as such by all and sundry. Indeed, references to the example set by and the lessons to be learnt from these economies abound. Scholars have written at length on the salient features of success and numerous conferences have been organised to disseminate the findings.[2] Policy oriented treatises, ranging from the efforts of the World Bank or the Asian Bank of Developement to individuals concerned that newcomers to the scene, such as independent Eritrea, must not repeat the mistakes of others but rather learn from positive example, have multiplied.[3] Yet few countries outside East and South East Asia appear to have consciously modelled attempts at full scale reform on the experience of the Dragons.

The very reason for this perhaps deplorable state of affairs is indicative of the difficulties in transferring experiences from one country to the next. For one thing, there is precious little agreement as to what constitutes the basic building blocs of East Asian economic success. At its most unrefined, two positions can be identified. On the one hand, the so called Washington consensus argues that the key to the success can be found in proper macro-economic management, export orientation and in avoiding undue government interference under the guise of industrial policy.[4] To the extent that East Asian governments have been found to interfere, they have done so in a market conform fashion.[5] On the other, from a variety of angles observers have come to the conclusion that the skilled implementation of ambitious yet selective industrial policies, in and of itself or in combination with a unique institutional and cultural setting, have served the Dragons much better than neo-classical prescriptions would have done. In fact, or so Amsden argues, the 'late learners' of East Asia have a proven track record of inducing industrialisation by, as it were, getting prices wrong.[6]

---

[1] Amsden (1994).
[2] Stein (1994), and (1995); ILO (1996); Wallace (1997), to mention but a few.
[3] Of which World Bank (1993) or ADB (1997) and Yohannes (1995), respectively, may serve as examples.
[4] World Bank (1993).
[5] Ibid., Chapter 2, and, e.g., Wang and Thomas (1993).
[6] Amsden (1989).

From the perspective of the adherents of universal principles, the problem of transferability is a minor one. It basically amounts to the willingness and ability of governments to adhere to prudent economic policies; indeed, the pursuit of such policies is what the East Asian experience is all about. Advocates of heterodox positions are less sanguine in this respect. Those arguing the importance and uniqueness of Asian culture are likely to find the proposition that it is possible to replicate the East Asian model highly disputable, but also others find it appropriate to raise question marks. Amsden, for her part, concludes that such a transfer 'cannot be done by force-feeding one East Asian model to all poor countries';[7] rather lessons have to be learnt at the level of individual institutions or policy areas. Others reject the claim that conditions are so special that a similar approach to industrialisation and development would not be feasible elsewhere.[8] Yet, it may well be the case that this can only be done under conditions where liberalisation, deregulation and privatisation is put on hold until the other features of the model are securely in place.[9]

This is precisely the point, we would submit, where both discussions on the lessons of Asia for Africa and on the pros and cons of structural adjustment programmes run into difficulties. Firstly, many countries have little choice but to stabilise. No matter one's position on whether reforms should be gradual and based on a real appreciation of national strengths and weaknesses, or whether basically universal prescriptions apply across the entire spectrum of developing economies, little can be achieved if not at least a modicum of stability is instituted. This is as true of macro-economic stability as of its political counterpart. Secondly, structural adjustment, while perhaps a dire necessity, is often conducted according to standard templates with little regard for individual characteristics. If at all adjusted to local conditions, it is typically the outcome of politically charged negotiations between the donors and the recipient country rather than of judicious assessments of institutional features and peculiarities.

Nowhere is the above line of argument more salient than in those polities that share a socialist legacy. Not only are these countries almost invariably in urgent need of putting their macro-economy in order. They also share an institutional set-up that by no stretch of the imagination can be considered an ideal platform from which to launch an exacting programme of private sector based growth and modernisation. Under such circumstances stabilisation and structural adjustment as typically conceived are likely to be useful in rectifying some, perhaps even most, of the distortions that central planning or kindred socialist economic policies have generated over the years. Yet, although institutional adjustment in the guise of institutional destruction may prove beneficial and perhaps a vital necessity, this is not likely to be enough. Rather, chances are that new, superior institutions will not emerge to fill the void automatically.

---

[7] Amsden (1994), p. 628. In fact, Amsden goes one step further still, questioning the notion of the existence of *one* East Asian model.

[8] E.g., Lall (1996).

[9] Bräutigam (1994), p. 137.

Therefore, it is argued in this volume, institutional adjustment also presupposes a concern for both the nature of the process of adjustment in itself and the outcome of that process. However, this insight must not be construed as an excuse for interventionist policies as such (which, depending on the circumstances, may or may not be useful or desirable), but rather admonishes us to evaluate current and past policies and institutions with, in Major's terms, institutional efficiency in mind.[10] This is done here with respect to one particular type of economic activity, the fortune of which is often regarded as a prerequisite for healthy economic development to take place: small and medium sized manufacturing.

To this end the case studies presented in Chapters Four to Seven describe the institutional and policy setting that small scale industries have been made to operate within. The case studies do so by employing a transaction costs approach and by comparing three sets of economies: China and Vietnam, which adopted a centrally planned economy before the reforms of 1978 and the mid-1980s, respectively; India and Taiwan, which did not; and finally two African socialist polities that went to great lengths to institute socialist economic policies without ever intending or being able to introduce central planning in full. In all cases, the initial comparative advantages lay in the existence of an abundance of labour. For all but one, this is still true. Furthermore, China, Vietnam and India as well as Ethiopia and Tanzania, our two African case studies, still belong to the low income countries, with agriculture invariably being the most important sector in terms of employment. Only Taiwan has been able to move from being labour rich and capital poor to being capital rich and labour poor. Indeed, Taiwan is often quoted as an example of an economy which successfully altered economic policy in response to shifting comparative advantages.

In these six countries, small scale industries have faced varied economic environments, including being subject to strongly protective policies, as in India, and having the status of a legally banned sector, as in pre-reform China. Elsewhere, small scale industries have been forced into the straightjacket provided by central planning, as in Vietnam, or have by and large been confined to the informal sector, as in Ethiopia and Tanzania. Within these diverse settings, small firms have developed a range of strategies aimed at reducing transaction costs and mitigating the disadvantages of being small and vulnerable. These strategies may have evolved over time and have often had to be adapted to a changing political and economic climate. In fact, confining one's activities to the informal sector appears to have been one of the most frequently employed strategies devised to this end.

The overall factors affecting transaction costs have their roots in economic, political and social institutions, past internal and external circumstances and developments. Factors currently causing high transaction costs are identified mainly with institutional rigidity in India, the uncertainty of policy in China and Vietnam, and the sheer weight of ideological prejudices and bureaucratic red tape in Tanzania and Ethiopia. Only in Taiwan are small scale manufacturers, while not parti-

---

[10] Major (1994), p. 323.

cularly favoured, at least for the most part left to their own devices to an extent not seen elsewhere outside the informal micro-enterprise sector. Then as now this has paid off as Taiwan has been able to capture benefits from dispersed industrialisation and flexibility in export activities. With much delay, the same phenomenon can nowadays be observed in China and, to a lesser extent, in Vietnam, but is yet to make an impact on the economic performance of India, Ethiopia and Tanzania.

The dynamics of small firms analysed in each of the six case studies point to the factors that have supported or hindered the range of action and decision making of the small firm. Some of these factors are part of each nation's historical heritage and some are the by-products of changing formal and informal institutions. Contingency rather than necessity is the hallmark of the varied experiences of our chosen cases, yet in most of them ideological preferences and political goals have conspired to create conditions which are unsettlingly similar across our cases. Outcomes that are almost invariably adverse or at least strikes the observer as suboptimal abound.

In what follows, a short list of factors that appear to be common to all or most of our cases is outlined. Drawing upon a comparison of the national traits of the environment within which firms operate, features that are typical (and at times unique) to a particular country can be specified in a more orderly fashion. These are of considerable interest to the analyst intent on clarifying the impact of a given institutional framework on the actions of economic agents. Arguably still more important, however, are the instances where factors generic in nature can be found, the existence of which in part can be made evident through systematic comparisons of contrasts and similarities. In this chapter, therefore, the focus is primarily set on factors that are shared by the six countries concerned, or that point in a common direction, without therefore neglecting the variety of experiences across these case studies.

Historical factors and strategies of development

The countries under consideration here are distinct in terms of natural resource endowments, historical development and development strategies pursued during the post-war era. Taiwan, a small country with poor natural endowment, gained from compensating for this deficiency through successful outward orientation, though this followed on a period of relatively mild import substitution. On the other hand, India and China are endowed with abundant natural resources. As far as mineral wealth, energy and soils are concerned, Ethiopia and Tanzania must be classified as relatively resource poor, if not as poorly endowed as Taiwan. The legacy of colonialism remains a contentious issue, but it may be safely stated that Taiwan was left in a better position than were India and in particular Tanzania. In Taiwan, the Japanese colonisation resulted in a relatively well-developed infrastructure that aided in the dispersed industrialisation, of which small firms were an important part.

As for the development strategies adopted, the two African states decided in favour of import substitution; following the Arusha Declaration of 1967 and the revolution of 1974, respectively, this strategy was made to go to ever greater lengths before reluctantly being modified and softened during the late 1980s and early 1990s. India opted for strict if standard import substitution combined with elements of central planning of producer goods industry. China and Vietnam established an extremely autarkic developmental strategy. In all instances, this implied an inward orientation, if to varying degrees. Furthermore, the nature of the developmental strategies adopted was biased towards heavy industry, which was pursued at the expense of other important sectors, especially agriculture. This inflicted heavy social and economic costs to the Indian, Chinese and Vietnamese economies. In Tanzania and Ethiopia, where industry was also favoured at the expense of agriculture, even under the more radical periods governments for the most part appear to have sensed the lack of realism in any plan to put too much emphasis on the producer goods sector. Yet modern and relatively large scale industrial manufacturing has taken priority throughout. In Taiwan, the developed state of agriculture and infrastructure was of considerable help during the initial period of industrialisation and this balanced development is an important factor in countries where a large part of the population depend on agriculture.

The role of agriculture

As noted above, agriculture has consistently taken second seat to industry. However, when better conditions have been granted, relative agricultural prosperity and rural development have accompanied high growth rates and healthy non-farm activities. China and Taiwan provide good cases in point. In both these countries established linkages with the rural sector in general and agriculture in particular proved advantageous to the efforts to industrialise. In Taiwan, a net transfer of resources out of agriculture to the benefit of industry did take place through fiscal means, without therefore stifling crop and animal husbandry production to the extent it happened in those countries where socialist agricultural policies were pursued with a vengeance. Once China turned its policies around in 1978, not only did agricultural production expand and rural incomes increase; rural, dispersed industrialisation also took off. In fact, rural industries absorbed most of the increases in rural purchasing power accruing from the early post-1978 reforms, thereby providing a healthy basis of expansion. In Tanzania and Ethiopia, this is yet to happen, while the record of Vietnam is mixed: production if not necessarily incomes have grown rapidly as a result of reforms instituted in the mid-1980s. It is noteworthy, however, that reforms made an impact only once macro-economic stability had been achieved a few years subsequent to the original launch of reform.

Historically, periods of agricultural neglect or natural disasters have had their impact on development of small firms and industrialisation in general. A healthy agriculture helped labour absorption in the non-agricultural sector through its forward linkages; and this in turn helped both agriculture, in terms of higher marginal productivity of existing inputs, and the non-farm sector in terms of growth. Neglect of agriculture often caused distress industries to be set up, without the required skills and market for further growth. The experiences of China during the collapse of the Great Leap Forward come to mind; Ethiopia, India and Vietnam are other examples.

The importance of infrastructure

The importance of physical and social infrastructure is clearly seen in aiding industrialisation, especially the small firm sector. India, China and Vietnam all have a large population living in rural areas and the poor state of infrastructure has hindered the flow of gains to the rural sector from the more resourceful urban sector. If anything, this would appear still more important in the cases of Tanzania and Ethiopia. Inadequate transport, unreliable communication and poor education have been constraints on the small firms in all of these countries. Being small, they suffer the disadvantages of not being able to internalise, or else compensate for, the deficiencies in the provision of public utilities, services and other forms of assistance. This has resulted in a lack of exposure to competitive units, discouraged growth and raised transaction costs to small operators no matter the industry. In China the extensive rural sector reforms launched in 1978 alleviated this problem somewhat but the geographical vastness, as in India, makes balanced regional development a difficult task since the investment in infrastructure has to come mainly from external sources as far as small firms are concerned.

Finally, we may note that literacy levels have been quite high in Taiwan, China and also Vietnam (compared to other low income countries). This has a bearing on the quality of entrepreneurial skills and imparts flexibility to the small firm. The reforms and transition periods provide opportunities as well as uncertainties and a high human capital endowment can go a long way in determining the timing of responses of the small firm. Taiwan benefited from the influx of skills from the mainland and from development assistance, whereas the Cultural revolution erased any such advantages China might have had as part of its pre-1949 or early socialist legacy.

Flexibility in labour markets

The efficiency of labour markets has helped in reducing transaction costs for the small firm. In the rapid industrialisation phase of Taiwan, competitive labour markets efficiently adjusted labour supply and demand, and without much intervention by the government, it served to minimise search costs. In China, immobility was policy induced and there was often an imbalance between supply and demand of certain skills. This was compensated by a reasonably good rural educational system and the enforced lack of large scale rural-urban migration which, at least in the short run, served to help local community governments bent on making the most of opportunities that came with economic reform. Vietnam and India suffer, as do Tanzania and Ethiopia, from concentration of skilled labour in a few urban centres and at least in the case of the former two this has been made worse by governmental intervention in the form of restrictive legislation.

While the smallest of the small firms do not depend on hired labour, labour regulations have resulted in firms operating on the borders of illegality or with an outright disregard for current safety standards and similar legislation. Labour unions were banned in Taiwan, and in India they were a problem of the larger of the small enterprises. In fact, there has been a high degree of inefficiency in the labour market, as expressed for instance by policy induced segmentation and the low productivity of labour through out much of the small scale industrial sector.[11]

The role of the state and small industry policy

Unlike what one is sometimes led to believe,[12] the role of the state has been very prominent in all the case studies presented and not only in the centrally planned economies among them. In China and Vietnam, until the advent of reforms, state intervention was direct and all-pervasive. In Taiwan government intervention was more indirect as far as the small firms are concerned, and in India the government assisted small firms both directly and indirectly. Small firms have been given the most promotional assistance in India, but the elaborate organisational structure built for serving small industry perpetuated an institutional rigidity that instead served to raise transaction costs for the small firm. Multiplicity of bureaucratic procedures and red tape gave way to corruption of government officials in securing approvals, permits, licenses and the like. While the product reservation and small industry policy in general was intended to achieve balanced small industry development, in reality the target groups were not reached fully. Although genuine ventures did avail themselves of the assistance provided, there were a number of ghost units that misdirected the resources to the large firms. This is all in marked contrast to Ethiopia and Tanzania, where socialistic distrust of small firms and entrepreneurs generally appears to have been interspersed with periods of, at best, benign neglect.

However, in all of the above cases the attitude towards small industry has been far from outright predatory, as was frequently the case during the height of socialist policies and central planning in China or in the Democratic Republic of Vietnam. In particular in China, the harsh measures taken during the socialisation drive created a vast amount of insecurity in terms of the government's attitude towards the private sector. This was arguably the most important factor raising

---

[11] For an illustrative case study, see the work by Mazumdar (1991) on the Indian textile industry.
[12] Most recently in Krueger (1997), pp. 9-10.

uncertainty for small firms; in fact, this situation has remained an important factor to be reckoned with well into the period of serious and substantive economic reforms. The small units in the communes or collectives, however, benefited from favourable linkages with the government and state enterprises.

In general, the heavy industry bias of China, Vietnam and India did adversely affect small scale manufacturing activities, and this was partly because the nature of products of heavy industry did not enable subcontracting with the smaller units. This is true of most countries pursuing the Big Push in steel and iron production. Indeed, it is a standard feature of the centrally planned or shortage economy. More specifically, in China the policy towards small scale manufacturing activities was anything between supportive and predatory. In Vietnam it was generally non-supportive, though the small scale sector was at times tolerated, at other times barely so. But also the relationship between small firms and the government in Taiwan was one of nonchalance; in India it was characterised by mutual distrust and contempt of the behaviour and performance of the other.

Instead, in China, Vietnam and India, as was the case in Tanzania and socialist Ethiopia, budgetary revenue was used to defray investment in state owned industry and for the recurrent expenditure of that sector. Little was deployed to the benefit of the private sector, presumably even less so for the benefit of small scale manufacturers. Also in Taiwan outlays on capital investment, physical and human capital have been high. Defence has been an important claimant on public funds in both Taiwan and China, perhaps even more so at times in Ethiopia. Unlike in the latter country, however, the budgets in Taiwan and China have shown surpluses for the most part and government savings have contributed to the impressive gross domestic savings ratio. This has had the beneficial effect of not inducing or contributing towards high levels of inflation, in itself a factor of uncertainty for producing firms. As such, it is in marked contrast to the other four, were soft budget constraints have led to public sector deficits, which in turn have necessitated large scale borrowing from internal and external sources in maintaining economic stability. To the extent that the state budget has been shielded from the ill effects of soft budget constraints, the banking sector may have been made to shoulder part of the burden, thus making access to formal finance difficult for small scale firms.

Arguably the most important role of state, however, is that it should allow a level playing field for small industry, and a passive role for the government would serve as well, if not better, than active involvement in small industry production. The cases of Taiwan and India serve to support this point of view. Harassment of small industry, as in pre-reform China, is definitely not part of a conducive environment. Indeed, in designing reforms a major issue to be resolved is the degree of intervention of the government in the dynamics of small firms. The other side of the story is to make small firms abide by the law, since most of them have hitherto existed on the border of legality, and avoided payment to government of any kind. Although the informalisation of the small scale sector is sometimes idealised as beneficial to the economy as a whole, we would concur with observers such as de

Soto that by and large formal sector activities are much to be preferred, not least on grounds of transactional efficiency.[13] Furthermore, a preponderance of formal sector activities would provide some help towards the end of rationalisation of the tax structure and a pressure to ease the regulatory framework for small scale enterprises. On the other hand, it goes without saying that the state has a considerable responsibility for making this a profitable and realistic proposition to the average entrepreneur.

Financial markets

One such sector where de Soto's argument is of particular relevance is finance. Informalisation denies entrepreneurs and firms the possibility of drawing on sources of formal credit. In fact, the case studies reveal that small firms have not relied on the formal financial markets in securing their credit needs. This is true of all the countries studied, since the financial markets are not well developed. The banking system has been captive to the dictates of the government in most cases, and monetary policy has not been used actively to aid the industrialisation process, except to finance government investment. Specialised banks have been established to cater to industry, including in some countries small industry (e.g., in India), with the intention of direct firm level assistance. The benefits appear not to have been very substantial, however, because of the elaborate procedures typically introduced and the correspondingly large room for subjective interpretation by the officials in charge. Lack of information regarding benefits available and inadequate transparency of allocation procedures have also led to a few firms cornering the benefits to the exclusion of the great majority. The dominant problem in most cases is not availability of capital as such, but access to capital as exists. This access has been denied to firms because of scant information and an insistence on too many formalities, formal licensing only being one of them. Even in the success story of Taiwan, in the absence of an efficient financial market high household savings have been a major source of enterprise capital.

The formal capital market has thus been out of reach of small industries and as in all six countries capital markets remain inadequately developed, they have been forced to turn elsewhere. Informal capital markets exist, for instance, in Vietnam which transact in assets like land and buildings in providing enterprise capital. There and elsewhere personal or family networks are actively used to raise funds for investment purposes, as are rotating savings associations and similar traditional institutions. The low reliance on formal financial markets has contributed to higher transaction costs on the one hand and prevented large scale expansion opportunities for the small firm on the other. In India, entry into modern small industry is easy, since the banking system has allocated a large share of resources for such technology intensive industries, but in the absence of well developed product mar-

---

[13] De Soto (1989), especially Chapters 5 and 8.

209

kets, repayment is a problem and the resulting closure of units implies that survival is difficult. The financial market has been dominated by the government, and savings, though quite high in countries such as India and Vietnam, have not been channelled into productive investment. In countries that do not have such an enviable record with respect to savings, such as Ethiopia and Tanzania, the difficulties facing the aspiring entrepreneur are of course worse still.

Political stability and policy certainty

Small firms have flourished under conditions of political and economic stability. The certainty that political stability may impart to the economic environment reduces transaction costs in that it permits medium to long term planning for the small firm. In the period under consideration here five out of the six countries considered (Ethiopia being the exception here) have experienced a reasonably stable political climate, with an absence of coups and insurgencies. However, as the case of India shows, political stability does not automatically warrant growth. It is at best a necessary condition. Macro-economic stability has not always been the top priority of the countries studied, with the more traditionally socialist among them suffering the most. In India and Taiwan, however, exogenous shocks have for the most part been quickly brought under control through appropriate internal adjustments. Increasingly, this insight has also spread to the socialist four among our six cases, with China and Vietnam stealing the march on Ethiopia and Tanzania.

This must not be taken to imply that political stability even as combined with prudent macro-economic policies automatically ensures the growth of small firms. Centralised political systems, with a rigid bureaucracy in charge of executing from the top down the decisions taken by the ruling party is an institutional constraint in its own right. It is so on account of being inflexible on the one hand and has a propensity to succumb to corruption at all levels on the other. In fact, small firms in China, Ethiopia, Tanzania and Vietnam have suffered this form of uncertainty, and until recently perhaps more so in China where also informal sector entrepreneurship was effectively circumscribed. Furthermore, in the case of long-standing one party states - four of which are represented among our case studies - political stability has not gone hand in hand with policy certainty in other vital areas. Waves of centralisation and decentralisation and sudden changes in attitudes towards the private sector have placed small firms in a vulnerable position and increased uncertainty as an integral part of the economic environment.

Horizontal and vertical linkages

A final point worth mentioning here is the benefits that linkages with larger firms may bring. Small firms in Taiwan have benefited enormously from both horizontal and vertical linkages. The role of MNCs in disseminating technology has been enhanced by the existence of the vertical linkages between larger firms and the small scale industrial sector. Although not universal, where links have been forged they have often served as a conduit for the diffusion of innovations. They have also served to make small scale manufacturers known to other producers and have often provided access to stable inter-firm relationships, thereby enhancing transactional stability and efficiency. For the smaller partner to the relationship, such links may also help mitigate the transactional disadvantages they often face simply by virtue of being small. State enterprises have also helped small industries through subcontracting and ancillarisation, but the poor payment record (as in India) has made it hard for the small firms to capitalise on this in full.

The centrally planned economies in our sample, including the two African ones, have proved less apt at making use of these linkages for the benefit of information flows and the dissemination of innovation to the small scale sector. For one thing, horizontal linkages were not developed; there is little need for such lateral links under central planning. To the extent that they existed beyond delivery and supply orders, they were informal in nature and primarily intended to alleviate shortages. For another, to the extent that it was permitted or encouraged, small scale industry was for the most part intended to serve local needs and to mobilise local resources. Only with the reforms has this situation begun to change, and not least in China the successful Township and Village Enterprise sector has found it advantageous to exploit the possibilities that vertical linkages with the large scale state owned sector brings.

This points to the importance of business associations and similar non-government agencies in contributing an organisational form through which institutional voids can be rectified. Not least important are organisations and institutions that allow the dissemination of information and improve the chances of contact and contract fulfilment over a wide range of enterprises of varying sizes and other characteristics. While the government can provide both the general economic stability under which small firms operate and an institutional setting conducive to entrepreneurship, quasi-government and private organisations can play a major role with respect to reducing transaction costs for the small firm.

In this regard, the Asian experience with business networks or networks of personal inter-relationships, such as captured by the Chinese concept of *guanxi*, may seem attractive if perhaps a typical feature that it is not possible to transfer. On a positive note, new start-ups in developed transition economies have been observed to make use of local network ties to counteract or reduce risk and uncertainty, thereby indicating that this may in fact provide for a way forward.[14] On the other hand, one must not jump to the conclusion that this is a panacea universal in character. For a start, even where conditions conducive to relational contracting exist, it is but seldom the case that it will help the small firm grow beyond the limits set by local relations based on trust. Similarly, it is not necessarily the case

---

[14] Kuczi and Makó (1996).

211

that ties based on proximity are of much help. This is so because the legacy of communism and shortages may well be an atmosphere of mistrust.[15]

Conclusion

The above list points to instances of convergence and divergence between our six case studies. In most respects it appears that the major dividing line is between unreformed central planners and those that, however reluctantly at times, may best be characterised as striving towards a market economy. It is quite clear that China at the time of Mao and Vietnam prior to the reforms of the mid-1980s did little to enhance the viability of the small scale industry. To the extent that it was not merely tolerated, the small scale industrial sector was assigned a secondary role with scant regard for the optimal conditions for their operations. As such, it frequently remained divorced from the economic and industrial mainstream.

Also in India, where official policy was much in favour of small scale production, small firms not only took second seat to the large scale ventures that we have come to associate with the development plans of the 1950s. The manner in which small scale manufacturing was promoted is indicative of a lack of understanding of the conditions under which small scale entrepreneurship is likely to flourish. Small firms where assigned, as it were, certain sectors or types of production where they enjoyed a high degree of protection. Little was done, however, to enhance the competitive strength of the entities so promoted.

This points to a general problem which to varying degrees can be detected across our full range of cases: little or no attention has been given to the fact that small scale industries suffer from diseconomies of scale at most stages of ordinary market transactions. Although there are considerable differences between economies, all fall short in this respect. What is more, in some instances politicians and planners in all six cases may, advertently or inadvertently, have contributed to the higher transaction costs of this particular sector. Not even Taiwan, where small and medium sized firms predominate, has the government refrained from adding obstacles to the progress of the small scale industrial sector. To put it in the language of the World Bank, the private sector in general and small scale firms in particular have been subject to the effects of a mild financial repression.[16] As a result, they were forced to rely upon informal credit or else consider other means to secure the requisite funds.

In fact, various institutional factors have worked to alter the threshold beyond which it has not been feasible to continue production. As compared to the centrally planned four in our sample, in Taiwan and to some extent in India the overall economic environment has helped keep this threshold at a reasonable level, but there has been a threshold none the less. In areas of governmental policy, infor-

---

[15] Gábor (1996).
[16] World Bank (1993), pp. 237-41.

mation bottlenecks have caused higher transaction costs to rural firms. Poor infrastructure has created a rural-urban fragmentation so as to minimise competition to the small firms. Although this may well have been thought of as desirable by entrepreneurs and regulators alike, it is likely to have been self-defeating in the long run. Not only does a local monopoly impair the ability of those so privileged to weather competition as and when it appears; it also raises transaction costs. Only in Taiwan, which is small in size, and those areas of the other five countries located in the immediate hinterland of major urban centres has this situation been avoided.

Underdeveloped technical and marketing support systems also raise transaction costs as do arbitrary legislation and an unreliable system of legal enforcement. Such a lack of transparency and predictability is often countered by the use of strong linkages with other firms; by resorting to relational contracting and drawing upon various forms of inter-personal trust transaction costs mitigating strategies can be devised. Thus, the control costs or the ex post transaction costs have been reduced through the use of informal institutions rather than legal systems. Although this is no doubt made easier, or more natural, where cultural norms stress trust and reputation, as in Chinese culture, a lack of resources and an ambiguous legal framework, as in India and Vietnam, have also strengthened the role of informal institutions, such as networking, kinship based associations and moral norms specific to defined sub-groups of society.[17]

The recourse to such institutions must be recognised as the second best solutions they actually are. As Platteau has observed, as expressions of particularised trust, networking and similar transaction costs mitigating devices are typically inferior to situations where generalised trust prevail.[18] African economies aspiring to emulate Asia's more successful policies therefore ought to consider policy action towards this end rather than resorting to the uncertain hope that particularistic networks will do the job for them. After all, as Fafchamps notes, this is one of the factors that tie micro-enterprises to the informal sector and that prevent these ventures from growing in the first place.[19] The same would be true of self-enforcing mechanisms, the linchpin of much of modern contract theory, which while clearly expedient would presumably be more effective from a transaction costs perspective were they to be extended also outside a specific group or contractual relationship.[20] If for no other reason, this is so simply because of the set-up costs implied by the need to repeatedly negotiate relevant clauses in contracts with a limited life span.

An increasingly favourable attitude toward small industry in previously centrally planned economies can go a long way in reducing ex ante transaction costs of the small firms. The large powers wielded by local governments in the pre-reform era

---

[17] Evidence to the effect that this is not merely a Chinese phenomenon, but also applies to India, is given by, e.g., Menning (1997).
[18] Platteau (1994b).
[19] Fafchamps (1994).
[20] Casson (1991), pp. 15-7.

can provide a useful resource for small industries, provided this does not encourage corruption and hence work to raise transaction costs. Especially in the period of transition, the increased competition and speculations about loss of previously well established markets creates a great deal of uncertainty, and as the case studies show, governmental and non-governmental agencies can help in the adjustment by improving availability and access to information. Above all, however, governments in the countries concerned face the challenge of convincing existing and prospective small scale manufacturers that the misplaced policies of the past will not once again appear on the agenda, let alone be repeated.

References

Abdela Jemal (1995), 'The Profile of Entrepreneurship in Ethiopia', in Ayalew Zegeye and Habteselassie Hagos (eds), *Proceedings of the First Annual Conference on Management in Ethiopia on the Theme Entrepreneurship*, Department of Management and Public Administration, Faculty of Business and Economics, Addis Ababa University, Addis Ababa, pp. 1-45.

ADB (1997), *Emerging Asia: Changes and Challenges*, Asian Development Bank, Manila.

Admit Zerihun (1994), 'Small and Rural Industries: an Area of Emphasis', in Getachew Yoseph and Abdulhamid Bedri Kello (eds), *The Ethiopian Economy: Problems and Prospects of Private Sector Development, Proceedings of the Third Annual Conference on the Ethiopian Economy*, n.p., Addis Ababa, pp. 91-123.

Admit Zerihun and Getachew Belay (1996), 'Private Sector Development in Ethiopia: an Assessment of the Enabling Environment and Incentive Structure', in Getachew Yoseph and Abdulhamid Bedri Kello (eds), *The Ethiopian Economy: Problems and Prospects of Private Sector Development, Proceedings of the Third Annual Conference on the Ethiopian Economy*, n.p., Addis Ababa, pp. 167-184.

Alem Abraha (1996), 'Trade Liberalisation and External Balance in Ethiopia: the Question of Sustainability', in Tadesse Abadi and Tekie Alemu (eds), *Adjustment in Ethiopia: Lessons for the Road Ahead*, n.p., Addis Ababa, pp. 1-22.

Alemayehu Lirenso (1990), 'Villagization: Policies and Prospects', in Siegfried Pausewang, Fantu Cheru, Stefan Brüne and Eshetu Chole (eds), *Ethiopia: Rural Development Options*, Zed, London, pp. 135-143.

Alemneh Dejene (1990), 'Peasants, Environment, Resettlement', in Siegfried Pausewang, Fantu Cheru, Stefan Brüne and Eshetu Chole (eds), *Ethiopia: Rural Development Options*, Zed, London, pp. 174-186.

Amsale Tshehaye (1996), 'Structural Adjustment and Legislation: a Lawyer's View', in Tadesse Abadi and Tekie Alemu (eds), *Adjustment in Ethiopia: Lessons for the Road Ahead*, n.p., Addis Ababa, pp. 201-208.

215

Amsden, Alice H. (1977), 'The Division of Labour is Limited by the Type of Market: the Case of the Taiwanese Machine Tool Industry', *World Development*, Vol. 5, No. 3, pp. 217-233.

Amsden, Alice H. (1988), 'Taiwan's Economic History: a Case of *Etatisme* and a Challenge to Dependency Theory', in Robert H. Bates (ed.), *Toward a Political Economy of Development: a Rational Choice Perspective,* University of California Press, Berkeley, CA, pp. 142-175.

Amsden, Alice H. (1994), 'Why isn't the whole world experimenting with the East Asian model to develop?: review of *The East Asian Miracle',* *World Development*, Vol. 22, No. 4, pp. 627-633.

Andargachew Tiruneh (1993), *The Ethiopian Revolution 1974-1987: a Transformation from an Aristocratic to a Totalitarian Autocracy*, Cambridge University Press, New York.

Andersen, Henny (1994), *Vietnam at the Crossroads*, Macroeconomic Studies 55/94, Swedish International Development Co-operation Authority, Stockholm.

Anderson, Dennis (1982), 'Small Industry in Developing Countries: a Discussion of Issues', *World Development*, Vol. 10, No. 11, pp. 913-948.

Åslund, Anders (1994), 'Lesson of the First Four Years of Systemic Change in Eastern Europe', *Journal of Comparative Economics*, Vol. 19, No. 1, pp. 22-38.

Åslund, Anders, Peter Boone and Simon Johnson (1996), 'How to Stabilize: Lessons from Post-communist Countries', *Brookings Papers on Economic Activity*, No. 1, pp. 217-313.

Assefa Admassie (1996), 'The Development of Small Scale Industries in Region 14 vis a vis Other Regions', paper for the Sixth Annual Conference on the Ethiopian Economy organised by the Department of Economics, Addis Ababa University, and the Ethiopian Economic Association, Nazret, 5-8 December.

Auty, Richard M. (1994a), 'Industrial Policy Reform in Six Large Newly Industrializing Countries: the Resource Curse Thesis', *World Development*, Vol. 22, No. 1, pp. 11-27.

Auty, Richard M. (1994b), *Economic Development and Industrial Policy: Korea, Brazil, Mexico, India and China*, Mansell, London.

Auty, Richard M. (1995), *Patterns of Development: Resources, Policy and Economic Growth*, Edward Arnold, London.

Ayalew Zegeye (1995), 'Entrepreneurial Development in Ethiopia: Some Notes', in Ayalew Zegeye and Habteselassie Hagos (eds), *Proceedings of the First Annual Conference on Management in Ethiopia on the Theme Entrepreneurship*, Department of Management and Public Administration, Faculty of Business and Economics, Addis Ababa University, Addis Ababa, pp. 46-73.

Bagachwa, Mboya S.D. (1993), 'Impact of Adjustment Policies on the Small-scale Enterprise Sector in Tanzania', in A.H.J. Helmsing and Th. Kolstee (eds), *Small Enterprise and Changing Policies: Structural Adjustment, Financial Policy and Assistance Programmes in Africa*, IT Publications, London, pp. 91-113.

Bagachwa, Mboya S.D. (1996), 'Macro Policy Framework for Small-scale Industries: a Tanzanian Case Study', paper prepared for the ILO Tripartite Policy Seminar on Macro-economic Policy Framework for Small-Scale Industries Development in Africa and Asia, Nairobi, 25-29 March.

Bagachwa, Mboya S.D. and T.L. Maliymkono (1990), *The Second Economy in Tanzania*, James Currey, London.

Bagachwa, Mboya S.D. and A. Naho (1995), 'Estimating the Second Economy in Tanzania', *World Development*, Vol. 23, No. 8, pp. 1387-1399.

Baker, Jonathan and Odd Eirik Arnesen (1992), 'The Challenges of Democratisation and Economic Transformation: a Situation and Perspective Analysis of Ethiopia', report for the Danish Ministry of Foreign Affairs, Copenhagen, March.

Bartholet, Jeffrey (1992), 'Ethiopia's Endangered Dream', *Newsweek*, 6 July, p. 19.

Baumol, William (1988), 'Is Entrepreneurship Always Productive?', *Journal of Development Planning*, No. 18, pp. 85-94.

Befekadu Degefe and Tesfaye Tafesse (1990), 'The Marketing and Pricing of Agricultural Products in Ethiopia', in Siegfried Pausewang, Fantu Cheru, Stefan Brüne and Eshetu Chole (eds), *Ethiopia: Rural Development Options*, Zed, London, pp. 111-120.

Ben-Ner, Avner and Egon Neuberger (1988), 'Towards and Economic Theory of the Firm in the Centrally Planned Economy: Transaction Costs, Internalization and Externalization', *Journal of Institutional and Theoretical Economics*, Vol. 144, No. 5, pp. 839-848.

Ben-Ner, Avner, Josef C. Brada and Egon Neuberger (1993), 'The Structure and Behaviour of Economic Organizations: Theoretical and Empirical Perspectives', *Journal of Comparative Economics*, Vol. 17, No. 2, pp. 201-206.

Beresford, Melanie (1989), *National Unification and Economic Development in Vietnam*, St. Martin's Press, New York.

Beresford, Melanie (1995), 'The North Vietnamese State-Owned Industrial Sector: Continuity and Change', *Journal of Communist Studies and Transition Politics*, Vol. 11, No. 1, pp. 56-76.

Berglöf, Staffan (1990), *Currency Devaluation and Adjustment Efforts in Tanzania,* Minor Field Study Series No. 14, Department of International Economic and Geography, Stockholm School of Economics, Stockholm.

Berhanu Abegaz (1994), 'A Late-industrialization Perspective on Ethiopian Manufacturing', in Berhanu Abegaz (ed.), *Essays on Ethiopian Economic Development,* Avebury, Aldershot, pp. 159-224.

Berry, Albert and Dipak Mazumdar (1991), 'Small-Scale Industry in the Asian-Pacific Region', *Asian-Pacific Economic Literature,* Vol. 5, No. 2, pp. 35-67.

Bhagwati, Jagdish (1993), *India in Transition: Freeing the Economy,* Clarendon Press, Oxford.

Bhagwati, Jagdish and Padma Desai (1970), *India: Planning for Industrialization. Industrialization and Trade Policies since 1951,* Oxford University Press, London.

Bowles, Paul and Gordon White (1993), *The Political Economy of China's Financial Reforms: Finance in Late Development,* Westview, Boulder, CO.

Brada, Josef C. (1993), 'The Transformation from Communism to Capitalism: How Far? How Fast?', *Post-Soviet Affairs,* Vol. 9, No. 2, pp. 87-110.

Bräutigam, Deborah A. (1994), 'What can Africa learn from Taiwan? Political economy, industrial policy, and adjustment', *Journal of Modern African Studies,* Vol. 32, No. 1, pp. 111-138.

Brietzke, Paul H. (1981), 'Socialism and Law in the Ethiopian Revolution', *Review of Socialist Law,* Vol. 7, No. 3, pp. 261-303.

Brunetti, Aymo and Beatrice Weder (1994), 'Political Credibility and Economic Growth in Less Developed Countries', *Constitutional Political Economy,* Vol. 5, No. 1, pp. 23-45.

Brus, Wlodzimierz (1993), 'Marketisation and Democratisation: the Sino-Soviet Divergence', *Cambridge Journal of Economics,* Vol. 17, No. 4, pp. 423-440.

Buiter, Willem H. and Urjit R. Patel (1992), 'Debt, Deficits and Inflation: an Application to the Public Finances of India', *Journal of Public Economics,* Vol. 47, No. 2, pp. 171-205.

Bukuku, Enos S. (1992), 'The Market and the Public Sector in Economic Development: the Case of Tanzania', paper presented at the Eight National Economic Policy Workshop, Dar es Salaam, 30 November - 2 December.

Cai Fang, Jin Hehui, Zhang Yuanhong, Du Zhixiong and Li Zhou (1991), *The Tradition and Structural Dynamics of Rural Industries in China,* Research Report No. 17, Department of International Economics and Geography, Stockholm School of Economics, Stockholm.

218

Cao, Andrew D. (1993), 'Privatization in Vietnam', in V.V. Ramanadham (ed.), *Privatization: A Global Perspective*, Routledge, London, pp. 459-469.

Carlsson, Jerker, Sverker Alänge, Kim Forss, Serve Malai and Sari Scheinberg (1988), *Sisterhood on Trial: an Evaluation of the Performance and Linkages of the Sister Industries in Tanzania*, SIDA Evaluation Report 1988/2, Swedish International Development Authority, Stockholm.

Caselli, Clara (1976), *The Banking System of Tanzania*, Cassa di Risparmio delle Provincie Lombarde, Milan.

Casson, Mark (1991), *The Economics of Business Culture: Game Theory, Transaction Costs, and Economic Performance*, Clarendon Press, Oxford.

Chadha, G.K. (1993a), 'Non-farm Employment for Rural Households in India: Evidence and Prognosis', *Indian Journal of Labour Economics*, Vol. 36, No. 3, pp. 296-328.

Chadha, G.K. (1993b), *Nonfarm Sector in India's Rural Economy: Policy, Performance and Growth Prospects*, Visiting Research Fellow Monograph Series No. 220, Institute of Developing Economies, Tokyo.

Chadha, G.K. (1994), 'Industrialization Strategy and the Growth of Rural Industry: the Past Experience', paper submitted to South Asia Multidisciplinary Advisory Team, International Labour Organisation, New Delhi.

China Economic Structural Reform Research Institute, Micro Research Department (1988), 'Market Structure and the Enterprise System in Microeconomic Reform', *Social Sciences in China*, Vol. 9, No. 4, pp. 42-66.

Chiu, C.H. Paul (1992), 'Money and Financial Markets: the Domestic Perspective', in Gustav Ranis (ed.), *Taiwan: From Developing to Mature Economy*, Westview, Boulder, CO, pp. 121-194.

Clapham, Christopher (1990a), *Transformation and Continuity in Revolutionary Ethiopia*, African Studies Series No. 61, Cambridge University Press, Cambridge.

Clapham, Christopher (1990b), 'Conclusion: Revolution, Nationality, and the Ethiopian State', in Marina Ottaway (ed.), *The Political Economy of Ethiopia*, Praeger, New York, pp. 221-231.

Clapham, Ronald (1985), *Small and Medium Entrepreneurs in Southeast Asia*, Research Notes and Discussions Paper No. 49, ASEAN Economic Research Unit, Institute of Southeast Asian Studies, Singapore.

Clarke, Donald C. (1992), 'Regulation and its Discontents: Understanding Economic Law in China', *Stanford Journal of International Law*, Vol. 28, No. 2, pp. 283-322.

Coase, Ronald H. (1937), 'The Nature of the Firm', *Economica*, New Series Vol. 6, pp. 386-405.

Cohen, Roberta (1987), 'Censorship Costs Lives', *Index on Censorship*, No. 5, pp. 15-18.

Coldham, Simon (1995), 'Land Tenue Reform in Tanzania: Legal Problems and Perspectives', *Journal of Modern African Studies*, Vol. 33, No. 2, pp 227-242.

Dahlman, Carl J. (1979), 'The Problem of Externality', *Journal of Law and Economics*, Vol. 22, No. 1, pp. 141-162.

Datt, Ruddar and K.P.M. Sundharam (1990), *Indian Economy*, S. Chand, New Delhi.

Dawit Wolde Giorgis (1990), 'The Power of Decision-making in Post-revolutionary Ethiopia', in Marina Ottaway (ed.), *The Political Economy of Ethiopia*, Praeger, New York, pp. 53-72.

Dejene Aredo (1990), 'The Evolution of Rural Development Policies', in Siegfried Pausewang, Fantu Cheru, Stefan Brüne and Eshetu Chole (eds), *Ethiopia: Rural Development Options*, Zed, London, pp. 49-57.

Deming, Angus and Ray Wilkinson (1986), 'Master Plan - Or Misery?', *Newsweek*, 5 May, pp. 32-34.

Desai, Ashok. V. and Nisha Taneja (1990), 'The Role of Small and Medium-Scale Industries in the Industrial Development of India', in *The Role of Small and Medium-Scale Manufacturing Industries in Industrial Development: the Experience of Selected Asian Countries*, Asian Development Bank, Manila, pp. 161-252.

Dessalegn Rahmato (1984), *Agrarian Reform in Ethiopia*, Scandinavian Institute of African Studies, Uppsala.

Dessalegn Rahmato (1987), 'The Political Economy of Development in Ethiopia', in Edmond J. Keller and Donald Rothchild (eds), *Afro-Marxist Regimes: Ideology and Public Policy*, Lynner Rienner, Boulder, CO, pp. 155-179.

Dessalegn Rahmato (1990), 'Cooperatives, State Farms and Smallholder Production', in Siegfried Pausewang, Fantu Cheru, Stefan Brüne and Eshetu Chole (eds), *Ethiopia: Rural Development Options*, Zed, London, pp. 100-110.

Diehl, Markus (1994), *Real Adjustment in the Economic Transformation Process: the Industrial Sector of Vietnam 1986-1992*, Kiel Working Paper No. 597, Kiel Institute of World Economics, Kiel.

Diehl, Markus (1995), 'Structural Change in the Economic Transformation Process: Vietnam 1986-1993', *Economic Systems*, Vol. 19, No. 2, pp. 147-182.

Dietrich, Craig (1994), *People's China: a Brief History*, Oxford University Press, New York.

van Dijk, Pieter Meine (1995), 'Flexible Specialization, the New Competition and Industrial Districts', *Small Business Economics*, Vol. 7, No. 1, pp. 15-27.

Dinh, Q. (1993), 'Vietnam's Policy Reforms and Its Future', *Journal of Contemporary Asia*, Vol. 23, No. 4, pp. 532-553.

Dollar, David (1994), 'Macroeconomic Management and the Transition to the Market in Vietnam', *Journal of Comparative Economics*, Vol. 18, No. 3, pp. 357-375.

Drabek, Zdenek (1990), *A Case Study of a Gradual Approach to Economic Reform: the Viet Nam Experience of 1985-88*, Internal Discussion Paper, Asia Regional Series, Report No. IDP 74, The World Bank, Washington, DC.

Eckstein, Alexander (1977), *China's Economic Revolution*, Cambridge University Press, Cambridge.

The Economist [London] (1991), 'The Men Who Follow Mengistu', 1 June, pp. 45-46.

The Economist [London] (1991), 'The Healing Touch', 14 December, p. 56.

The Economist [London] (1994), 'Voting, of a Sort', 4 June, p. 50.

The Economist [London] (1994), 'Red Terror Relived', 30 July, pp. 37-38.

The Economist [London] (1994), 'Ethiopia's State Terror on Trial', 17 December, pp. 39-40.

Eggertsson, Thráinn (1990), *Economic Behavior and Institutions*, Cambridge University Press, New York.

Eggertsson, Thráinn (1994), 'The Economics of Institutions in Transition Economies', in Salvatore Schiavo-Campo (ed.), *Institutional Change and the Public Sector in Transitional Economies*, World Bank Discussion Paper No. 241, The World Bank, Washington DC, pp. 19-50.

Eriksson, Gun (1991), *Economic Programmes and Systems Reform in Tanzania*, Macroeconomic Studies No 18, The Planning Secretariat, Swedish International Development Authority, Stockholm.

Eriksson, Gun (1993a), *Market Oriented Reform in Tanzania: an Economic System in Transition*, Research Report No. 18. Department of International Economics and Geography, Stockholm School of Economics, Stockholm.

Eriksson, Gun (1993b), *Incidence and Pattern of the Soft Budget Constraint in Tanzania*, Part One: *Suggestion from Data on Loss Makers and Budget Sof-*

tening Mechanisms via the Government, Macroeconomic Studies No. 44, The Panning Secretariat, Swedish International Development Authority, Stockholm.

Eriksson, Gun (1995), *Incident and Pattern of the Soft Budget Constraint in Tanzania,* Part Two: *Suggestions from Budget Softening Mechanisms via the Donors: the Case of Import Support,* Macroeconomic Studies No. 60, The Planning Secretariat, Swedish International Development Co-operation Authority, Stockholm.

Eriksson, Gun and Mats Lundahl (1993), 'Economic Recovery under Institutional Constraints: Tanzania Facing the Economic Crisis' in Magnus Blomström and Mats Lundahl (eds), *Economic Crisis in Africa: Perspectives on Policy Responses,* Routledge, London, pp. 268-287.

Eshetu Chole (1987), 'Constraints to Industrial Development in Ethiopia', *Eastern Africa Social Science Research Review,* Vol. 3, No. 2, pp. 1-24.

Eshetu Chole (1994), 'Reflections on Underdevelopment: Problems and Prospects', in Abebe Zegeye and Siegfried Pausewang (eds), *Ethiopia in Change: Peasantry, Nationalism and Democracy,* British Academic Press, London, pp. 95-117.

Eshetu Chole and Makonnen Manyazewal (1992), 'The Macroeconomic Performance of the Ethiopian Economy', in Mekonen Taddesse (ed.), *The Ethiopian Economy: Structure, Problems and Policy Issues, Proceedings of the First Annual Conference on the Ethiopian Economy,* n.p., Addis Ababa, pp. 3-42.

Esubalew Demissie (1991), 'Employment and Labour Productivity in Ethiopian Small-scale Manufacturing Industries', Addis Ababa University, Addis Ababa.

Fafchamps, Marcel (1994), 'Industrial Structure and Micro-enterprises in Africa', *Journal of Developing Areas,* Vol. 29, No. 1, pp. 1-30.

Fforde, Adam and Stefan de Vylder (1988), *Vietnam - an Economy in Transition,* Swedish International Development Authority, Stockholm.

Friedman, Eric J. and Simon Johnson (1995), *Complementarities and Optimal Reform,* Working Paper No. 109, Stockholm Institute of East European Economics, Stockholm School of Economics, Stockholm.

Gábor, István R. (1996), 'Too many, too small: small entrepreneurship in Hungary', in Gernot Grabher and David Stark (eds), *Restructuring Networks in Postsocialism: Legacies, Linkages and Localities,* Oxford University Press, Oxford, pp. 158-175.

Galenson, Walter (ed.) (1979), *Economic Growth and Structural Change in Taiwan: the Postwar Experience of the Republic of China,* Cornell University Press, Ithaca, NY.

Gates, Carolyn L. and David H.D. Truong (1992), *Reform of a Centrally-Managed Developing Economy: the Vietnamese Perspective*, NIAS Report No. 9, Nordic Institute of Asian Studies, Copenhagen.

Gates, Carolyn L. and David H.D. Truong (1993), 'Transition of a Developing Socialist Economy to a Developing Mixed Economy: the Case of Vietnam', *International Journal of Political Economy*, Vol. 23, No. 1, pp. 65-85.

Getachew Minas (1995), 'Impacts of Government Policies on Entrepreneurship in Ethiopia', in Ayalew Zegeye and Habteselassie Hagos (eds), *Proceedings of the First Annual Conference on Management in Ethiopia on the Theme Entrepreneurship*, Department of Management and Public Administration, Faculty of Business and Economics, Addis Ababa University, Addis Ababa, pp. 140-166.

Ghelawdewos Araia (1995), *Ethiopia: the Political Economy of Transition*, University Press of America, Lanham, MD.

Gibbon, Peter (1996), 'Structural Adjustment and Structural Change in Sub-Saharan Africa: Some Provisional Conclusions', in Peter Gibbon and Adebayo O. Olukoshi, *Structural Adjustment and Socio-economic Change in Sub-Saharan Africa: Some Conceptual, Methodological and Research Issues*, Research Report No. 102, Nordiska Afrikainstitutet, Uppsala, pp. 9-47.

Gilkes, Patrick (1975), *The Dying Lion*, Davison, Blandford.

Girma Kebbede (1992), *The State and Development in Ethiopia*, Humanities Press, Atlantic Highlands, NJ.

Goss, David (1991), *Small Business and Society*, Routledge, London.

Government of China (1956), *First Five Year Plan for Development of the National Economy of the People's Republic of China in 1957-61*, Foreign Languages Press, Beijing.

Gray, Jack (1990), *Rebellions and Revolutions: China from the 1800s to the 1980s*, Oxford University Press, Oxford.

Gunnarsson, Christer (1993), 'Dirigisme or Free-trade Regime? A Historical and Institutional Interpretation of the Taiwanese Success Story', in Göte Hansson (ed.), *Trade, Growth and Development: the Role of Politics and Institutions. Proceedings of the 12th Arne Ryde Symposium 13-14 June 1991, in honor of Bo Södersten*, Routledge, London, pp. 154-183.

de Haan, H.H. (1980), *Rural Industrialization in India: the Contribution to Labour Absorption and to Curbing Rural-Urban Migration*, Discussion Paper No. 54, Centre for Development Planning, Erasmus University, Rotterdam.

Hansson, Göte (1995a), *The Ethiopian Economy 1974-94: Ethiopia Tikdem and After*, Routledge, London.

223

Hansson, Göte (1995b), *Ethiopia 1995*, Macroeconomic Studies No. 1995:64, Swedish International Development Co-operation Agency, Stockholm.

Hansson, Göte, Stefan Hedlund and Mats Lundahl (1983), 'Tanzania - socialistland med bekymmer', *Tiden*, No. 2, pp. 91-99.

Harbeson, John W. (1990), 'State and Social Transformation in Modern Ethiopia', in Marina Ottaway (ed.), *The Political Economy of Ethiopia*, Praeger, New York pp. 73-91.

Hart, Keith (1973), 'Informal Income Opportunities and Urban Employment in Ghana', *Journal of Modern African Studies*, Vol. 2, No. 1, pp. 61-89.

HASIDA (n.d.), *Aims and Functions*, Handicrafts and Small Industries Development Authority, Addis Ababa.

Havnevik, Kjell J., Rune Skarstein and Samuel M. Wangwe (1985), *Small Scale Industrial Sector Study - Tanzania. Review of Experiences and Recommendations for the Future*, Scandinavian Institute of African Studies, Uppsala.

Hedlund, Stefan and Mats Lundahl (1987), *Tanzanias ekonomi*, Världspolitikens Dagsfrågor No. 1987:3, Utrikespolitiska Institutet, Stockholm.

Hedlund, Stefan and Mats Lundahl (1989), *Ideology as a Determinant of Economic Systems: Nyerere and Ujamaa in Tanzania*, Research Report No. 84, Scandinavian Institute of African Studies, Uppsala.

Ho, Samuel P.S. (1978), *Economic Development of Taiwan, 1860-1970*, Yale University Press, New Haven, CT.

Ho, Samuel P.S. (1980), *Small Scale Enterprises in Korea and Taiwan*, World Bank Staff Working Paper No. 384, The World Bank, Washington DC.

Ho, Samuel P.S. (1982), 'Economic Development and Rural Industry in South Korea and Taiwan', *World Development*, Vol. 10, No. 11, pp. 973-990.

Hsiao, Katherine Huang (1987), *The Government Budget and Fiscal Policy in Mainland China*, Mainland China Economic Series No. 5, Chung-Hua Institution for Economic Research, Taipei.

Hydén, Göran and Bo Karlström (1993), 'Structural Adjustment as a Policy Process: the Case of Tanzania', *World Development*, Vol. 21, No. 9, pp. 1395-1404.

Hyuha, M., M.O. Ndanshau and J.P. Kipokola (1993), *Scope, Structure and Policy Implications of Informal Financial Markets in Tanzania*, EARC Research Paper No. 18, African Economic Research Consortium, Nairobi.

Ibrahim Abdullahi Zeidy (1994), 'The Impact of Monetary Control and Fiscal Contraction on Private Sector Development in Ethiopia'a Stabilization and Adjustment Programme', in Getachew Yoseph and Abdulhamid Bedri Kello (eds), *The Ethiopian Economy: Problems and Prospects of Private Sector De-*

224

velopment. Proceedings of the Third Annual Conference on the Ethiopian Economy, Addis Ababa University, Addis Ababa, pp. 143-159.

ILO (1974), *Sharing in Development: a Programme of Employment, Equity and Growth for the Philippines*, International Labour Office, Geneva.

ILO, World Employment Programme (1990), *Informal Sector Employment in Ethiopia: An Analysis of a Survey in Addis Ababa, Dire Dawa and Harar*, Jobs and Skills Programme for Africa (JASPA), Addis Ababa.

ILO (1996), *Macro Policy Framework for Small-Scale Industries Development in Africa and Asia: Report of an ILO Tripartite Seminar, Nairobi, Kenya, 26-29 March 1996*, Eastern Africa Multidisciplinary Advisory Team/South Asia Multidisciplinary Advisory Team, International Labour Organisation, Addis Ababa/New Delhi.

Inoue, Kyoko (1992), *Industrial Development Policy of India*, IDE Occasional Paper Series No. 27, Institute of Developing Economies, Tokyo.

Islam, Rizwanul (1991), *Growth of Rural Industries in Post-reform China: Patterns, Determinants and Consequences*, ILO/ARTEP Working Paper, Asian Regional Team for Employment Promotion, International Labour Organisation, New Delhi.

Itana Ayana (1994), 'Credit Policy, Financial Institutions and Private Investment in Ethiopia', in Getachew Yoseph and Abdulhamid Bedri Kello (eds), *The Ethiopian Economy: Problems and Prospects of Private Sector Development. Proceedings of the Third Annual Conference on the Ethiopian Economy*, Addis Ababa University, Addis Ababa, pp. 237-253.

James, C.V. (ed.) (1989), *Information China*, Vol. 2, Pergamon Press, Oxford.

Jiang, Yiwei (1980), 'The Theory of an Enterprise-based Economy', *Social Sciences in China*, Vol. 1, No. 1.

Jin-Sang, Lee (1995), 'Entrepreneurship Development in Ethiopia: Lessons from Korean Experience', in Ayalew Zegeye and Habteselassie Hagos (eds) *Proceedings of the First Annual Conference on Management in Ethiopia on the Theme Entrepreneurship*, Department of Management and Public Administration, Faculty of Business and Economics, Addis Ababa University, Addis Ababa, pp. 332-366.

Jinyan Li (1991), *Taxation in the People's Republic of China*, Praeger, New York.

Johansson, Sara and Per Ronnås (1995), *Rural Industrialization: a Review of Selected Asian Experiences*, Working Paper Series in Economics and Finance, Working Paper No. 46, Stockholm School of Economics, Stockholm.

Joshi, Vijay and I.M.D. Little (1989), 'Indian Macroeconomic Policies', in Guillermo Calvo, Ronald Findlay, P. Kouri and J.B. de Macedo (eds), *Debt,*

225

Stabilization and Development: Essays in Memory of Carlos Diaz-Alejandro, Blackwell, Oxford, pp. 286-308.

Joshi, Vijay and I.M.D. Little (1994), *India: Macroeconomics and Political Economy: 1964-1991,* The World Bank, Washington, DC.

Joskow, Paul L. (1995), 'The New Institutional Economics: Alternative Approaches, Concluding Comment', *Journal of Institutional and Theoretical Economics,* Vol. 151, No. 1, pp. 248-259.

Jowitt, A.J. (1989), 'China: the Demographic Disaster of 1958-1961', in John Clarke, Peter Curson, S.L. Kayastha and Prithvish Nag (eds), *Population and Disaster,* Institute of British Geographers Special Publication Series No. 22, Blackwell, Oxford, pp. 137-158.

Kamarck, Andrew M. (1976), *The Tropics and Economic Development: a Provocative Inquiry into the Poverty of Nations,* The World Bank, Washington, DC.

Kashyap, S.P. (1988), 'Growth of Small-size Enterprises in India: Its Nature and Content', *World Development,* Vol. 16, No. 5, pp. 667-681.

Kashyap, S.P. (1993), 'Emerging Tendencies in Rural Manufacturing Sector: Role of Policy', *Indian Journal of Labour Economics,* Vol. 36, No.3, pp. 387-395.

Keller, Edmond J. (1993), 'Government and Politics', in Thomas P. Ofcansky and LaVerle Berry (eds), *Ethiopia: a Country Study,* Federal Research Division, Library of Congress, Washington, DC, pp. 207-266.

Khalil, Elias L. (1995), 'Organizations versus Institutions', *Journal of Institutional and Theoretical Economics,* Vol. 151, No. 3, pp. 445-466.

King, Kenneth (1979), 'Petty Production in Nairobi: the Social Context of Skill Acquisition and Occupational Differentiation', in Ray Bromley and Chris Gerry (eds), *Casual work and Poverty in Third World Cities,* John Wiley, New York, pp. 217-228.

Kokko, Ari and Mario Zejan (1996), *Vietnem 1996: Approaching the Next Stage of Reforms,* Macroeconomic Report No. 1996:9, Swedish International Development and Co-operation Authority, Stockholm.

Kornai, János (1979), 'Resource-constrained versus Demand-constrained Economies', Econometrica, Vol. 47, No. 4, pp. 801-819.

Kornai, János (1980), *The Economics of Shortage,* Vol. A-B, North-Holland, Amsterdam.

Kornai, János (1992), *The Socialist System: the Political Economy of Communism,* Oxford University Press, Oxford.

Kornai, János (1995a), 'Eliminating the Shortage Economy: a General Analysis and Examination of the Developments in Hungary', *Economics of Transition,*

Vol. 3, No. 1, pp. 13-37.

Kornai, János (1995b), 'Eliminating the Shortage Economy: a General Analysis and Examination of the Developments in Hungary: Part 2', *Economics of Transition*, Vol. 3, No. 2, pp. 149-168.

Krauss, Willy (1991), *Private Business in China: Revival between Ideology and Pragmatism*, Hurst, London.

Krueger, Anne O. (1993), *Political Economy of Policy Reform in Developing Countries*, MIT Press, Cambridge, MA.

Krueger, Anne O. (1997), 'Trade Policy and Economic Development: How We Learn', *American Economic Review*, Vol. 87, No. 1 (1997), pp. 1-22.

Kuczi, Tibor and Csaba Makó (1996), 'Towards industrial districts? Small-firm networking in Hungary', in Gernot Grabher and David Stark (eds), *Restructuring Networks in Post-socialism: Legacies, Linkages and Localities*, Oxford University Press, Oxford, pp. 176-189.

Kuo, Shirley W.Y. (1975), 'Effects of Land Reform, Agricultural Pricing Policy and Economic Growth on Multiple Crop Diversification in Taiwan', *Philippines Economic Journal*, Vol. 14, Nos. 1/2, pp. 159-164.

Kurths, Kristina (1995), *Private Small Scale Industries in Vietnam: Development Environment and Empirical Results*, Working Paper Series in Economics and Finance, Working Paper No. 57, Stockholm School of Economics, Stockholm.

Kuznets, Simon (1979), 'Growth and Structural Shifts', in Walter Galenson (ed.), *Economic Growth and Structural Change in Taiwan: the Postwar Experience of the Republic of China*, Cornell University Press, Ithaca, NY, pp. 15-132.

Kweka, A.N. (1995), 'One Party Democracy & the Multi-Party State,' in Colin Legum and Geoffrey Mmari (eds), *Mwalimu - The Influence of Nyerere*, James Currey, London.

Lal, Deepak (1988), *The Hindu Equilibrium*, Vol.1, Clarendon Press, Oxford.

Lall, Sanjaya (1996), *Learning from the Asian Tigers: Studies in Technology and Industrial Policy*, Macmillan, Basingstoke.

Le Dang Doanh (1994), 'Vietnam: Country Report', paper presented at the Asian Transitional Economies Project International Conference, Osaka, 30-31 October.

Lefort, René (1983), *Ethiopia: an Heretical Revolution?*, Zed, London.

Leibenstein, Harvey and Dennis Ray (eds) (1988), 'Entrepreneurship and Economic Development', special issue of *Journal of Development Planning*, No. 18.

Levitsky, Jacob (ed.) (1989), *Microenterprises in Developing Countries*, IT Publications, London.

Levy, Brian (1990), 'Transactions Costs, the Size of Firms and Industrial Policy: Lessons from a Comparative Case Study of the Footwear Industry in Korea and Taiwan', *Journal of Development Economics*, Vol. 34, Nos. 1-2, pp. 151-178.

Levy, Brian (1993), 'Obstacles to Developing Indigenous Small and Medium Enterprises: an Empirical Assessment', *The World Bank Economic Review*, Vol. 7, No. 1, pp 65-83.

Levy, Brian, Albert Berry, Motoshige Itoh, Linsu Kim, Jeffrey Nugent and Shujiro Urata (1994), *Technical and Marketing Support Systems for Successful Small and Medium-Size Enterprises in Four Countries*, Policy Research Working Paper No. 1400, The World Bank, Washington, DC.

Liedholm, Carl (1993), 'Small- and Microenterprise Dynamics and the Evolving Role of Finance', in A.H.J. Helmsing and Th. Kolstee (eds), *Small Enterprises and Changing Policies: Structural Adjustment, Financial Policy and Assistance Programmes in Africa*, IT Publications, London, pp. 261-273.

Lin, Jan (1989), 'Beyond Neoclassical Shibboleths: a Political-economic Analysis of Taiwanese Economic Development', *Dialectical Anthropology*, Vol. 14, No. 4, pp. 283-300.

Little, I.M.D. (1979), 'An Economic Renaissance', in Walter Galenson (ed.), *Economic Growth and Structural Change in Taiwan: the Postwar Experience of the Republic of China*, Cornell University Press, Ithaca, NY, pp. 448-508.

Little, I.M.D. (1981), 'The Experience and Causes of Rapid Labour-intensive Development in Korea, Taiwan Province, Hong Kong and Singapore and the Possibilities of Emulation', in Eddy Lee (ed.), *Export-led Industrialisation and Development*, Maruzen Asia, Singapore, pp. 23-45.

Little, I.M.D., Dipak Mazumdar, and John Page (1987), *Small Manufacturing Enterprises: a Comparative Study of India and Other Economies*, Oxford University Press, New York.

Little, I.M.D, Tibor Scitovsky and Maurice Scott (1970), *Industry and Trade in Some Developing Countries: a Comparative Study*, Oxford University Press, London.

Lundberg, Erik (1979), 'Fiscal and Monetary Policies', in Walter Galenson (ed.), *Economic Growth and Structural Change in Taiwan: the Postwar Experience of the Republic of China*, Cornell University Press, Ithaca, NY, pp. 263-307.

Ma Jisen (1988), 'A General Survey of the Resurgence of the Private Sector of China's Economy', *Social Sciences in China*, Vol. 9, No. 3, pp. 78-92.

Maddison, Angus (1990), 'The Colonial Burden: a Comparative Perspective', in Maurice Scott and Deepak Lal (eds), *Public Policy and Economic Development: Essays in Honour of Ian Little*, Oxford University Press, New York, pp. 361-375.

Mahalanobis, P.C. (1963), *The Approach of Operational Research to Planning in India*, Asia Publishing House, Bombay.

Major, Iván (1994), 'The Decay of Command Economies', *East European Politics and Societies*, Vol. 8, No. 2, pp. 317-357.

Makau wa Mutua (1994), 'Ignoring the Lessons of History: Ethnocracy and Human Rights Violations in Ethiopia', *Ethiopian Review*, December, pp. 23-27.

Markakis, John and Nega Ayele (1986), *Class and Revolution in Ethiopia*, Red Sea Press, Trenton, NJ.

Mazumdar, Dipak (1991), 'Import Substituting Industrialization and Protection of the Small Scale: the Indian Experience in the Textile Industry', *World Development*, Vol. 19, No. 9, pp. 1197-1213.

McCrory, James T. (1956), *Small Industry in a North Indian Town*, Ministry of Commerce and Industry, Government of India, New Delhi.

McKinnon, Ronald (1994), 'Financial Growth and Macroeconomic Stability in China, 1978-1992: Implications for Russia and Other Transition Economies', *Journal of Comparative Economics*, Vol. 18, No. 3, pp. 438-469.

Mekdes Aklilu (1995), 'Financial Handicaps of Small Enterprises in Ethiopia: Some Paradoxes with Government Policy Gospels', in Ayalew Zegeye and Habteselassie Hagos (eds), *Proceedings of the First Annual Conference on Management in Ethiopia on the Theme Entrepreneurship*, Department of Management and Public Administration, Faculty of Business and Economics, Addis Ababa University, Addis Ababa, pp. 262-303.

de Melo, Martha and Alan Gelb (1996), 'A Comparative Analysis of Twenty-eight Transitions Economies in Europe and Asia', *Post-Soviet Geography and Economics*, Vol. 37, No. 5, pp. 265-285.

Mengistu Haile Mariam (1983), 'Mengistu Haile Mariam's Central Report to COPWE Second Congress', *BBC Summary of World Broadcasts*, Part 4, Second Series, ME/7224/B, 6 January, pp. 8-12.

Menning, Garrett (1997), 'Trust, Entrepreneurship and Development in Surat City, India', *Ethnos*, Vol. 62, Nos. 1-2, pp. 59-90.

Ministry of Finance, India (1989), *Economic Survey 1988-89*, Government of India Press, New Delhi.

Ministry of Foreign Affairs, Sweden (1992), *In Support of Asian Development. Asian Development Trends: Lessons Learned and the Experience of Donors - a Basis for a Swedish Agenda*, Department for International Development Co-operation, Ministry of Foreign Affairs, Stockholm.

Moshi, H.P.B. (1990), 'Tanzania's Public Enterprises and the Economic Recovery Programme: Is Re- and Privatization the Answer?', paper presented at the Sixth Economic Policy Workshop, Dar es Salaam, 2-4 January.

Msambichaka, L.A. (1992), 'Economic Reforms in Tanzania: Major Reform Questions, Successes, and Expectations' paper presented at the Eight National Economic Policy Workshop, Dar es Salaam, 30 November - 2 December.

Mukandala, Rwekaza S. (1995), 'State Power and Political Institutions,' in Gabriel Winai Ström (ed.), *Change in Tanzania 1980 - 1994*, Swedish International Development Authority, Stockholm.

Mulatu Wubneh (1990), 'Development Strategy and Growth of the Ethiopian Economy: A Comparative Analysis of the Pre- and Post-revolutionary Period', in Marina Ottaway (ed.), *The Political Economy of Ethiopia*, New York, Praeger, New York, pp. 197-219.

Mulatu Wubneh (1994), 'Manufacturing Productivity in Ethiopia, 1960-88', in Berhanu Abegaz (ed.), *Essays on Ethiopian Economic Development*, Avebury, Aldershot, pp. 255-297.

Mulatu Wubneh and Yohannis Abate (1988), *Ethiopia: Transition and Development in the Horn of Africa*, Westview, Boulder, CO.

Murrell, Peter (1993), 'What Is Shock Therapy? What Did It Do in Poland and Russia?', *Post-Soviet Affairs*, Vol. 9, No. 2, pp. 111-140.

Myers, Ramon H. (1985), 'The Economic Development of the Republic of China in Taiwan, 1965-81', in Lawrence J. Lau (ed.), *Models of Development: a Comparative Study of Economic Growth in South Korea and Taiwan*, Institute for Contemporary Studies, San Fransisco, CA, pp. 13-64.

Myers, Ramon H. (1995), 'Chinese Debate on Economic Reform: Can China Create a Socialist Market Economy?', *Asian-Pacific Economic Literature*, Vol. 9, No. 2, pp. 55-68.

Naughton, Barry (1992), 'Implications of the State Monopoly over Industry and its Relaxation', *Modern China*, Vol. 18, No. 1, pp. 14-41.

Ndulu, Benno (1988), *Stabilization and Adjustment Policies and Programmes: Tanzania,* Country study No. 17, WIDER, Helsinki.

Negarit Gazeta [Official gazette, Addis Ababa], various issues.

230

Negussay Ayele (1990), 'The Ethiopian Revolution: Political Aspects of the Transition from PMAC to PDRE', in Marina Ottaway (ed.), *The Political Economy of Ethiopia*, Praeger, New York, pp. 11-29.

Ngwira, Austin B.A. (1995), '"Small Enterprise" or the "Informal Sector"?', *Small Enterprise Development*, Vol. 6, No. 1, pp. 49-52.

Nooteboom, Bart (1992), 'Small Business, Institutions and Economic Systems', paper presented at the 2nd EACES Conference, Groningen, 24-27 September.

Nooteboom, Bart (1993), 'Firm Size Effects on Transaction Costs', *Small Business Economics*, Vol. 5, No. 4, pp. 283-295.

Nooteboom, Bart, Peter S. Zwart and Tammo H.A. Bijmolt (1992), 'Transaction Costs and Standardisation in Professional Services to Small Business', *Small Business Economics*, Vol. 4, No. 2, pp. 141-152.

Norrman, Leif (1991), 'Hopp om ljus framtid', *Dagens Nyheter* [Stockholm], 13 November, p. 11.

North, Douglass C. (1981), *Structure and Change in Economic History*, Norton, New York.

North, Douglass C. (1990), *Institutions, Institutional Change and Economic Performance*, Cambridge University Press, Cambridge.

North, Douglass C. and John J. Wallis (1994), 'Integrating Institutional Change and Technical Change in Economic History: a Transaction Cost Approach', *Journal of Institutional and Theoretical Economics*, Vol. 150, No. 4, pp. 609-624.

Nove, Alec (1986), *The Soviet Economic System*, Allen and Unwin, Boston, 3rd rev. ed.

Nyirabu, Mohabe (1994), 'New Parties in Tanzania: Structure and Practice', paper presented at the 2nd State of Politics Conference organised by the Department of Political Science and Public Administration, University of Dar es Salaam, 4-6 July.

Odesola, Segun N. (1988), 'Ethiopia's Unfulfilled Revolution', *Journal of African Studies*, Vol. 15, Nos 1-2, pp. 10-15.

Ody, Anthony J. (1992), *Rural Enterprise Development in China, 1986-90*, World Bank Discussion Paper No. 162, The World Bank, Washington, DC.

Osmani, S.R. (1995), *Macroeconomic Policy and Small Scale Industry in Developing Asia*, SAAT Working Papers, South Asia Multidisciplinary Advisory Team, International Labour Organization, New Delhi.

231

Osoro, Nehemiah E. (1993), *Revenue Productivity Implications of Tax Reform in Tanzania*, EARC Research Paper No. 20, African Economic Research Consortium, Nairobi.

Pack, Howard (1992), 'New Perspectives on Industrial Growth in Taiwan', in Gustav Ranis (ed.), *Taiwan: From Developing to Mature Economy*, Westview, Boulder, CO, pp. 73-120.

Page, John M. (1994), 'The East Asian Miracle: an Introduction', *World Development*, Vol. 22, No. 4, pp. 615-626.

Papola, T.S. and R.S. Mathur (1979), *Inter-sectoral Linkages in Manufacturing: a Study of Metal Engineering Industry in Kanpur, India*, unpublished paper, Giri Institute of Development Studies, Lucknow.

Park, Yung Chul (1994), 'Concepts and Issues', in Hugh T. Patrick and Yung Chul Park (eds), *The Financial Development of Japan, Korea and Taiwan: Growth, Repression, and Liberalization*, Oxford University Press, New York, pp. 3-26.

Parker, Ronald L., Randall Riopelle and William F. Steel (1995), *Small Enterprises Adjusting to Liberalization in Five African Countries*, World Bank Discussion Papers, Africa Technical Department Series No. 271, The World Bank, Washington DC.

Patrick, Hugh T. (1994), 'Comparisons, Contrasts and Implications', in Hugh T. Patrick and Yung Chul Park (eds), *The Financial Development of Japan, Korea and Taiwan: Growth, Repression, and Liberalization*, Oxford University Press, Oxford, pp. 325-371.

Pausewang, Siegfried (1990a), '"Meret Le Arrashu" Land Tenure and Access to Land: a Socio-historical Overview', in Siegfried Pausewang, Fantu Cheru, Stefan Brüne and Eshetu Chole (eds), *Ethiopia: Rural Development Options*, Zed, London, pp. 38-48.

Pausewang, Siegfried (1990b), 'The Peasant Perspective', in Siegfried Pausewang, Fantu Cheru, Stefan Brüne and Eshetu Chole (eds), *Ethiopia: Rural Development Options*, Zed, London, pp. 213-226.

Pedersen, Poul Ove, Arni Sverrisson and Pieter Meine van Dijk (eds) (1994), *Flexible Specialization: the Dynamics of Small-scale Industries in the South*, IT Publications, London.

Perkins, Dwight H. (1994), 'China's "Gradual" Approach to Market Reforms', in Andrés Solimano, Osvaldo Sunkel and Mario I. Blejer (eds), *Rebuilding Capitalism: Alternative Roads after Socialism and Dirigisme*, University of Michigan Press, Ann Arbor, MI, pp. 177-206.

232

Pernia, Ernesto M. and Joseph M. Pernia (1986), 'An Economic and Social Impact Analysis of Small Industry Promotion: a Philippine Experience', *World Development*, Vol. 14, No. 5, pp. 637-651.

Pham Van Thuyet (1995), *The Emerging Legal Framework for Private Sector Development in Viet Nam's Transitional Economy*, Policy Research Working Paper No. 1486, The World Bank, Washington, DC.

Piore Michael J. and Charles F. Sabel (1984), *The Second Industrial Divide: Possibilities for Prosperity*, Basic Books, New York.

Platteau, Jean-Philippe (1994a), 'Behind the Market Stage Where Real Societies Exist - Part I: the Role of Public and Private Order Institutions', *Journal of Development Studies*, Vol. 30, No. 3, pp. 533-577.

Platteau, Jean-Philippe (1994b), 'Behind the Market Stage Where Real Societies Exist - Part II: the Role of Moral Norms', *Journal of Development Studies*, Vol. 30, No. 4, pp. 753-817.

Pyke, Frank and Werner Sengenberger (eds) (1992), *Industrial Districts and Local Economic Regeneration*, International Institute for Labour Studies, Geneva.

Qian, Yingyi and Joseph Stiglitz (1996), 'Institutional Innovations and the Role of Local Government in Transition Economies: the Case of Guangdong Province of China', in John McMillan and Barry Naughton (eds), *Reforming Asian Socialism: the Growth of Market Institutions*, University of Michigan Press, Ann Arbor, MI, pp. 175-193.

Rainnie, Al (1989), *Industrial Relations in Small Firms*, Routledge, London.

Ramamurthy, Bhargavi and Per Ronnås (1995), *Small Industries and Institutional Framework: a Transaction Costs Approach*, Working Paper Series in Economics and Finance, Working Paper No. 83, Stockholm, Stockholm School of Economics.

Ranis, Gustav, (1979), 'Industrial Development', in Walter Galenson (ed.), *Economic Growth and Structural Change in Taiwan: the Postwar Experience of the Republic of China*, Cornell University Press, Ithaca, NY, pp. 206-262.

Ranis, Gustav (1992a), 'From Developing to Mature Economy: an Overview', in Gustav Ranis (ed.), *Taiwan: From Developing to Mature Economy*, Westview, Boulder, CO, pp. 1-14.

Ranis, Gustav (ed.) (1992b) *Taiwan: From Developing to Mature Economy*, Westview, Boulder, CO.

Rao, Sudhakara B. (1985), 'Rural Industrialisation and Rural Non-farm Employment in India' in Swapna Mukhopadhyay and Chee Ping Lim (eds), *Development and Diversification of Rural Industries in Asia*, Asian and Pacific Development Centre, Kuala Lumpur, pp. 149-248.

Rasmussen, Jesper, Hubert Schmitz and Pieter Miene van Djik (1992), 'Exploring a New Approach to Small Scale Industries: Introduction', *IDS Bulletin*, Vol. 23, No. 3, pp. 2-7.

Ray, Dennis (1990), 'Introductory Essay: the Role of Entrepreneurship in Economic Development', *Journal of Development Planning*, No. 18, pp. 3-18.

RBI (1990), *Reserve Bank of India Annual Report, 1989-90*, Reserve Bank of India, Bombay.

Riedel, James (1988), 'Economic Development in East Asia: Doing What Comes Naturally?', in Helen Hughes (ed.), *Achieving Industrialization in East Asia*, Cambridge: Cambridge University Press, Cambridge, pp. 1-38.

Riskin, Carl (1971), 'Small Industry and the Chinese Model of Development', *China Quarterly*, No. 46, pp. 245-273.

Riskin, Carl (1991), *China's Political Economy: the Quest for Development Since 1949*, Oxford University Press, New York.

Roman Habtu (1994), 'Small-scale Industry in Ethiopia', in Berhanu Abegaz (ed.), *Essays on Ethiopian Economic Development*, Avebury, Aldershot, pp. 227-253.

Ronnås, Per (1992), *Employment Generation Through Private Entrepreneurship in Vietnam*, Asian Regional Team for Employment Promotion, International Labour Organisation, New Delhi.

Ronnås, Per (1993), 'Economic Diversification and Growth in Rural China: the Anatomy of a "Socialist" Success Story', *Journal of Communist Studies*, Vol. 9, No. 3, pp. 216-244.

Ronnås, Per and Örjan Sjöberg (1991), 'Introduction: a Socio-economic Strategy for Vietnam', in Per Ronnås and Örjan Sjöberg (eds), *Socio-Economic Development in Vietnam: the Agenda for the 1990s*, Swedish International Development Authority, Stockholm, pp. 1-17.

Ronnås, Per and Örjan Sjöberg (1996), 'Township Enterprises: a Part of the World or a World Apart?', in Per Ronnås (ed.), *Rural Industries in Post-Reform China: an Inquiry into their Characteristics*, South Asia Multidisciplinary Advisory Team, International Labour Organization, New Delhi, pp. 177-206.

Rosati, Dariusz K. (1994), 'Output Decline During Transition from Plan to Market: a Reconsideration', *Economics of Transition*, Vol. 2, No. 4, pp. 419-441.

Rothermund, Dietmar (1993), *An Economic History of India: From Pre-Colonial Times to 1991*, Routledge, London.

Rweyemamu, J.F. (1979), 'The Historical and Institutional Setting of Tanzanian Industry,' in Kwan S. Kim, Robert B. Mabele and Michael J. Schultheis (eds),

Papers on the Political Economy of Tanzania, Heinemann Educational, Nairobi, pp. 69-77.

Sachs, Jeffrey D. (1985), 'External Debt and Macroeconomic Performance in Latin America and Asia', *Brookings Papers on Economic Activity*, No. 2, pp. 523-575.

Sachs, Jeffrey and Wing Thye Woo (1994), 'Structural Factors in the Economic Reforms of China, Eastern Europe and the Former Soviet Union', *Economic Policy*, No. 18, pp. 101-145.

Saith, Ashwani (1992), *The Rural Non-farm Economy: Processes and Policies*, International Labour Office, Geneva.

Sandesara, J.C. (1980), 'Small Industries in India: Evidence and Interpretation', Presidential address, Gujarat Economic Association, Ahmedabad.

Sandesara, J.C. (1988), 'Institutional Framework for Promoting Small-Scale Industries in India', *Asian Development Review*, Vol. 6, No. 2, pp. 10-40.

Sandesara, J.C. (1992), *Modern Small Industry, 1972 and 1987-88: Some Aspects of Growth and Structural Change*, unpublished paper, IIM, Ahmedabad.

Sarris, Alexander H. and Rogier van den Brink (1993), *Economic Policy and Household Welfare during Crisis and Adjustment in Tanzania*, New York University Press, New York.

Schmieding, Holger (1993), 'From Plan to Market: On the Nature of the Transformation Crisis', *Weltwirtschaftliches Archiv*, Vol. 129, No. 2, pp. 216-253.

Scitovsky, Tibor (1985), 'Economic Development in Taiwan and South Korea: 1965-81', *Food Research Institute Studies*, Vol. 19, No. 3, pp. 215-264.

Schmitz, Hubert (1982), 'Growth Constraints on Small-scale Manufacturing in Developing Countries: a Critical Review', *World Development*, Vol. 10, No. 6, pp. 429-450.

Schmitz, Hubert (1989), *Flexible Specialisation - a New Paradigm for Small Scale Industrialization*, Discussion Paper No 261, Institute for Development Studies, Brighton.

Schmitz, Hubert (1990), 'Small Firms and Flexible Specialization in Developing Countries', *Labour and Society*, Vol. 15, No. 3, pp. 257-287.

Schwab, Peter (1985), *Ethiopia: Politics, Economics and Society*, Pinter, London.

Scott, Maurice (1979), 'Foreign Trade', in Walter Galenson (ed.), *Economic Growth and Structural Change in Taiwan: the Postwar Experience of the Republic of China*, Cornell University Press, Ithaca, NY, pp. 308-383.

Scully, Gerald W. (1987), 'The Choice of Law and the Extent of Liberty', *Journal of Institutional and Theoretical Economics*, Vol. 143, No. 4, pp. 595-615.

Scully, Gerald W. (1988), 'The Institutional Framework and Economic Development', *Journal of Political Economy*, Vol. 96, No. 3, pp. 652-662.

Sengenberger Werner and Frank Pyke (1991), 'Small Firm Industrial Districts and Local Economic Regeneration: Research and Policy Issues', *Labour and Society*, Vol. 16, No. 1, pp. 1-22.

Shea, Jia-Dong (1994), 'Taiwan: Development and Structural Change of the Financial System', in Hugh T. Patrick and Yung Chul Park (eds), *The Financial Development of Japan, Korea, and Taiwan: Growth, Repression, and Liberalization*, Oxford University Press, New York, pp. 222-287.

Shibusawa, Masahide, Zakaria Haji Ahmad and Brian Bridges (1992), *Pacific Asia in the 1990s*, Routledge, London.

Shiferaw Bekele (1994), 'Small and Medium Enterprises Development in Ethiopia: Opportunities and Challenges under a Structural Adjustment Programme', paper presented at the 7th International Conference of the World Assembly of Small and Medium Enterprises (WASME), Addis Ababa, 7-12 March.

Shirokov, G.K. (1980), *Industrialization of India*, Peoples' Publishing House, New Delhi.

SIDO [1984?], *Ten Years of the Small Industries Development Organizaion (SIDO) 1973-1983*, Small Industries Development Organisation, Dar es Salaam.

Skarstein, Rune and Samuel M. Wangwe (1986), *Industrial Developement in Tanzania: Some Critical Issues*, Scandinavian Institute of African Studies, Uppsala.

Smith, Heather (1995), 'Industry Policy in East Asia', *Asian-Pacific Economic Literature*, Vol. 9, No. 1, pp. 17-39.

Solinger, Dorothy J. (1989), 'Urban Reform and Relational Contracting in Post-Mao China: an Interpretation of the Transition from Plan to Market', *Studies in Comparative Communism*, Vol. 22, Nos 2/3, pp. 171-185.

Solomon Wole (1992), 'The State of Small-scale Industries in Ethiopia: Problems and Policy Issues', in Mekonen Taddesse (ed.), *The Ethiopian Economy: Structure, Problems and Policy Issues, Proceedings of the First Annual Conference on the Ethiopian Economy*, AAU Printing Press, Addis Ababa, pp. 171-182.

Solomon Wole (1994), 'Profile of the Private Sector in Ethiopia', in Getachew Yoseph and Abdulhamid Bedri Kello (eds), *The Ethiopian Economy: Problems and Prospects of Private Sector Development, Proceedings of the Third Annual Conference on the Ethiopian Economy*, n.p. Addis Ababa, pp. 21-32.

Solomon Wole (1996), 'Adjustment and Private Sector Investment in Ethiopia: an Overview', in Tadesse Abadi and Tekie Alemu (eds), *Adjustment in Ethiopia: Lessons for the Road Ahead*, n.p., Addis Ababa, pp. 157-166.

de Soto, Hernando (1989), *The Other Path: the Invisible Revolution in the Third World*, Harper and Row, New York.

Späth, Brigitte (1992), 'The Institutional Environment and Communities of Small Firms', *IDS Bulletin*, Vol. 23, No. 3, pp. 8-14.

Staley, E. and R. Morse (1965), *Modern Small Industry for Developing Countries*, McGraw Hill, New York.

Steel, William F. (1993), 'Analyzing the Policy Framework for Small Enterprise Development', in A.H.J. Helmsing and Th. Kolstee (eds), *Small Enterprises and Changing Policies*, IT Publications, London, pp. 39-49.

Stein, Howard (1992), 'Desindustrialization, Adjustment, the World Bank and the IMF in Africa', *World Development*, Vol. 20, No. 1, pp. 83-95.

Stein, Howard (ed.) (1995a), *Asian Industrialization and Africa: Studies in Policy Alternatives to Structural Adjustment*, Macmillan, Basingstoke.

Stein, Howard (1995b), 'Policy Alternatives to Structural Adjustment in Africa: an Introduction', in Howard Stein (ed.), *Asian Industrialization and Africa: Studies in Policy Alternatives to Structural Adjustment*, Macmillan, Basingstoke, pp. 1-29.

Stewart, F. (1990), 'Macro-policies for Small-scale Industry and Appropriate Technology', *Small Enterprise Development*, Vol. 1, No. 3, pp. 4-16.

Strömberg, Tove (1995), *Tanzania: Transaction Costs in the Small Scale Industry*, unpublished Bachelor of Arts Thesis in Economics, Department of Management and Economics, Linköping University, Linköping.

Svenska Dagbladet [Stockholm] (1995), 'Anklagelser om fusk i etiopiska vallokaler', 9 March, p. 7.

Taye Berhanu (1995), 'Entrepreneurship and the Development of the Private Sector in Ethiopia', in Ayalew Zegeye and Habteselassie Hagos (eds), *Proceedings of the First Annual Conference on Management in Ethiopia on the Theme Entrepreneurship*, Department of Management and Public Administration, Faculty of Business and Economics, Addis Ababa University, Addis Ababa, pp. 228-261.

Taye Berhanu (1996), 'The Reform Process and SSE Development (synopsis)', paper prepared for the Sixth Annual Conference on the Ethiopian Economy Organised by the Department of Economics, Addis Ababa University and the Ethiopian Economic Association, Nazret, 5-8 December.

Taye Mengistae (1990), 'Urban-rural Relations in Agrarian Change: an Historical Overview', in Siegfried Pausewang, Fantu Cheru, Stefan Brüne and Eshetu Chole (eds), *Ethiopia: Rural Development Options*, Zed, London, pp. 30-37.

Teshome Mulat (1994), *Institutional Reform, Macroeconomic Policy Change and the Development of Small-scale Industries in Ethiopia*, Working Paper Series in Economics and Finance, Working Paper No. 23, Stockholm School of Economics, Stockholm.

Teshome Mulat (n.d.), 'Some Notes on Employment in Small-scale Manufacturing and Handicraft Industries', preliminary draft paper.

Thorbecke, Erik (1992), 'The Process of Agricultural Development in Taiwan', in Gustav Ranis (ed.), *Taiwan: From Developing to Mature Economy*, Westview, Boulder, CO, pp. 15-72.

Tripp, Aili Mari (1989), *Defending the Right to Subsist: the State vs. the Urban Informal Economy in Tanzania*, WIDER, Helsinki.

Turner, John W. (1993), 'Historical Setting', in Thomas P. Ofcansky and LaVerle Berry (eds), *Ethiopia: a Country Study*, Federal Research Division, Library of Congress, Washington, DC, pp. 1-67.

Tyabji, Nasir (1989), *The Small Industries Policy in India*, Oxford University Press, Calcutta.

UNECA (1994), *Improvements in Legal and Regulatory Constraints to Private Sector Development (Country Case Study: Ethiopia)*, Development Management Series No. 6, Public Administration, Human Resources and Social Development Division, United Nations Economic Commission for Africa, Addis Ababa.

UNIDO (1991), *Ethiopia: New Directions of Industrial Policy*, Industrial Development Review Series, United Nations Industrial Development Organization, Addis Ababa.

United Nations (1995), *World Economic and Social Survey*, United Nations, New York.

Upsala Nya Tidning [Uppsala] (1995), 'Etiopien visar vägen', 10 May, p. 2.

Vo Nhan Tri, (1990), *Vietnam's Economic Policy Since 1975*, Institute of Southeast Asian Studies, Singapore.

Vyasulu, Vinod (1995), *The Indian Economy in 1995: Looking Ahead on the Basis of Experience of The New Economic Policy*, South Asia Multidisciplinary Advisory Team, International Labour Organisation, New Delhi.

de Vylder, Stefan (1993), *Vietnam: State and the Market*, Macroeconomic Studies No. 38/93, Swedish International Development Authority, Stockholm.

Wade, Robert (1990), *Governing the Market: Economic Theory and the Role of Government in East Asian Industrialization*, Princeton University Press, Princeton, NJ.

Wagao, Jumanne H. (1992), 'Multi-partyism and the Tanzanian Economy: Some Challenges', paper presented at the Eight National Economic Policy Workshop, Dar es Salaam, 30 November-2 December.

Wallace, Laura (ed.) (1997), *Deepening Structural Reform in Africa: Lessons from East Asia. Proceedings of a Seminar held in Paris, May 13-14, 1996*, International Monetary Fund, Washington, DC.

Wang, Yan and Vinod Thomas (1993), 'Market supplanting versus market fostering interventions: China, East Asia and other developing countries', *China Economic Review*, Vol. 4, No. 2, pp. 243-258.

Weingast, Barry R. (1993), 'Constitutions as Governance Structures: the Political Foundations of Secure Markets', *Journal of Institutional and Theoretical Economics*, Vol. 149, No. 1, pp. 286-311.

Williamson, Oliver E. (1975), *Markets and Hierarchies: Analysis and Antitrust Implications*, Free Press, New York.

Williamson, Oliver E. (1981/82), 'The Economics of the Transaction Cost Approach', *American Journal of Sociology*, Vol. 87, No. 3, pp. 548-577.

Williamson, Oliver E. (1985), *The Economic Institution of Capitalism: Firms, Markets, Relational Contracting*, Free Press, New York.

Williamson, Oliver E. (1993), 'Transaction Cost Economics and Organization Theory', *Industrial and Corporate Change*, Vol. 2, No. 2, pp. 107-156.

Williamson, Oliver E. and William G. Ouchi (1981), 'A Rejoinder', in Andrew H. van de Ven and William F. Joyce (eds), *Perspectives on Organization Design and Behavior*, John Wiley, New York, pp. 387-390.

Winiecki, Jan (1989), 'CPEs' Structural Change and World Market Performance: a Permanently Developing Country (PDC) Status?', *Soviet Studies*, Vol. 41, No. 3, pp. 365-381.

Winiecki, Jan (1991), *Resistance to Change in the Soviet Economic System: a Property Rights Approach*, Routledge, London.

Woo, Wing Thye (1994), 'The Art of Reforming Centrally Planned Economies: Comparing China, Poland, and Russia', *Journal of Comparative Economics*, Vol. 18, No. 3, pp. 276-308.

Wood, Adrian (1989), 'Deceleration of Inflation with Acceleration of Price Reform: Vietnam's Remarkable Recent Experience', *Cambridge Journal of Economics*, Vol. 13, No. 4, pp. 563-571.

Worku Aberra (1987), *The Import Substitution Policy of Haile Selassie's Government: an Assessment*, Discussion Paper No. 45, Centre for Developing Area Studies, McGill University, Montreal.

World Bank (1988), *Parastatals in Tanzania: Towards a Reformed Program*, Report No. 7100-TA, The World Bank, Washington, DC.

World Bank (1990), *China: Revenue Mobilization and Tax Policy*, The World Bank, Washington, DC.

World Bank (1992), *World Development Report 1992: Development and the Environment*, Oxford University Press, New York.

World Bank (1993), *The East Asian Miracle: Economic Growth and Public Policy*, Oxford University Press, New York.

World Bank (1994), *Adjustment in Africa: Reforms, Results, and the Road Ahead*, Oxford University Press, New York.

World Bank (1995a), *Trends in Developing Economies*, The World Bank, Washington, DC.

World Bank (1995b), *Viet Nam: Economic Report on Industrialization and Industrial Policy*, Report No. 14645-VN, Country Operations Division, The World Bank, Washington, DC.

Yang, Ya-Hwei (1994), 'Taiwan: Development and Structural Change of the Banking System', in Hugh T. Patrick and Yung Chul Park (eds), *The Financial Development of Japan, Korea, and Taiwan: Growth, Repression, and Liberalization*, Oxford University Press, New York, pp. 288-324.

Yeager, Rodger (1989), *Tanzania: an African Experiment*, Westview, Boulder, CO, 2nd rev. ed.

Yohannes, Okbazghi (1995), 'Reflections on the political economy of transition in Eritrea: lessons from Asia's newly-industrializing countries', in John Sorenson (ed.), *Disaster and Development in the Horn of Africa*, Macmmillan, Basingstoke, pp. 93-111.

Yojana [Ministry of Information and Broadcasting, New Delhi], 1-15 March 1988.

Zewdie Shibre and Zekrie Negatu (1995), *Problems and Constraints of Industrialists in Addis Ababa and Regions*, Ethiopian Private Industrialists Association/Friedrich Ebert Stiftung, Addis Ababa.

Zhang Gang and Örjan Sjöberg (1992), *Institutions and Managerial Strategies in China: a Transaction Costs Approach to the Study of Rural Industries*, Research Report No. 13, Department of International Economics and Geography, Stockholm School of Economics, Stockholm.

Zhao Ziyang (1986), 'Report on the Seventh Five-year Plan (Delivered at the

Fourth Session of the Sixth National People's Congress on March 25, 1986)', *The Fourth Session of the Sixth National People's Congress (Main Documents)*, Foreign Languages Press, Beijing, pp. 1-61.

For Product Safety Concerns and Information please contact our EU
representative GPSR@taylorandfrancis.com Taylor & Francis Verlag GmbH,
Kaufingerstraße 24, 80331 München, Germany

Printed and bound by CPI Group (UK) Ltd, Croydon, CR0 4YY
08/05/2025
01864370-0007